TIME OUT

TAKING A BREAK FROM SCHOOL,
TO TRAVEL, WORK, AND STUDY
IN THE U.S. AND ABROAD

Robert Gilpin with Caroline Fitzgibbons

A FIRESIDE BOOK
Published by Simon & Schuster

New York   London   Toronto   Sydney   Tokyo   Singapore

Fireside
Simon & Schuster Building
Rockefeller Center
1230 Avenue of the Americas
New York, New York 10020

First Edition

FIRESIDE and colophon are registered trademarks
of Simon & Schuster Inc.

Manufactured in the United States of America

10 9 8 7 6 5 4 3 2 1

Library of Congress Cataloging-in-Publication Data

Gilpin, Robert (Robert Peyton)
    Time out : taking a break from school to travel, work, and study in the U.S. and abroad /
Robert Gilpin with Caroline Fitzgibbons.
        p.   cm.
    Includes bibliographical references and indexes.
    1. Non-formal education—United States.   2. Experiential learning.
3. Internship programs—United States.   I. Fitzgibbons, Caroline.
II. Title.
LC45.4.G55   1992
371'.04—dc20   91-20981
                                                                                                    CIP

ISBN 0-671-76118-8

Contents

III · APPENDIXES

Foreword

◇ ◇ ◇

One cannot have spent any significant amount of time admitting students to college without being struck by the lock-step nature that characterizes such a large part of the college process in this country.

Having just completed my twenty-fourth season as an admission dean (formerly at Swarthmore and Stanford, and now at Princeton), I'm frequently asked what observations I might make as a result of my experience. The one that comes most often to mind is this: If we had to pick precisely the wrong age at which to select students for college, we have, it seems, nailed it down—eighteen years old, give or take a year.

It won't come as a surprise to many parents when I suggest that eighteen year olds are still growing and developing, and, in fact, develop at different rates in the various aspects of their lives. Some mature at a faster rate academically than socially, while others, heaven knows, mature faster socially than academically. Or, as one mother described her eighteen year old, "she's going on twenty-five socially but heading toward fourteen academically."

I am not talking about good students on the one hand and mediocre students on the other. Rather, I am talking about the differences one perceives among young men and women, many of whom present excellent academic credentials when they apply for admission to college.

I don't find any of this very surprising. Different people simply develop at different rates in different aspects of their lives. Nowhere is it writ in stone that it all comes together for everyone at age eighteen or at the time one graduates from high school, and—Shazam!—everyone is ready at that point to begin college.

Ironically, I suppose, given my particular occupation, I have mixed feelings about the length of time many of our young people spend in educational institutions. For some, it now begins with preschool "schooling" and goes on through graduate or professional school, representing a good portion of one's life, spent with adults many of whom have spent all of *their* lives in educational institutions.

I am not antischool. In fact, my greatest wish for every young man and

woman, when he or she is ready for it, is access to a first-rate college education. College is life's great sabbatical. Yes, it has its practical side. But as
someone once reminded me, and as I now remind each incoming class at
Princeton, "the person each of you will spend most of the rest of your life
with is yourself, and therefore you owe it to yourself to use your college
years to become as interesting a companion as possible."

But I am also convinced that one's college education is greatly enhanced
by the more maturity, experience, and perspective a student can bring to
it. Alas, it also strikes me that these three traits are the very ones that are
most difficult for most young people to come by given the lock-step nature
that currently characterizes such a large part of the school-to-college
process.

Can we change this? Probably not in any major way. In other countries,
particularly the European ones, it is not unusual for even the very best
students to make it a part of their educational plans to spend a year between
high school and college, either working or traveling. Americans have generally been reluctant to consider not going right on to college or taking time
off while in college, both of which are quite acceptable socially.

Some American students of course do take a break between school and
college and it has been my good fortune in my role as an admission dean
to be able both to encourage them in their decisions and to welcome them
a year (sometimes two years) later as incoming students. Some spend time
between school and entrance to college working, some with organized programs such as the American Field Service (AFS), some pursuing an avoca-
tion (for example, dance or music) in greater depth, and some living and
working on their own in a foreign country simply in order to get a better
grasp on the language of that country. At Princeton, in recent years, out
of each freshman class of just more than 1,100 students, only about 30
entering students have spent a year or more between high school and college. That is a small number.

And I suspect it is a small number for two reasons. First, it's probably
the case that not very many students and their families are aware that taking
a year off between school and college is a real option. While I certainly
can't speak for all of the more than 3,000 colleges and universities in the
country, the ones I am familiar with have no hesitation in deferring a
student's entrance to college for a year or two. Indeed, of all of the enthusiastic letters I send to students in one year, none are more enthusiastic than
those I send in response to students requesting to defer their entrance to
college.

Second, it is also the case that it often has been difficult for students who
are interested in taking a break between school and college, or even a break
sometime during college, to know what sorts of options or programs exist
that can provide them with excellent opportunities for using their time in
rewarding and productive ways. Which is why I not only very much welcome the publication of *Time Out* but enthusiastically recommend it. It is
chock full of just the sort of information I am often asked for by students

and their parents, but rarely have I been able to put my hands on when I needed it most.

I commend the authors for the thoroughness with which they have set out to answer just about every conceivable question that might occur to someone contemplating taking some time out from their schooling.

—Fred A. Hargadon
Dean of Admission, Princeton University

Introduction

◈ ◈ ◈

How many times have you said, "I need a break" or perhaps instead squealed, "Gimme a break"? A thousand, maybe? Actually, probably more than that, because the phrase is . . . horrors . . . a cliché. But, you know, like most clichés, it means something. When you say, I need a break, what you mean is "ease off," or "I need to take time out." If you combine these definitions, you will begin to have a sense of what this book is all about. One "breaker" (as we occasionally will refer to those people who have taken time out of mainstream education) said that a break is the pause that refreshes. Yes, another cliché. But when pressed, that individual went on to explain that time out was a chance to learn from a different perspective and often a different place, and to do so out of the structure and the pressure of mainstream education. What we hope to do in this book is to tell you what you need to know to find the right "break" for you.

First, we'll explain how the book works, and tell you something about ourselves.

What you will find in the following pages:

(1) Two "letters"—one to parents, one to students. Every person considering taking a break from traditional education needs to examine the reasons for doing so. In these two letters, we address that issue. We hope our letter to parents will help them understand the rationale for and advantages of taking time out. We hope our letter to students will resolve some of the doubts and fears they may have about taking a break.

(2) Student and parent questionnaires. These questionnaires will give you some direction as you consider taking time out. They should help clarify your thoughts, although they probably won't solve all your problems, so please don't expect them to. Your answers to the questions will guide you to various sections of the book by the references that accompany most of the choices provided.

(3) "Questions Everyone Has and We Can Answer." In this section, we address many of the questions you probably have considered as you approached the idea of taking a break.

(4) "Taking a Break: How to Decide, Where to Start, What to Plan On."

This section contains some personal advice about taking your break. While you might have already considered much of what it says, there's always the chance something might be mentioned that you've forgotten—or just haven't thought about.

(5) Listings of the programs themselves. These listings are done by topic, for example, Environment or Internship, with subheadings such as Federal Government. It would be wise to leaf through all the chapters, since many contain helpful information at the beginning of the section. For example, you will find several pages of discussion on going abroad—both philosophy and nuts and bolts advice. Within each chapter, programs are listed alphabetically, and the appendixes provide the page reference for each program, so you should have no problem locating the program that interests you. Some programs are explained in more detail than others. Where possible, the authors have visited the program in question or spoken with alumni. Thus, we have tried to provide ample detail about it. Even when this was impossible, you should find in the statistical or descriptive material all necessary details. If you don't, write or call the program itself. One final reminder: Although all statistical data have been checked and rechecked, your best bet is always to do it yourself. Due dates, particularly, are subject to change. So be aware of that possibility and don't delay contacting any program you're interested in.

(6) A series of appendixes. These breakdowns of the programs explained within are meant to help you see what's available once you've made some preliminary decisions. For instance, if you come from Caribou, Maine, and you desperately want to spend some time in a warmer climate—just to see what it's like—then Appendix 4 (List of Programs by Location) should help you see what programs are available south of the snow zone. If you know you want to be in a situation in which you will be with your peers but not in a classroom, then you can check the appendix of programs by type (Appendix 2 [Alphabetical Listing of Programs]). If you know you can't afford to spend much money to get into that situation, then you should check Appendix 3 (List of Programs by Cost).

(7) An annotated bibliography to the materials available on specific aspects of programs and opportunities around the world. We feel that the Introduction is also the place for us to introduce ourselves to you. We're going to do this one at a time so you'll have a sense of what brought us together and how the book evolved.

BOB GILPIN:

I'm reminded as I write this of those ads for books proclaiming "Millionaire Salesman Reveals His Secrets to Wealth and Fame." I suppose you could call some of what is in this book "secrets." But it isn't guaranteed to bring you wealth and fame. Nor will it necessarily bring you happiness. What this book should do for you is get you thinking and suggest some possibilities for broadening your horizons.

As for the millionaire part, well, I'm certainly no millionaire. What I am is a teacher. I've been one for over twenty years; I've taught in high school and in college. Moreover, and I think this is important, I've spent the last fifteen years of my life working and living in a boarding school. That means I've been living in dormitories full of adolescents. That's where this book began. After observing, listening to, and advising students on their way to college year after year, I began to wonder about the advice I was giving. I wasn't interested in leading them to financial success. I was more interested in human success, in helping students find college, and life after college, fulfilling.

But was what I was telling students helping them feel successful? After all, when I started teaching high school, I knew why I was there—to prepare students for college. I teach in a preparatory school—and what else is that for? Likewise, as I counseled students getting ready to attend college or already in college, I advised them to get on with it. That was what I had done (and, I'm sure, what most adults in my generation had done). The only reasons students might stop their education in the "old days" (that's before 1965 . . . honestly; it was in the 1960s that many of the programs described in this book got started) were lack of money or a run-in with the college disciplinary system. And when commencement was over, life commenced—the real world, a job, a career beginning.

I don't think the world has changed. But certainly my perspective on it has. I saw students who needed to look beyond the classroom, and so I decided to look out there myself and see what existed. Now, almost two years later, I can say that I have discovered a multitude of ways to engage, to enrich, to fulfill the young people I teach. In the last two years, I've discovered that education extends well beyond the classroom. One of the first persons to make me aware of that was my coauthor.

CAROLINE FITZGIBBONS

I am, for the most part, a product of mainstream education. I went to high school and then straight to college. I did what I was supposed to do . . . no stops, no delays, no breaks. But a funny thing happened on the race through school: I forgot to learn. I guess I don't believe I really began learning until the summer after my sophomore year in college when I took an internship with Governor Madeleine Kunin's campaign staff in Vermont. Don't get me wrong. The years I spent in class did something, just not as much as they could have if there had been some practical life experience to go with them. My summer in Vermont taught me that lesson in all its glory. Here I was a political science major really watching the wheels of democracy turn. Suddenly things like voter-pattern theories that had seemed dull and dreary in a textbook came alive and had meaning. Suddenly I knew why I was learning! The one thing I can promise you about experiential education is that it will make you see the classroom in a completely different way. Whether you spend a summer as an intern on a campaign or as a student in another country, you will never view your classes the same way. And that experiential part of your education will help form the backbone of your base of knowledge.

Preliminaries

Letter to Users/ Students

◇ ◇ ◇

You wouldn't have bought this book if you weren't considering doing something: traveling, working, studying ... anything but being in school next term or next year. Well, be aware of two things. First, this book is packed with choices—hundreds of programs and individual opportunities around the world. Second, having grasped the breadth of opportunity, you now need to stop and translate your desire into practice. You have to plan carefully if your time out is to become a worthwhile experience. This book is designed to explain some ways to do that, but first, let's talk about the idea itself.

If you're thinking about alternative opportunities, remember that you will be suspending your regular educational existence. That may sound easy, but it's probably something you've never done before. Think about it. Most of the people you know go directly from high school to college and then on to graduate school or into a career. You are thinking of doing something different. Be ready for people's reactions to that difference. If older adults are going to be involved in your decision, parents or counselors for example, it might a good idea to alert them to the situation early. Have them look at the Letter to Parents that follows this letter—and you should read it, too.

At the moment, though, you're only considering a break. OK. If a break is just a possibility, what does "break" really mean, and what are its advantages? Well, first of all, taking a break doesn't really have much to do with what the term implies. You're not going to be sitting on the sidelines of life, resting. At least, that's not what this book is for—and it's not what a break is all about.

The break has to do with stepping out of mainstream education. You are going to challenge the idea that you and every other student need to go through sixteen years of education from first grade to college graduation in an unbroken sequence. You probably don't think you're exactly like anybody else. You may not even think you're exactly like you were six months or a year ago. That's because people change a lot from fifteen to twenty-five. If that is so, then how could streaming everyone through the same system make any sense? Why force every student to stay in school? Shouldn't that be just one choice, particularly if neither economics nor career potential is disturbed by alternatives? That question poses an even bigger one: What does a break do to your life?

The obvious answer is that it liberates you. And if it's college or career that you're concerned about, just take a look at the problem from a historical perspective for a minute. A century or so ago, few went to college. Indeed, many young men left school long before high school graduation, and many young women did not attend high school at all. The drive in this country to educate our young produced a mind-set by the 1940s and '50s that not only ensured a high school education for virtually every youth but also made a college education available and affordable for millions. Fundamentally, none of these realities have changed since.

But society has changed. Whether white or blue collar, our society is entirely different from what it was in 1950. These changes may be good or bad, but the fact of change is a reality. Equally real are the astronomical costs of attending college; the variety of educational experiences available in high schools, public and private; the ferocity of competition for college places, graduate school places, and career places. America still sends its youth to high school. It still sends millions to college. But in the last two decades, the notion of choosing other experiences within a student's whole educational experience has become more and more popular. Why?

There are several answers. The first has to do with pressure. The college process—getting in and staying in—has been a big deal for decades. But in the last ten years, the odds have increased. Now it's SAT prep courses, speed reading courses; even the media has hyped us up. Simply put, today the pressure is intense; it breeds burnout. And so, you might need the maturing advantage time out of the mainstream of education could give you. You might need the experience of a noncurricular setting, the reality of "real world" employment, the encounter with challenges that lead you to greater self-understanding or to an enriched sense of the wider communities in which you live, or the fulfillment of having served others.

And you know what else? A break might just make you a better candidate, a better achiever, a more "successful" person. How? Well, that's simple. Maybe you're burned out because you've achieved great things in school and just need a break, or you're burned out because you just can't put it all together, despite a whole lot of effort—or you're burned out because you just hate school. Whatever the reason, the evidence from those who have done it seems to indicate that taking a break makes you appreciate both what you've done and where you're headed.

The following are examples of people who chose to spend some "time out" of the educational mainstream.

School had been tough for Sharon. She wanted to go to college, but money was tight and she was afraid. She feared that college would gobble her up, even if she could afford it. She saw herself carried along by life without the ability to decide for herself. So Sharon decided to take a year off, make some money—enough to survive on—and see something different. Sharon also had a couple of things going for her. She wasn't afraid of work, and she liked children a lot. Having heard about working exchange programs, she looked for, and found, a way to go to Europe as an au pair. She got together the airfare, convinced her parents she would be all right, and flew to Europe. She ended up working as an au pair for five months, learned Italian, and made enough money to spend the next three months seeing Europe on a shoestring. Next, she got a job as a maid. Then she toured Europe for another month before heading home. She was ready to go to school, but "it felt as if I'd added another lifetime to the one I'd had."

Leo had no problems in school. He was into college, but he just wanted to do something different. He had been involved in community service in high school and had really felt fulfilled working with less-advantaged people. So Leo found out about an internship, one with a small circus, which also appealed to his sense of adventure. The circus served disadvantaged youth, teaching them how to tumble. Leo found this internship put him in touch with a world he had never known and also gave him a chance to help others. Before the circus, he'd never given a thought to "living in a trailer in the Midwest." He went back to school saying that it gave him a perspective he'd not imagined.

Dan just couldn't make it. He barely graduated from high school—he joked about paying off one of his teachers in order to get that passing grade. He knew he wasn't stupid; he'd just done some stupid stuff. He'd had run afoul of some controlled substances in junior high, some turnoff teachers . . . and he had turned off. Maybe he'd go to college someday—his parents were willing to send him—but right now they'd given up the idea. So what was there? No mailroom, no pumping gas; Dan couldn't deal with that. It wasn't that he minded working with his hands. No, he actually liked that. But he felt closed in. Then a friend told him about an apprenticeship program, building boats. That sounded sort of cool to him. He'd always been near the water. But build a boat? Well, Dan ended up going to Maine, and he built a boat. It took him most of a year. He spent another year there working. Now, Dan is in school part-time because he discovered he needed to learn some things to go on with his life. But next fall he's off with boats again. This time on one, sailing on a semester program. And life looks pretty good to him.

A break can and should be exciting, energizing—and it can give you a new perspective on education and learning. There aren't too many moments in life when you can stop and look at yourself without serious cost. You may not believe this. Your parents may not believe this, but taking that time during the educational process is likely to be the least costly of all. A break serves you by giving you a chance to look around, to learn to value yourself and your world. Oddly enough, taking that break also serves you by the simple chronological process you undergo. By adding that time to your life, you send a message to those with whom you will be dealing at the next stage of your life: I'm older now. Unquestionably, our society places a value on age. So it doesn't hurt to be a little bit older—and it helps a lot if that time has been well spent.

You've been mulling this idea over for a while now. What do you think? Presume for a moment that you've come to a tentative decision about taking time out, that you find the possibilities exciting. But your name isn't Rockefeller or Trump, so how are you going to afford this time? Is it fair to ask your parents to support you?

That's a question to discuss with your parents. They might be willing, if not enthusiastic, to take that burden on. But it may be more sensible (and mature) to think about ways of making yourself self-sufficient during this planned-for year. It's conceivable that you can do all *you* want to do in addition to earning the funds to do it. Wouldn't it be nice to give Mom and Dad a year of no bills to pay?

There are some ways to do that. But they begin with the word "plan." So if you want to go ahead with this idea of a break, turn to the questionnaire on p. 000. Once you've worked through that, and plugged in the answers as directed, then you can find out what sorts of possibilities await you. Don't ever lose sight of the fact that you have at least seven and probably fifteen months to play with here. If it's the latter—if you're breaking for a year—then planning out that time carefully means the difference between spending money and being self-sufficient. If you're careful and thoughtful, this break can be everything you hope it will be.

Letter to Parents

Chances are that this book now rests in your hands impelled there by a volition other than your own. Or perhaps you've picked it up to see what the fuss is about. Can there possibly be a rationale for taking time out between kindergarten and the end of college? There is, after all, a symmetry about that process of education, one in which we as parents (and products of the system) believe. These days education begins with the socializing process of preschool and concludes with the career-launching noises of commencement speeches. The structure is designed so that students are carried from one step to the next. Skills learned at each level are designed to carry one's education forward. Finally, armed with a college degree, and perhaps some exposure to the ideas of a particular field, the young graduate sets out.

At least this is the way the process might seem to an outside observer. To a participant, particularly in the eighties, the process is often irrelevant, unfocused, and grueling. The more competent are caught by the paradox of success. Although they may be attracted to the stuff of education, they soon find that learning for its own sake isn't a premium value in this system. Instead, all valuable results must be quantifiable. Only the tallysheets ultimately matter, because it is their measure that determines whether and where the student will move to the next stage, particularly the ultimate passage, from high school to college.

Today, getting into college is serious business. The "highly motivated" students apply to the "highly selective" colleges. The less motivated are discouraged from doing so. Notice that while discussing motivation and selectivity we have not mentioned intellectual interest. The reason for that omission is quite simple—academic success in the form of good grades often overshadows the real reason for attending school: learning and the appreciation of knowledge.

We feel that education should be both process and substance. For students today, it too often loses that second value. All too often, then, the educational system is an educational assembly line that propels our children through at least twelve years of schooling and, as we press on them the idea of self-improvement, creates strong expectations of at least four more years.

But what if the student doesn't succeed? Because there is another element crucial to this process, you see, and that is the procedure by which the student's response to education is measured. In other words, what has the student learned? As we've noted, the standard is a quantitative measurement. What if many of those measurements are arbitrary ones, based less on accuracy than on the need to produce a measurable result?

All students, therefore, hew to a system that may support the ongoing process but often is a less accurate reflection of stuff actually learned. The consequence is that some great learners are not seen as good students, and so the system rejects them as failures. Lest that word "failure" seem too strong, it is important to realize that, from the students' point of view, an inability to compete on the highest level is a failure. Moreover, in less competitive environments, a student's reluctance to go to college is perceived as abject failure. In short, our educational system puts a significant premium on a college education and further on the value of an education at certain colleges. The graduating high school senior who chooses a slightly different course of action is viewed, at best, as less than successful. Similar recognition is often given to the college undergraduate who chooses to take time out. In both cases, the public perception is identical: Once you stop, you might never get back. Stepping out of the system equals failure. We trust the system and its products; we are wary of the "failures" and demand of them stark and often unobtainable proofs.

Might it be possible that we overlook in our children the presence of another element in the greater process of education, one that we ourselves likely came to willy-nilly? That element, of course, is maturity. Maturity has proven impossible to codify and equally impossible to teach as part of a curriculum. But its existence often seems the catalyst for making learning for its own sake worthwhile—and for endowing the process of learning with worth. But if maturity can't be taught or learned from a book, how does one get it?

We believe that part of the answer to that question comes from investing the student with responsibility. In the pages that follow, hundreds of opportunities are listed. All share a single characteristic: They break with the continuum of education from kindergarten to graduate school. By allowing a student the opportunity for taking time out, parents, guardians, and advisers invest that student with responsibility. How to structure that time out, how to use that year outside the educational system, becomes the student's obligation. For the academically "successful," this is a challenge they had not experienced because it forces them to look at their lives in a different and often rather risky way. For the "unsuccessful," this opportunity is a welcome one because it offers them a chance to participate in a process that may be measured in very different ways than by the standards of measurement used in the educational process. For all students, the opportunities within this volume offer two other rewards: (1) Each opportunity gives the participant the chance to view himself or herself from a new and different perspective; (2) each opportunity also carries with it an exposure to a reality different from that to which the student is accustomed. In other words, the opportunities within should teach participants about themselves and about the world in which they live. These are neither radical claims nor trivial ones. Indeed, they are claims that educators would be happy to make about their part of the educational system. Unfortunately, for many students, the educational system does not produce these results.

Instead, what the educational system often produces today is a phenomenon known to adults as "burnout." As adults well know, career burnout is not restricted to the successful. And so educational burnout affects students across the spectrum from success to failure. It is not coincidental that in the last two decades, the notion of choosing other experiences within a student's whole educational experience has become more and more popular. Why? There are several answers. One lies in the quality of the changes in the educational system referred to above. That quality is intensification: Costs have intensified; competition has intensified, particularly as the variety of experiences available has intensified. Looking back, we of an earlier generation quickly realize that we did not have to contend with the system that exists today. Today many young people need the maturing advantage that time out of the mainstream of education might give them. They need the experience of a noncurricular setting, the reality of "real world" employment, the encounter with challenges that lead them to greater self-understanding or to an enriched sense of the wider communities in which they live, the fulfillment of having served others.

And by choosing an individual alternative to the mainstream of education for a period of time, the chooser may well enhance his or her ability to proceed along the mainstream. In other words, success in an alternative program might enhance the chances of admission to college or graduate school or career. As we become older as a people, we allow, in fact expect, maturity to come gradually. Age alone does not bring maturity, but decisions that reflect opportunities given and used effectively often seem to say: "This person is growing as an individual." So the decision to choose an alternative to the mainstream today is not only a logical one but one that can help its maker grow and succeed in life. If this concept seems a foreign one, consider for a moment the wave of encouragement for sabbaticals for adults, for the support we give those who change their career patterns in midlife, in short, for the concept of flexibility in shaping one's life. As parents, you might find it remarkable that we have given so little attention to the strains and pressures of adolescence and young adulthood. Only parents and teachers know how agonizing growing up can be. Perhaps adults collectively repress the painful parts of adolescence. When that problematic period of life is coupled necessarily with the competitive tensions of high school and college, isn't the individual who strides through all of those years exceptional? Surely it's only normal to expect adolescents and young adults to be subject to the same needs as careerists in their forties. But while sabbaticals for adults are seen as recovery for burnout, alternative programs for young people should be regarded as experiential learning, relieving tensions principally because those programs are not mainstream.

As for the economics of such a decision, that, too, may have become more judicious today. Setting aside for the moment that group who can afford the spiraling costs to which we refer, what follows is meant for those who wonder how they can face the cost of what seems to be an "extra" year. To begin with, you shouldn't pay for it, at least not alone. This book contains descriptions of programs and suggestions and books that recommend paying jobs around the world for any young person who takes the time and trouble to apply for them. But what's more important is that anyone considering an alternative year—or any other amount of time out of the system— needs to do the planning for it. In that process is one of the lessons to be learned, after all. That planning should include ways to generate income to cover the costs of whatever is chosen. But you should also consider the interests and needs of your child or children. This book was written to alert the consumer to the enormous variety of programs available. On the next few pages, the authors have made up two questionnaires that should help you reach some conclusions about what direction this alternative year should take. Please take the time to go through the appropriate form, and have your son or daughter do the same. Not only will it clarify what choices need to be made, it should also help make the economics of those choices clearer. Among the appendixes provided in this book is one that sorts programs by cost (Appendix 3). As you complete the questionnaire and apply your answers to the key provided, what you can afford vis-à-vis the programs available will become much clearer.

If you've read all this and you still are having trouble with the notion of an alternative year, please flip through the rest of the book before you reach a conclusion. After reading the summaries of some of the programs available, we'd be surprised if you weren't a little envious of the opportunities afforded your child. Here's your chance to do vicariously what you weren't allowed to consider for yourself. For your child's sake and for yours, then, we hope you will find what follows useful. Please write and tell us of your reactions. Our address is: Time Out; Box 7561; Quincy, MA 02169.

Questionnaires, with Cross-References to Text

◈ ◈ ◈

Following are questions that will help in the decision to take time off. Answer them on a separate piece of paper.

STUDENT QUESTIONNAIRE

Part A:
1. How do you want to spend this time (semester/year) off? Please put an X on all lines that apply.
Do you want to . . . . study? [See Academic Programs in the United States, p. 29; Academic Programs Abroad, p. 43]

. . . . volunteer? [See Environmental Programs, p. 232; Community Service Programs, p. 258]

. . . . work? [See Work Opportunities in the United States, p. 138; Work Opportunities Abroad, p. 151]

. . . . have an Internship? [See Internships, p.163; Apprenticeships, p. 194; See Environmental Programs, p. 232]

. . . . be outdoors? [See Environmental Programs, p. 232; Travel/Study Programs, p. 199 (other programs have an outdoor dimension: see index under outdoor.)]

. . . . learn a specific skill? [See index for the specific skill you want to investigate]

. . . . learn a foreign language? [See Language Study Programs, p. 204; some programs listed in Academic Programs Abroad, p. 43, also have a linguistic focus]

. . . . travel? [See Travel/Study Programs, p. 199; see index for other programs that have a focus on travel]
2. Where do you want to spend this year off (or a portion of it)? Check any that might apply.
[Check the Listing of Programs by Location, p. 301; you will discover that there are programs and opportunities all around the world]

Do you want to be in . . . . The USA
                         . . . . North
                         . . . . South
                         . . . . Midwest
                         . . . . Far West
                         . . . . Southwest
                         . . . . Northwest
                         . . . . Hawaiian Islands
                         . . . . Alaska
Do you want to be in . . . . a city?
                         . . . . the country?
Do you want to be in . . . . a foreign country?
If you answered yes, please list all countries you would like to live in or travel to during this break.
3. What about living arrangements? Please check all below that would be acceptable to you.
Would you live with . . . . a family? [Check Index under "Homestay"]
                       . . . . students in a dormitory?
                       . . . . students in an apartment?
                       . . . . coworkers?
4. What about finances? Please answer yes or no to the following:
. . . . Is money an issue for you?
. . . . Do you need financial aid?
. . . . Do you need to make money during your break?
5. How much money can you spend? Please check off which of the following best fits your situation:
. . . less than $5,000   . . . $5,000–$10,000   . . . more than $10,000
Part B:
1. Briefly describe your vision of a dream year off.
2. Why are you taking this time away:
3. What do you most want to gain during this time out?
4. Name some of your favorite activities, for example, reading, horseback riding, mountain climbing, playing with your computer, gardening.
(Since there are so many programs and opportunities out there, you will be surprised to find how relevant this question is.)
5. Are you interested in an individual experience or a group experience?
6. Are you fluent or near fluent in another language? Please specify.
(See Language Study Programs, p. 204, for listings and descriptions of programs and opportunities for perfecting your linguistic skills.)
7. Is there a field that you are particularly interested in investigating, as a career, for instance?
8. Do you like children? Are you willing to work with them?

PARENT QUESTIONNAIRE

1. Why is your child taking time out?
2. How do you feel about that?
3. What do you hope your child gains from this time out?
4. If you were your child, what is the experience you would most like to have?
5. What, if anything, are you dead set against your child doing? Why?
6. What do you consider your child's greatest strengths? Greatest weaknesses?

Questions Everyone Has and We Can Answer

1. What is experiential education?
Simply put, experiential education is learning by doing. Remember the first time you rode a bicycle? No matter how anyone described it, you had to be there, right? That is education through experience. Experiential education can include learning a language through immersion in a culture, discovering a career through an internship, or mastering a life skill through living it.

2. What is mainstream education?
Students in the mainstream experience four years of high school without an interruption and then continue directly to college for another four years. Usually, the phrase implies attending high school and college.

3. What is alternative education?
Alternative education is the catchall phrase used by educators when they want to label anything that doesn't fall into the framework of mainstream education. In fact, alternative programs can parallel mainstream education, but most often they take place in a physical framework different from the mainstream—or are conceived in a different way. For example, a program might provide a year of education, with appropriate credits, but that year might be spent in the wilderness. Both location and concept differ widely from the classroom. But the educational goals and the quantitative result might be the same as a year in the classroom. If Bill returns from a year in France a fluent French speaker and is able to demonstrate that fluency in a written test, hasn't he achieved the same result French study in the classroom was designed to achieve?

4. If I take a year off, am I really going to want to go back to school?
Obviously, we can't predict the future. But every shred of evidence we have says that students finish their time of, whether a semester or a year, with a renewed desire to return to school and continue their studies. Another way to answer this question is to consider what's really being asked. Clearly, an

education is a prerequisite for all sorts of opportunities today. If you appreciate that fact, you will return to school. Part of the reason for taking a year off is to gain perspective. Surely that perspective should create the renewed desire to return to school we describe above.

5. How do I know if a program is a good one?
For the most part, there are no bad programs, there are only bad fits. If you use the tools provided in this book, you should be able to narrow the options until they include the programs that will work for you. One legitimate concern here is that programs not give you what they have advertised. In fact, however, the essence of experiential education rests with you. If you invest yourself in the opportunity you choose, in an analogous but very different way from the investment mainstream education might demand, then you should find the program works for you. Part of the problem with your choices initially is that they may lead you to a level of investment of self you hadn't planned on. Experiential education encourages, indeed demands, a level of involvement you might have avoided in mainstream education.

6. Is financial aid available for programs?
In most cases, yes, but there are important exceptions. Please refer to Appendix 3. There you will find programs broken down by cost. Individual listings will include information on financial aid.

7. Will taking a year off help me get into a better college?
No, probably not, and yes. All these answers apply in the following order. Lets try to understand the problem by breaking it down into each of the possible answers: (a) No, because taking a break in order to better your college chances is not a good "if . . . , then . . ." relationship. The time you spend away from school may be great for you. But that's no guarantee that College X will appreciate you any more than it had before your break. In fact, most college admissions officers will maintain that your previous record in mainstream education, whether high school transcript or previous experience in college, will be the only significant experiential determinant in the admissions or transfer process. Perhaps you can write a better essay after a superb experience away, but that experience has little value otherwise. (b) Probably not, because if you're taking a year off, you're only halfway through when you apply to College Y (or reapply to College X). Your numbers haven't changed, even if you have. (c) Yes. Have you changed? Can what you've done be represented on paper? If so, then your year off can help you. Let's say your heart is set on a particular college. You applied to that college and were rejected or put on a waiting list. It doesn't hurt to ask that college if there is anything you could do to make you more attractive to them. If that college, when asked *politely* and *after* the admissions process, says that you are a viable candidate but need something more to enhance your candidacy, then you're on your way. In return, you tell them

your plans (Hint: Here's one reason why a plan is so important). Their response may be in this case to encourage you—with no guarantees—to resubmit with details of your accomplishments, even as they might be in process.

In the same way, if you're out on probation—or if you've been asked to leave your college—then you have options. Make sure you understand them, and make sure the college understands what you intend to do.

In other words, don't plan on having your break catapult you into college—or into a different college. "Getting in" isn't the purpose of taking that break. And don't plan on having your year turn you into Superperson in the collective eyes of the colleges to which you aspire. What you think and feel is the important issue; what they perceive may not be the same thing. For instance, those university systems that base admissions on scores and numbers certainly won't find your accomplishments on your break easily quantified.

But if you have chosen a college—and if that college finds you almost acceptable (those are two very big conditions)—then proposing a break in specific terms might make the difference. And there's one other possibility to consider: that a break may just change the way you look at College X. So go into the process for *you*, not to change your college expectations.

8. Do alternative programs provide adequate college advising or academic advising?
As in No. 7, there are several answers to this question, but the most important is to check on the program's track record before you enroll. If you are joining a program designed for thirteenth-year students, find out how students previously enrolled in the program have found colleges after their thirteenth year. Had most of them deferred before entering the program? Had most of them used their high school counselors for continuing advice about college aplications? Or does the program have a trained counselor who provides college advice, is knowledgeable about deadlines, and related matters?

Indeed, the best answer to this question is to rely on yourself. If you must apply to college during your break, then take the responsibility for applications and deadlines yourself. If academic advice is the issue, because you want to apply credits to your transcript for graduation, then make sure you have talked through the possibilities with your academic adviser and have in writing whatever guarantees your school or college is willing to give. Don't rely on a single person's verbal guarantee. Situations like this become problems when not certified on paper.

9. What's the most important thing to consider when planning a break?
Remember that it probably doesn't begin until January or June, so make sure you finish the semester or year you're in as strongly as possible. And make sure you close that semester or year out neatly. Don't burn any bridges. Tell your college, if you're enrolled, that you want a leave of absence. Almost every college will respond positively. If you're in high school, make

sure your high school counselor understands your plans. The counselor doesn't need to agree, just understand. But if the counselor doesn't agree, make sure you understand why.

10. What are the benefits of taking a year off?
This is tough to answer because the answers will vary from individual to individual. However, some common answers appear again and again, and they are: increased self-confidence, increased desire to learn, happier attitude, feeling more comfortable with yourself, having a better picture of what you want to do . . . and satisfaction, that comfortable feeling that comes from having done something you know was a once in a lifetime opportunity.

Finally, a few questions about program features:

11. What is a homestay?
Quite literally, it means staying in a home; that you live with a family instead of in a dorm. It is often an option in foreign programs. Homestays mean constant exposure to the language of the country in which you're staying. A homestay also should give you have a much better chance to become involved in another culture.

12. What is an internship?
An interiship is, for the most part, a job. You agree to work for very little money, if any, in exchange for getting to see the ins and outs of a particular field, profession, place of business, or surroundings. The point of taking an internship is twofold: to learn about the job and to consider the career potential in it for you.

13. What is an apprenticeship?
An apprenticeship is only partly a job. True, you will be working, possibly doing some portion of a project for the skilled craftsman from whom you are learning. True, that portion will grow as you learn. But, in the meantime, you will be going through a process ages old—hands-on learning under the eyes and direction of a master of whatever skill you have chosen to take as your own. Whereas internships usually involve so-called professional positions, like law, medicine, or business, and apprenticeship implies a skilled craft or trade. The learning period in the case of apprenticeships is likely to be longer than for internships.

14. What is PG?
The term PG applies principally to students in their thirteenth year, a year inserted between high school and college. This particular insertion is a logical one because it comes at a time when a break with school is easily made. Not only do most colleges happily defer students who have been accepted, but socially you are in between also.

Taking a Break

HOW TO DECIDE, WHERE TO START, WHAT TO PLAN ON

If you've read to this point, then you should have some idea about what a break should mean to you. But maybe you've just thumbed around to this page. Maybe you've looked at a few program descriptions, or read the Letter to Users/Students, or maybe you're just starting here. It doesn't matter where you've been; this section will tell you how you to determine where to go next.

(1) The Rules. There are really five and a half rules to follow once you've begun to consider taking a break. The first is the easiest. It applies to everyone.

Rule 1: Think about what you would do during your break if you could do anything you wanted.
See? That's not hard. Just indulge your fantasies, but only in terms of things: Would you build a boat? Sail a boat? Ski? Speak fluent Urdu? Help the homeless? Take the case of Laura O, who desperately wanted to study art during her break. But she wanted to do so in a way that would also expose her to the language of her choice. Whatever your dream is, no matter how involved or esoteric, start with that. But a corollary to this rule also holds. Don't just pick something convenient. Make sure that your dream choice is just that. The reason you want to be so careful about Rule 1 is because of Rule 2.

Rule 2: Think about where you would live if you could live anywhere.
Now do you understand? Rules 1 and 2 could be in agreement. It's also possible that place rather than subject is what interests you. Mel G. wanted to be in Italy. Once he had arrived at that conclusion, it was easy to figure

out what to do. But it's just as likely that your desire to speak fluent Urdu might have to be satisfied in San Francisco, if you have your choice. That's not impossible, but you quickly can see the probable complications here.

Those complications are likely to be increased when you work on Rule 3.

Rule 3: Figure out how much you can afford to spend on your break.
We began with fantasy; now we come crashing down to reality. If Rule 3 leads to an answer of limited means, then the result is further complications. But that result shouldn't dictate despair. If living in San Francisco and speaking fluent Urdu is your goal, then perhaps your limited resources might be supplemented by gainful employment: a job. Not only do the authors of this book advise you elsewhere to factor employment into your break if possible, we also suggest that a job might be exactly what you might find most fulfilling. Tracy got a job abroad teaching English. She claimed her English teachers would have been most surprised at her choice of employment. But the job was just what she needed. It helped her respond to rules 1 and 2. Perhaps Rule 4 can be the deciding component.

Rule 4: Consider with whom you want to spend your break.
This is an important condition of your break, but one you may not deal with until it's too late. Can you stand taking your break in the rain forest of the Amazon, where you won't speak to another American between the ages of eighteen and twenty-five for six months? Or do you mind being alone for a month or two? Clearly, we all have preferences here; the issue is to decide what—or, rather, whom—you can live with. When Bryony and Samantha decided to live together for their break, they solved that problem. On the other hand, for Lawrence the most important thing was being with people his own age. Since many programs offer small group involvement, he had lots of choice. However, Tim's unwillingness to be alone for any prolonged amount of time led him to soften his desire to trek by himself. In fact, balancing among options is the issue with all the rules above. The next rule makes that a little more complicated.

Rule 5: Compare your goals with those your parents have for you.
Obviously, there are situations—and people—that make this rule inapplicable. But, like it or not, your parents probably have made significant contributions to your education, including making or influencing your decisions about your future in that milieu. They may not share your enthusiasm for this decisions (the authors hope this book will help convince them of its worth), but you should get the benefit of their experience before finalizing your decisions about your break. Lila's parents were opposed to her taking any time off from school. They were worried about the expense; they were afraid she wouldn't return; and they couldn't conceive of what she would do. But when she openly discussed the idea, offering them the option of convincing her of the fallacies in it, the discussion led to comments from

both parents of their thwarted desires to do something or go somewhere during their educational careers. Lila also showed them how she had planned out her time off, how much her college counselor was in agreement with the concept, and why the experience should help her focus in the future.

Your responses to rules 1 through 5 above are likely to lead to someplace in the middle, hence Rule 5½.

Rule 5½: Compromise.
Perhaps the most amazing thing about taking a break is the fact that you stand a very good chance of realizing a substantial part of all your desires, no matter how contradictory they may seem at this point. This book has been designed to help you achieve that compromise by sorting programs according to subject, location, cost, and constituency. Please use the appendixes accordingly.

Before we start, a piece of advice: Remember that you're going somewhere else to learn from that place. If you try to take your home with you, you won't get the full experience. And "going" doesn't just mean physical travel. This break is a separation from your education. You're leaving the classroom and going somewhere else. Go with your arms and mind open; that way the learning will be much easier.

MAKING A CHOICE

If you considered your answers to the questionnaire on page 11, then you have realized that how you choose your break depends on your preferences in at least two categories: what to do and where to do it. Most of the rest of this book is devoted to helping you make choices about what to do. From those choices will come the answers to questions of when and how to take your break. Obviously, your choice of opportunity will also be dictated by where you go. So what follows is a discussion of where, with special attention to the issues involved in going abroad.

1. Where do you want to go?
Everybody has a preference here. Whether you want to go to Africa, Asia, Europe, Central and/or Latin America, Australia and/or New Zealand, or even just someplace else in the United States, there is a possibility of its happening. But you need to make some choices *before* you think about the steps below, because every step narrows your options. Therefore location should be among the first of the choices you will make—at least we think so. Obviously, you can be more specific than simply choosing a continent or a city or region in the United States, as we suggest above. But if you focus in on, say, Bulgaria, make sure you have an alternative or two, because

you might find as you go through the steps below that Bulgaria is virtually impossible given the other conditions you pose for yourself.

2. Deadlines
Almost every program has deadlines. Once you've chosen a location or locations, check out what the deadlines are. Most are predictably early spring for the following fall, fall for the following spring, midwinter for the summer. But there is no single date. You can't depend on April 1, for example, as a designation of early spring. In fact, when we do give specific dates in the book, it is best to confirm them with the program, because due dates change from year to year. Don't send your application in three days late by mistake. Call or write the programs you're interested in.

3. Prerequisites
You've found you can meet the deadline, but can you meet the prerequisites? Many programs have a variety of conditions: a minimum average; a language requirement; some previous coursework. The possibility of requirements is less true for programs in the United States, at least beyond qualifications of age and academic standing. You need to make sure that you can meet those conditions before you begin to consider the program. And make sure that you can meet the other requirement many programs abroad put forward: orientation time. This demand ranges from a meeting or two on the home campus of the program to a semester in residence on that campus. The semester is often during the summer, and the rationale is valid: to send you abroad with a thorough grounding in language and culture. But the sacrifice of time and money will be yours (often the longer orientations carry the reward of credits, but whether or not these transfer is a question to add to No. 4 below).

BEFORE YOU GO

Let's get down to basics and make a list. You've decided to take a break, right? It doesn't matter whether it will last a year or month. Now that you've made the commitment, you have to deal with several issues.

1. Give yourself enough time to plan your break.
Impulse and spontaneity are great qualities; but taking a break needs some forethought, some time for serious planning. This is true for two reasons: (a) You need lead time to look at your options and choose from among them; (b) one purpose in taking a break is to reinforce your ability to go through exactly that process—the process of planning, and then executing, a series of decisions. It just isn't something that you can do in a day or a week. So, once again, give yourself enough time to make the kinds of plans a responsible break demands.

2. Inform your educational institution of your intentions.

Are you in school? If the answer is yes—and that means intending to be in school during the supposed break, whether school is high school, your first year in college, any year in college, or graduate school—you've got an easy next step. Tell your school what you're doing. That seems obvious. It's also easy. But beware of a pitfall. Your educational institution may not be happy about your decision. There is a variety of hidden agendas here. Some are the school's—we'll get to those in a minute—some are yours. Are you "in good standing" academically, as the phrase goes? Don't just assume that you are. Let the school tell you. If you're not, the chances of the school's official unhappiness increase significantly. If your record is OK, fine. If your record is shaky, and the registrar—or your adviser, or your counselor, or whoever—gives you a hard time about leaving, then you need to do the following:

Find out from that person or someone *official* exactly what you have to do to be able to leave in good standing. If leaving in good standing is impossible with your record, or—and this is equally possible—if the "official" you talk to is discouraging because he or she isn't well informed about alternative opportunities, show them this book and/or descriptions of what you're considering. If, for example, the opportunities you've picked out have credit attached to them, then their value goes up for most people. If credit isn't the issue—if your institution is simply set against leaves—then you have a choice. Forget it, or try to get a realistic appreciation of your chances if you had to reapply. Again, you have some decisions to make, but I'd suggest you keep in mind the accessibility of most colleges. It is the unusual institution that would deny a student the right to return within a reasonable period of time (for example, a year or less).

Another suggestion is to contact the program or situation you intend to be involved with during your break and ask if they might (1) write a letter outlining their credentials and (2) provide the name of one or two individuals who have done what you have (whether any of this is possible depends on what you intend to do). Then contact those individuals, find out to what educational situation they returned and what their school thought of their experience. All of this can be evidence you can use in your behalf. (3) Write a careful letter spelling out your intentions, your reasons for choosing the path you have, and provide the information you've obtained, plus whatever information you have about your plans, including any printed descriptions of your opportunity. None of this might help, but, in fact, most educators are impressed by people who have done their homework—and that's what you will be demonstrating by all this.

So where are you? You've told your school what you intend to do and you've been given permission to leave—or an understanding of what conditions you must meet to gain that permission.

There's an exception to all of this: those people who don't intend to go on to school at any level. For you, the above discussion is irrelevant. What you need to consider first is what you will be returning to. If you intend to spend this break learning a skill, finding out about your interest in cooking, for example, or farming, or boat building, you might consider giving some thought to potential employment after your break. You've probably already thought about working for someone. In fact, it's likely that interest helped push you to think about a break. Regardless, take the time to inquire about your employability after and because of your break. Chances are that prospective employers may find your experience valuable to them and thus be predisposed to look favorably on your application later. Don't forget, of course, that you should keep in touch with those prospects during your break.

3. Get your affairs in order.

Here's where the nitty-gritty paperwork comes in: checking on your driver's license renewal date; getting a social security card if you don't have one; getting a passport if you don't have one; figuring out how you will do your banking, especially if you're going abroad. This is only a very partial list, and it includes things you needn't worry about if you're not leaving the United States. The program you will be taking part in should provide you with a more detailed and specific list of things to take care of as well.

4. Research your destination carefully.

Just where do you think you're going? If you leave home, you need to make sure you will be safe, secure, and with at least the potential for happiness wherever you're going. So find out what you can about where you're headed. Before you go see that reservation agent, make sure you are clear on what alternative ways you have of getting there. Note, for example, the descriptions of the quarterly magazine *Transitions Abroad* (see Bibliography) and the organization CIEE (see page 70) included in this book. Both could be extremely helpful in supplying necessary information about the process of getting to your destination and about the destination itself. This is particularly true if your destination is outside the United States. Clearly, there are some basic reasons why you need to go to all this trouble. Two obvious ones are cold and hot. If it's either one of those, or both, and you're not prepared, then suffering is likely. In other words, does destination X require special clothing?

Another issue is budgeting. If you're considering alternative destinations, which is cheaper? If you don't know, find out. If your choices lie in the United States, travel guides will tell you something of what you want to know. If you're looking abroad, contact the local consulate or the Washington embassy of the nation under consideration. You might also talk to the State Department about traveling and living in these places. Finally, in the Bibliography we've suggested several books that can help answer some of these questions. Don't take the usual approach to bibliographies and ignore this one. We want to see you take advantage of opportunity; we don't want to see you done in by it. Good and specific advice will help to prevent trouble. So do your homework.

5. Consider the conditions of your return.

Finally, there is the issue of returning. We've alluded to this issue above, but for many the return is likely to be into changed circumstances. The best time to plan for this is before you leave. You simply don't know what can occur. Some experiences will change the way you think about where and how you will return; others will not. One constant is the date for application to college, either for initial admission or for transfer. You will have to meet this date if you intend to go to school in which you're not currently enrolled. So make a note of it.

Also remember that if you've been away for any appreciable time, things will be different. Your perceptions may have changed; so may other conditions. So before you go on an extended break, don't commit yourself to future situations that may change in the interim.

A NOTE ABOUT CREDIT

Getting course credit could be likened to winning your state lottery. Sure, it's easy to buy a ticket. But the odds are against you. Still, as a friend of mine once said, "You can't win if you don't play." What that translates into is this: Whether or not you get credit for your break, it's always worth trying to. The reasons for trying are functional and economic. First, it will show up on your transcript—and that's always positive. Second, if you get credit from the institution you attend or at which you plan to matriculate, you will save some money. How do you get that credit? Let's begin with the in-school scenario. You decide you want to join an established academic program abroad. It may be a program sponsored by another college, or perhaps connected with an institution abroad. First, read your present school's catalogue carefully to be sure what conditions your college sets for getting credit for programs abroad. Then read the program literature. If it's a program sponsored by an American college, you may be required to attend that school for the semester previous to your departure. What would your school say to such a departure? By "say" here the issue is one of credit. Will your school give you credit for going to another school for a semester? Chances are they won't. But it doesn't hurt to ask—in writing—and to get an answer in writing from at least a middle-management official (read: dean of something). Next, or at the same time, ask in writing about credit for the program you have in mind abroad, and include in the letter (which you will follow up with a visit or phone call) a request for acceptable substitutes. Remember, such a request requires you to specify your reasons for wanting this kind of break. As this exchange goes on, don't forget your goal: to find out whether your institution will give you credit for what you do. Otherwise, as fulfilling as your break may be, in terms of credit it will not yield a specific return. That's okay as long as you know about it in advance. But make sure you have a clear picture, from your institution, in writing.

What if you're not in school currently? What's likely to be the effect of that situation on your possibilities for credit? Well, bluntly, your chances resolve themselves into two categories: never and hardly ever. But in the current climate, you do have certain advantages. If you have deferred matriculation, it might be best simply to sit on whatever you do on your break until after you've matriculated—and even spent a semester or year at your prospective institution. If you are simply out of school at the moment, credit per se may become less valuable than an alternative use for your break successes: their value in strengthening your application to wherever. Whatever you decide, make sure you have documented thoroughly your successes during your break. Documentation should include letters, testimonials as to your incredible talent, kindness, wit, etc. Any more quantitative evidence also should be husbanded. Then you will have something to show when the time comes. The exception to this rule is language. Any language program will yield not only immediate benefits in terms of fluency but also should give you the ability to take language placement tests when you enter (or return) to school. The essential predictability of these results make language programs the only reliable credit bet.

If this all sounds pessimistic, that's because schools simply don't want to give you credit unless you pay them for it—not an entirely unreasonable attitude. The results, however, can be frustrating. Take the case of Jim, a junior at a highly prestigious institution. Jim wanted to spend a semester at Oxford. What could be more respectable? Moreover, Jim understood the system. He consulted everyone he could think of; his school had no program of its own. The coast looked clear. All officials agreed that Jim was acting responsibly and wouldn't lose anything by going abroad. Note that phrase 'lose anything." There's another catch to reckon with. If you aren't taking a break but want to stay enrolled, make sure everyone official agrees. Jim thought he had; he even took some courses by tutorial abroad for his home institution. What happened? Well, Jim hadn't gotten the institution's commitment in writing. He also lost credit—both for what he did and for some of the time in which he did it. Not good? You're right; it wasn't. So get in writing what your institution proposes; then you can be better assured of getting what they promised. Also, keep in mind what else Jim got—as he did. As Jim remarked about this incident: "I'd do it all again, knowing the consequences. It just would have been a little less frustrating if I'd known them in the beginning."

The Programs

Academic Programs in the United States

The programs that follow have an unusual characteristic—and it's not that they're located in the United States. Rather, what these programs share is a unique approach to education, to the possibilities and problems of an academic experience.

Academic Year in New York City
5 Carmine Street, Townhouse C
New York, NY 10014
(212) 228-2210
Contact persons: Alison Baker or Renwick Jackson, directors
Program length: semester or year
Cost: $7,500 per semester
Financial aid: available
Housing: provided, apartment living
Age range of participants: PG; high school and college
Number of participants: 12 per semester
Application process: application forms; interview; faculty letter of reference
Application due date: rolling admissions until May 1 for fall; November 1 for spring
Program location: New York City

The Academic Year in New York City was designed around a simple principle: exposure to the day-to-day life and culture of New York City would cause students to grow and learn much as would a year spent abroad. To complete this task, the directors divided the Year into three components:

1. An academic course taken at one of New York City's colleges. Most courses are taken through the City University of New York, although occasionally other schools are used.

2. An individual research project in a particular field of interest.

3. A seminar on New York City entitled The City as Text and led by the two program directors, Alison Baker and Renwick Jackson. In this part of

the program students explore the nature of New York City. Required reading includes the *New York Times* and the *Village Voice*. Field trips and city exploration are stressed here.

One of the foundations of the Year is that students may choose the direction they want to take during their time in New York. They choose the course that interests them most and design a research project that in some way connects to their coursework. Often, research projects take the form of internships in a field of interest, and the directors aid students in securing placement with a professional in the field.

While this freedom to allow students to explore their individual interests is what is so compelling about the program, it is also its downside. By its nature, Academic Year in New York City is a minimally structured program. While the directors meet regularly with the students to check on how everything is going, the success of any program relies on the participant's initiative. The program's dynamic is individually fueled. Students do not meet together, even for meals, except by their own choosing. They may live in one of two program-owned apartments in Greenwich Village, or in the home of one of the directors. It is possible that each student will be pursuing a field of study different from roommates or program mates. Given this freedom, the program resembles a collection of individual opportunities held together by the directors and the common seminar. So if the possibility of spending a year in the fascinating metropolis of New York piques your imagination, remember that to get full value from the opportunity, you must be ready to generate much of your own enterprise, select your own goal, and push yourself toward it.

Appalachian Semester

Coordinator, Appalachian
  Semester
Union College
Barbourville, KY 40906
(606) 546-4151
Program length: semester
Cost: $3,600
Financial aid: work/study program
  available
Housing: provided

Age range of participants: college
  sophomore, junior, or senior
Number of participants: 15
Application process: application;
  transcript and essay; teacher
  recommendation; photos
Application due date: June 1
Program locations: Barbourville,
  Kentucky and southern
  Appalachia

In the words of the program's director, L. James Cox, "through an intergration of classroom and community, theory and experience, the program gives the student the opportunity to develop an understanding of the changing patterns of culture, society, and political economy within the Appalachian region." By so doing, one can appreciate its differences and understand how our larger society is forcing change upon this subculture. The Appalachian Semester integrates classroom study with fieldwork; you will go from seminar to field trip on a rotating basis for the first five weeks. After that, you select an internship or study project, while continuing the seminar/fieldwork cycle around the weekly edges of your remaining time in Kentucky. Internships include Frontier Nursing Service (see p. 264), various sectarian and state social services, as well as other federal and local service agencies. And you'll be given insights into those internships as you listen to visiting lecturers for the first several weeks. "What was fascinating to me was that I found out not only how social service programs were supposed to work but how they did work: who was and who wasn't doing what."

If an internship is unappealing, you may choose a directed study project learning about traditional music, collecting oral histories, or folklore. Finally, you can pursue other issues related to the political economy of Appalachia and its impact on poor people.

While there, you will be living at Union College, a small liberal arts college in southeastern Kentucky. For some, that may take some getting used to. "I found that there were some very different ideas from what I was used to about the social privileges for men and women.... But we were all students, and living at the college. If you were to live outside the college, you would be even more shaken up than we were by just the differences.... Life there made me understand what I was doing majoring in sociology, what I'd been studying about. For those people [in Appalachia], the whole structure of society was making their lives what they were."

"I've been to Latin America: Costa Rica, Guatemala, Peru ... but [the Appalachian Semester] is the best thing I've ever done in college."—"As a student, I was isolated from what I was learning about; Appalachian Semester was a hands-on experience."

Applied Environmental Science Program

W. H. Miner Research Institute
Chazy, NY 12921
(518) 846-7144
Program length: semester or
  summer
Cost: $1,000 for tuition for
  semester; $1,000 for room and
  board
Financial aid: none
Housing: efficiency apartments
  available

Age range of participants:
  primarily college seniors
Number of participants:
  approximately 20
Application process: 2.5 GPA;
  junior/senior standing in
  ecology/environmental science;
  letter of application; interview
Application due date: April 15
Program location: Chazy, New
  York

The key to understanding this program is the word *applied* in its title. Because of the existence of the Miner Research Institute, the Applied Environmental Science Program there has a distinct quality: it affords access to diverse ecosystems entirely under the control of the institute. The result is a study in diversity: "chunks of days spent in everything from fieldwork to analysis." And it's tough work, as one student noted. "It was all hands on." This is a "serious place ... you have to work hard." Consequently, any student interested in a real opportunity to apply accrued knowledge in environmental science has in the Miner Research Institute approximately eight thousand acres to work with. The Applied Environmental Science Program is a "totally integrated program. . . . You are exposed to everything: you are out in the field; you're getting your hands dirty; you're learning the bookwork, and you're working in the lab with equipment and stuff you'd never touch at a university." This opportunity is enhanced by the ease with which this program deals with questions of room and board. Because students are housed at the institute, the program is affordable. "They are very flexible about your life there." And there are "great people. That's what is great about it—the contact with wonderful people."

The Center for Northern Studies
Wolcott, VT 05608
(802) 888-4331
Contact person: Steve Young, director
Program length: semester or full year; summer trip
Cost $5,600 a semester
Financial aid: available
Housing: available
Age range of participants: college, graduate students

Number of participants per session: 5–12
Application process: essay; transcript; interview at the center strongly encouraged
Application due date: rolling admissions
Program location: northern Vermont

Nestled in rural Vermont, the Center for Northern Studies is perhaps one of Vermont's best-kept secrets. The center specializes in the study of the circumpolar North (the area of the earth nearest to a pole, in this case the North Pole) and provides intense and exciting academics complemented by related fieldwork. Originally developed in conjunction with Middlebury College's Department of Northern Studies, the center provides a setting where fieldwork as well as academics in this major can take place. Now an independent institution, the center strives to have its students gain a broader and deeper understanding of all aspects of the Circumpolar North. Coursework includes "integrated courses dealing with interrelated physical, biological, social, economic, and political systems" of the northern environment as well as specific courses that focus on paleoenvironment and prehistory, northern ecosystems, political economy of natural resources, traditional peoples and cultures of the North, community development, northern law, northern policy studies, and more. Academic work is supplemented with two major field trips, one in the fall, and one in the spring, to Newfoundland and Canada.

Students and faculty alike stress the interdisciplinary nature of the center's academics. Science is studied in conjunction with politics, culture, and history. Due to the small number of students at the center at any given time, individual attention and independent study are the rule rather than the exception. Students are serious about the center and why they are there. This dedication to the center and its purpose serves to create a strong sense of community for the individuals studying and working there. This is enhanced by the student living arrangements—coed houses in the town of Wolcott. Students say that this is a bonus, and a nice change from dormitory living, but caution interested individuals to remember that this living arrangement combined with the small number of program participants causes constant interaction with the same group of people. Yet, while it is not always easy, current residents clearly are thriving in the program. The center provides an interesting educational opportunity for anyone interested in the field of northern studies.

Haystack Mountain School of Crafts

Deer Isle, ME 04627
(207) 348-2306
Contact person: Candy Haskel
Program length: summer, 2- or 3-week sessions
Cost: $210–$690 depending on length of time and type of accommodations
Financial aid: available
Housing: dormitory
Age range of participants: 18 and up

Number of participants per session: 80
Application process: application; short statement of intent; $20 application fee
Application due date: rolling admissions
Program location: Deer Isle, Maine

Haystack Mountain offers serious artists and art enthusiasts a place to explore their medium or try a new one. The classes are small, and the instructors top-notch. Everyone at Haystack is committed to art and its development, but you will not find classical painting or drawing here. Haystack focuses on crafts as art. Each two- to-three-week period has a particular theme that structures the individual courses. The courses offered include glassblowing, basketmaking, woodworking, quilting, weaving, and clay working. The area of focus and the degree of proficiency needed to complete each course successfully vary according to the workshop theme. The instructors vary according to the sessions and always include several visiting artists. Haystack offers those already involved in crafts, or those interested in beginning an involvement, a fabulous learning retreat.

While at Haystack you can expect comfortable living arrangements. Rooms are available in single, twin, triple, and quad sizes. There is also an open bunkhouse. One may choose to have a bathroom attached or use a central washroom. And your tuition will vary according to your accommodation choice. Meals are taken in a central dining hall. Haystack is much like camp for the serious artist, complete with a beautiful view. By all accounts this island retreat is a neat place to spend some time, perhaps best summed up in the words of one Haystack faculty member: "Haystack—twenty-four-hour studios, breathtaking geographical beauty, good friends, thought-provoking conversations . . . those are my memories of summers past. And the chance to do it all again is one that can't be missed." It is clear that Haystack on Deer Isle is a magnificent setting that lends itself well to the creation of artistic pieces, knowledge, and peace of mind.

The Maine Coast Semester

The Chewonki Foundation
Wiscasset, ME 04578
(207) 882-7323
Contact person: Scott Andrews
Program length: fall or spring
  semester
Cost: $6,750
Financial aid: available

Housing: dormitory
Age of participants: junior or
  senior in high school
Number of participants: 40
Application process: essay;
  transcript; references
Application due date: March 1
Program Location: Maine

The Chewonki Foundation's Maine Coast Semester combines a semester of rigorous academics with an environment that allows the students to become involved with the natural sciences and environmental education. Located on four hundred acres of oceanfront property, the Maine Coast Semester offers students a working classroom. It is owned in part by twelve private "member" schools that regularly send students to the program. The member schools include the Taft Schools, the Charlotte Country Day Schools, Deerfield Academy, Miss Porter's school, Noble and Greenough School, the Packer Collegiate Institute, Phillips Andover Academy, Shady Side Academy, the Thatcher School, Waynfleet School, the Westminster Schools, and the Princeton Day School. While these schools regularly send students to participate in the Maine Coast Semester, anyone may apply for a space. MCS regularly maintains a set number of places each semester for interested, nonmember students.

Because the students who attend member schools are quite talented, the Maine Coast Semester offers challenging academics that maintain the standards set for those schools. Participants take five courses, two of which, English and Environmental Issues, are required. Students then choose three of the following to round out their course of study: Natural Science; U.S. History; various levels of mathematics, French, and Spanish; and Art and the Natural World. "Academics are basically the same as at your member school. You can take U.S. History, French, Math and it's the same course that they teach at Nobles, what's different is the way you learn. I didn't feel like I was working as hard. I was relaxed and I had time to think about things but looking back, I learned twice as much as any other semester before."

The most exciting coursework offered include options such as Environmental Issues, Natural Science, and Art and the Natural World. All these courses exploit the unique setting of the Maine coast and make best use of the facilities and opportunities Chewonki offers. As one former student noted, commenting on the special course on Environmental Issues, "One of our projects was to fight for a bill that abolished plastic six-pack holders. I spoke in front of the Maine House of Representatives against the six-pack yokes. The bill passed and we won."

Student life at Chewonki is different than at any other boarding school. There are no sports, and students are required to use what would be sports time to do extramural work. Since the community is so small, it is essential that students help keep the school running; they work in the kitchen, chop wood, clean up common areas and bathrooms, and take responsibility for a myriad of tasks that need to be completed. "There was no janitor—we did all the cleaning, some of the building, and all the chores. We cleaned the bathrooms and split the wood for our fires. We helped out in the kitchen and it made the school our home because of it."

But in return, students have a real say in how issues are decided. The faculty allows the school to be run in a consensual fashion. To date, no student decision has been overruled. When entrusted with the responsibility for making the community work, students seem to rise to the occasion and really help it along. At Chewonki, the faculty provides support and stability rather than manifestations of authority.

Housing exists in the form of dorm rooms and winterized cabins. Rooms are comfortable but fairly spare; the cabins are decidedly rustic but, unsurprisingly, are the most desired living quarters. "It's important that people know it's not tents and woods. There *are* showers; you can take as many as you want. It really is a home." No formal study halls exist, and students can be found studying in faculty offices every evening. This informality extends to demeanor and approach of the staff. The faculty at Chewonki lives primarily on campus. Partially as a result of the increased student-faculty contact such propinquity creates, students enjoy an unusual rapport with their teachers. One faculty member described his job as part teacher, camp counselor, and big brother.

Chewonki offers a wonderful option to students interested in an academic challenge in a unique learning environment. Students grow in and out of the classroom as a result of being an important part of a small, tightly knit community in which they hold a fair degree of responsibility. "It was great because of the community involved, the people and the atmosphere. When you have thirty kids all there because they want to be, it's great ... it became a second family." And, while the environment at Chewonki nurtures personal growth, the unique classroom opportunities provide students with the fuel to stretch their minds in unaccustomed ways.

The Mountain School Program of Milton Academy

RR1, Box 123F
Vershire, VT 05079
(802) 685-4520
Contact persons: David and Nancy
   Grant, directors

Program length: semester
Cost: approximately $7,500;
   miscellaneous account deposit
   of $300
Financial aid: available

Housing: provided

Age range of participants: high school junior, senior

Number of participants: 41

Application process: application with fee; transcript; 3 teachers' recommendations

Application due date: March 1

Program location: Vershire, Vermont

As its codirectors explain, "This is a place that cajoles, exhorts, and even demands that students look carefully and affectionately at the world around them and ask, 'What can I do?' " Place that vision on a three-hundred-acre working farm spread across the Vermont hills and you have a sense of the Mountain School. It is customary for students who go on programs to return with positive feelings. But this program enjoys not only good press from its alumni, it also has its member-school constituencies clamoring for admission.

"My brain is constantly in high gear. All my learning is connected—it all seems to fit together"—"Before I came here I didn't know what kale was or what chickens ate. . . . I think I'm learning how connected everything in the world is."—"I think that the Mountain School has reinforced what I've always felt an education should be—a learning of techniques and ideas that help you get involved in the world around you."

These plaudits aside, the Mountain School also provides a semester of education, both traditional and experiential. Beyond the acknowledged environmental focus of its English and environmental science courses, all disciplines are biased toward the landscape in which the school is set. But all also manage to carry their students through a normal curriculum. What enriches this academic experience also keeps the community functioning, because it is the student population, assisted and supervised by faculty and staff, that maintains the farm and sustains the community. Finally, such efforts have a measurable impact on the individuals carrying them out. "Seeing your own physical work materialize into visual results really gives a tremendous feeling of pride in yourself. If I am unable to do something I am not afraid to ask for help, because I feel secure that everyone around me will help me learn. I don't have inhibitions about things I 'should' know."

The spirit such work engenders extends to after hours. Although there is no organized athletic program, the terrain avails students of the opportunity for hiking in fall and spring, skiing in winter, and informal gatherings whenever. The performing arts, again both organized and not, sustain the community at other moments.

If you want what the codirectors call "both the challenge and the opportunity inherent in our size and structure," the Mountain School has given you a reason to spend a semester in Vermont.

Salt Center for Field Research
19 Pine St.
P.O. Box 4077
Portland, ME 04101
(207) 761-0660
Contact person: Pamela Wood
Program length: semester
Cost: $3,780; room and board *not* included
Financial aid: available
Housing: none provided

Age range of participants: college and up, 19–65
Number of participants: 12 per session
Student to teacher ratio: 3:1
Application process: essay; interview; portfolio or work; recommendation
Application due date: rolling admissions
Program location: Portland, Maine

Salt is a program that evokes passion from participants and alumni. Those admitted to the program are—indeed, they have to be—passionate about their fields—journalism and photojournalism—and the Salt faculty is passionate about imparting its extensive knowledge of these fields to the students. The result is an intense hands-on learning experience for the participants. Salt students, under the direction of the faculty, also work to create a magazine from start to finish. So it's fair to say that Salt's student body and faculty comprise a group of dedicated writers and photographers. In other words, Salt is a school, a place at which students learn, a program in which each person works with every other member of the program, faculty and student, to create and polish stories and photo essays that explore Maine culture. Participants take part in classroom as well as field study, and a great deal of time is spent one-on-one with faculty members. Classroom time at Salt is held in seminar fashion; and students freely discuss photography, literature, and reporting techniques as they relate to the task of creating a magazine. This style of teaching allows students to sink their teeth into their subject, understand its relevance to their lives, and as a result take responsibility for their own learning. The end product is knowledge, heightened skills—and their manifestation in a highly polished, thoroughly professional magazine dedicated to Maine and Maine-oriented issues.

Salt is run more like a job than a school, and its participants are dedicated to its mission. Competition for one of the twelve spaces is fierce, and applicants often negotiate with Salt for a period of time before actually enrolling in the program. It is important to note that in most cases students arrange for their own housing and are always responsible for their own board. Salt's location in metropolitan Portland does simplify the issue of housing to a degree. Amenities aside, Salt provides a unique opportunity for interested and motivated students to have the benefit of both classroom and practical experience.

Sea Semester

Sea Education Association Box 6
Woods Hole, MA 02543
(508) 540-3954
Program length: semester (there
    are sessions year round; all 12
    weeks in length)
Cost: $6,000 tuition; $1,750 room
    and board while at sea; house
    rental while in Woods Hole
    approximately $450
Financial aid: available
Housing: provided

Age range of participants: college
Number of participants: 24 per
    program
Application process: application
    with fee; high school and
    college transcripts; 2 teachers'
    recommendations; an
    interview report
Application due date: rolling
    admissions
Program locations: Woods Hole,
    Massachusetts, and at sea

Sea Semester is a unique blend of six weeks of classroom instruction and six weeks of shipboard life. In the first unit, students are introduced to academic programs that include oceanography, maritime, and nautical studies. During that time, they work in small groups, using not only the facilities of the school but those of the Woods Hole Oceanographic Institute. Within this curriculum are lectures, seminars, field trips, and laboratories and hands-on workshops. Then, it's seaward. "I went as a sociology major who had never set foot on a boat before. Coming here and knowing nothing, the first two weeks at sea was the most humbling experience I've ever had."—"There is no question that the Sea Semester is the most exciting educational experience which I have ever had during college." You sail on either a 125-foot schooner or a 134-foot brigantine. And you sail to Bermuda, the Caribbean, or Nova Scotia, among other ports of call. During that time, you continue in class aboard, as well as doing research and other projects. One look at the pictures of life aboard ship, and if Masefield or Conrad or Melville mean anything at all to you, this program will be appealing.

However, applying to it might seem daunting initially. You do need to have taken either an AP science course in high school (and done reasonably well in it) or have done some science in college, unless your interest is in the Maritime Semester. With the exception of that program track, which is history oriented, Sea Semester is heavily biased toward science. Oceanography accounts for ten of the seventeen credits you will earn by completing the program. You also need a handful of references, including one from a nonacademic source. Finally, after essays and transcripts, you have to have a personal interview with an alum of the program. This is actually really helpful for you, since it's the only way to clear up any of your misapprehensions, as well as a way to get some real insights into the program.

Whitney Museum Independent Study Program

384 Broadway, 4th Floor
New York, NY 10013
(212) 431-1737

Contact person: Edie Locke
Program length: full academic
    year

Cost: $1,800
Financial aid: available
Housing: none provided
Age range of participants: 18 and up
Number of participants: approximately 30

Admissions requirements: artists: 15–20 slides; 2 letters of recommendation. Museum studies: writing sample; 2 recommendations
Application due date: April 1
Program location: New York City

The Whitney program was devised to give art history students and studio artists a chance to work and study together in the belief that such a combination will promote a better understanding of the complete art world. The program attempts to eliminate the mystery between artist and critic and to allow each a glimpse of the other. The program is analytical, and participants spend a great deal of time exploring critical and cultural theory within the art world. Program staff cautions that one must be prepared for the intellectualization of art. Called a "think-tank year" by one of its administrators, this is not a program that fosters production of art, rather it is a year of fostering thought. Yet all agree that the creative stimulus thus provided has enormous value for the future. The Whitney program draws upon a wealth of guest lecturers, many of whom are well known artists and critics.

While the Whitney program is intellectually directed, it does offer practical experience. Museum studies participants have the opportunity to arrange a show that will hang in the Whitney or at one of its branches during the course of their year. Whitney students take care of all the details, from locating crucial paintings to the opening night. It is a tremendous experience for anyone interested in museum work. Studio artists and photographers receive studio space at the program's Broadway location for a full twelve months and so are able to enjoy a most stimulating environment.

The Whitney program offers a unique opportunity for serious artists and museum studies students to combine forces, thus gaining a stronger sense of each other and of the art world as a whole.

The Williams-Mystic Program
Mystic Seaport, Inc.
Mystic, CT 06355
(203) 572-0711, ext. 359
Contact person: Ellen Anderson
Program length: fall or spring semester
Cost: $7,950
Financial aid: can carry it from home institution
Housing: 4 student houses
Age range of participants: college sophomore and up—must be in college to do the program; cannot have graduated.

Number of participants per program: 21
Application procedure: essays; interview; transcript; 2 faculty recommendations
Application due date: February 10 for early decision; April 10 for regular decision. These dates apply to *both* semesters.
Program location: Mystic, Connecticut

Set on the grounds of the Mystic Seaport Museum, the Williams-Mystic Program in Maritime Studies offers an exciting way to spend an academic semester. The Maritime Studies program is an interdisciplinary approach to the sea and our nation. At Williams-Mystic, students study the relationship between America and the sea. Each student takes the following courses: Literature of the Sea, American Maritime History, Marine Policy, and either Oceanography or Marine Ecology. The point of the Williams-Mystic Program is to provide its students with a "whole" education in which the courses complement one another, and in which discovery in one field carries over into the others. One alum says of the interdisciplinary nature of this program: "Trying to keep up with four unrelated courses back here at college makes me appreciate the integrated academics of Mystic. It is definitely a much more successful way to get an education."

Courses are taught by outstanding teachers, most affiliated with Williams College or with one of the other sponsoring schools: Amherst, Bates, Bowdoin, Colby, Colgate, Connecticut College, Dartmouth, Hamilton, Middlebury, Mount Holyoke, Oberlin, Smith, Trinity, Tufts, Union College, Vassar, Wellesley, Wesleyan, or Wheaton. Professors from other universities also teach their specialties at the Mystic program. At this point, it is important to note that while the above schools sponsor the program, you do not need to attend these schools in order to participate. Anyone enrolled in college is eligible. Classes at Mystic are small, and the student-teacher ratio is 3:1. The twenty-one students take their maritime history class together and then break into sections for the other classes. The classes encourage open dialogue and lots of exploration. One alum says of the Marine Ecology course: "I've rarely come away from a course feeling like I learned how to look at things, how to think, or how to solve problems in a better way than I knew before . . . this class was one of, if not the, most profound learning experience of my life." While the classroom experience at Mystic is wonderful, it is greatly enhanced by the program's experiential component. The program uses the facilities of the Seaport Museum brilliantly to teach its coursework. Students spend two afternoons a week involved at the museum in a course called Maritime activities. Here students become part of the living history that the museum is famous for by apprenticing as a boat builder, learning celestial navigation, working as a guide on the ships, or learning to sail. Students can also expect to spend time working with the "living exhibit," a squad of actors who wander the museum grounds playing out scenes from life in a coastal town or on a sailing vessel during the nineteenth century. Yet, perhaps the biggest chunk of experiential education is done away from the museum—offshore during a two-week-long research cruise on a schooner. All twenty-one students, the entire program, spend two weeks together with faculty engaged in scientific research while they cook, stand watch, and sail the vessel. Most students select the trip as the high point of their semester. The trip serves to bind the twenty-one students and put them in touch with their studies in ways previously unrealized. As one graduate says: "The trip was definitely one of the most memorable aspects of the entire semester! We all got to know each other better and were able to understand more about the people who went to sea in the literature we read and the history we studied. Although I don't think we are all intrepid sailors now, the trip accomplished so much by putting us in touch with what we learned."

Perhaps one of the greatest aspects of the program is how quickly students absorb so much. One student recalled taking her parents through the museum during parents' weekend. She was amazed at how much she could tell them about American maritime history and said: "I hadn't even realized how much I'd learned. Somehow I would open my mouth and just know it." The Williams-Mystic Program gives its students the opportunity to "live and breathe" the ocean for a semester. It will provide you with a rigorous academic program, embellished by a unique experiential component that will excite and enlighten. This is a great way to spend a semester, studying and experiencing a new world, without leaving the old one entirely.

Cooking Schools

The New England Culinary Institute
250 Main Street
RR #1, Box 1255
Montpelier, Vermont 05602
(802) 223-6324
Contact person: Ellen McShane, director of admissions
Program length: 2-year degree program
Cost: $12,400 per year: possible stipends for internships
Financial aid: available
Housing; available

Age range of participants: 18 and up
Number of participants: 112 per session
Application process: essay; two recommendations; interview encouraged
Application due date: rolling admissions
Program location: Montpelier, Vermont

The New England Culinary Institute describes itself as a "two-year comprehensive, hands-on, production-based chefs' training program." And by all accounts they deliver what they promise. The institute strives to combine theory taught in classrooms (with a student-teacher ratio of 7:1) with practical application to the restaurant business. In order to accomplish this the institute owns and runs two restaurants, a catering business, and a bakery, staffed by its students, all in downtown Montpelier. Students are on a rotating schedule that allows them to spend six weeks in each location. During each rotation students experience firsthand the options and problems associated with each of the restaurant environments. This rotation process is augmented by two six-month internships at "real" restaurants. These internships take place during the second half of the first and second years. During their internships students gain the insight that only working in true environments, without the structure of the institute, can provide. Students also receive a stipend during their internships. The stipends usually range from $240 to $320 per month, depending on the location and degree of student expertise.

Students live on campus or in institute-owned housing during their stay in Montpelier. During their internships, students are aided both by the school and their internship employer in the search for housing. Meals obviously take care of themselves most of the time. The institute concentrates on providing students with a solid foundation in gourmet cooking for the restaurant business. As a result the program is fixed and there is little time for experimentation. Students are encouraged to master the basics during their time at the institute and then, in internship or on their own, explore the specialized and creative sides of the business. Anyone who tastes the goods served at their Montpelier restaurants can be guaranteed that there's always something yummy cooking at the institute.

There are many other cooking schools in the United States that accept students for long- and short-term programs. Two worth noting are:

LaMaison Meridien
1252 Peabody Avenue
Memphis, TN 38104
(901) 722-8892
Cost: 10-week basic professional course: $2,950; 40-week grand diploma course: $3,550
Application process: application with fee

Courses are offered at the Memphis Culinary Academy on a ten-week basis for basic professional training; a forty-week program is also available. Students enrolled in the Diplome program will receive practical instruction in the academy's restaurant, Chef, as well as in the teaching kitchen.

Tante Marie's Cooking School
271 Francisco Street
San Francisco, CA 94133
(415) 788-6699
Cost: 3-month certificate: $4,600; 6-month certificate: $8,500; 9-month certificate: $12,000

Tante Marie's offers a nine-month course, with beginning, intermediate, and advanced segments, each three months long. The program includes the daily preparation of a complete meal.

Academic Programs
Abroad

◇ ◇ ◇

On the pages that follow you will find just the merest hint of the wealth of academic opportunities available outside the United States. Two references mentioned in the Bibliography, *The International Schools Directory 1989* and *Academic Year Abroad*, contain comprehensive listings respectively of secondary school and PG and college programs abroad.

Make sure you have read and understood what it takes to go abroad (see Before You Go, p. 21). The programs described below are going to have some connection to the academic institution you are leaving, either because these programs are academic or because you are making an academic connection between them yourself—in other words, you're looking for credit. Make sure you've done your homework to ensure that connection exists *and* continues after you leave here for there.

The same considerations are in force for "there." As you examine the programs abroad that you're interested in, give careful consideration to what they are asking of you. For example, college-level programs particularly often have a requirement for orientation time. This demand ranges from a meeting or two on the home campus of the program to a semester in residence on that campus.

SOME WARNINGS ABOUT OVERSEAS PROGRAMS

With exceptions—and that's an admonition that applies to all comments below—American programs abroad tend to fall into three categories:

A. Specific school programs. These programs are restricted to a school's own students or to in-state residents. If you attend the college or university that runs the program, fine. If not, you probably need to keep shopping—or move to that state, if the program is operated by a state institution. Many schools that run overseas programs will demand that you apply and be accepted in order to attend the program, yet the admitting institution realizes you won't be staying once the program is over. You may be admitted as a special student. But this is an issue to be considered and to raise with your home institution.

B. Programs with significant requirements. This condition covers the majority of extant programs. By requirements, we mean grade point average (usually at least 2.5, but more likely 2.75 to 3.0) and, if relevant and possible, some language facility. Depending on the program, this latter condition usually means about two years of college-level study of the language of your chosen country. You'll probably need to have some college standing, i.e., to be an undergraduate of record, and most likely you'll have to be at least a sophomore. If you don't meet all qualifications but can pass at least the GPA and the language requirements with ease, you may be able to work something out.

C. Programs with minimal or no requirements. You probably can find a program that will allow you to go abroad even if you are without a foreign language, without a sufficient GPA, and without the appropriate educational experience. But you may not be able to go where you want, and you may want to examine the program's credentials carefully and ask questions.

As the late Lily Von Klemperer argued in a brief essay entitled "How to Read Study-Abroad Literature" (in *Academic Year Abroad* [New York: Institute for International Education, 1989], p. 358), programs abroad "should reflect quality, selectivity, and effective academic control." The literature for any program should resolve a variety of questions. The more ambiguity, the more suspect the program. For instance, as Ms. Von Klemperer points out, promotional statements like "study at a famous university," "international student body," and "college credit available" seem reasonable. But upon closer examination, each can be misleading. The "famous university" indeed exists, but whether you will be taking classes under its aegis is another question. Schools all over the world rent space to outside groups who have no other affiliation with them. How "international" is the student body? If it includes Americans resident abroad, perhaps not very. Or the school might have a special affiliation with a particular nation or area, so it is international but not diverse. The biggest question is: Will your college acknowledge the coursework you do in this program? "College credit" may be "available," but not to you. Many American colleges and universities are quite choosy about accepting credit from other institutions. So check with your school before finalizing any application procedure. The bottom line is this; If you read through the literature of any program and come away without knowing exactly where it is, where you will be living and with whom, what it will cost in dollars and cents, what you will get out of it and how you will get it, how you get in and, by implication, the logic of those requirements, and who you can write and call, preferably in the United States—if you can't find out all that, then be wary. Yes, there are exceptions; yes, some programs are so other-worldly as to eschew such detail, but therein lie risks that you must be prepared to take. The word *prepared* here is the important one.

TRANSFERABILITY

Does your program have transferability with your college? Are you going to go off for a semester or a year and find out on your return that what you did is unrecognized by your college? And while we're at it, how are you leaving your college? Will they recognize the program and simply regard you as taking time elsewhere but still enrolled? Will they give you a leave of absence? Or do you have to reapply upon your return? These are important questions, and ones you must consider—which means you need to confront the dean of students office and/or the registrar and/or the off-campus programs office (or whatever it's called) before you act.

STUDYING IN THE UNITED KINGDOM

"Because admission to universities in England and Wales is highly competitive, and because many American students are not interested in [degree work there] . . . private entrepreneurs have developed a number of special programs which cater to American students. Some are located in university towns, and imply that they are affiliated with, or part of, a regular English or Welsh university. A student who is considering enrollment in one of these programs should take special care in making arrangements for transfer of credit with a U.S. institution prior to making any financial commitment. If at all possible, the arrangements for transfer of credit should be confirmed in writing by the U.S. college official involved. [From James S. Frey, "Education in England and Wales," in *Transitions Abroad*, vol. 3, no. 2 (winter 1979), pp. 8ff.]

NOTIFICATION DATE

While you're looking at deadlines, find out when the program says they will notify you of acceptance. If you're in college, your school is going to want to know whether you're returning for fall or spring or the year at a certain time. Your school is going to want a deposit. And they're not going to wait for Program X to notify you. This information is not readily available, although we have noted it whenever possible. You may have to call the program to find out. Don't hesitate; it could be financially important to you later on.

GETTING THE FACTS ON YOUR PROGRAM—AND YOUR DESTINATION

We've gone through all the bureaucratic niceties above, so everything seems great, right? Bulgaria, here we come. Wait a minute. What courses will you be able to take in Bulgaria? Where will you live in Bulgaria? Is that living situation guaranteed? What about extras? Do you pay for room and board or just your coursework through the program? How those charges are broken down can become important when you arrive in your promised land. So let's take a few minutes and consider all this carefully.

A. What are the course offerings like? Where are they offered? Who are the offerers? Are you going to Bulgaria to be taught by Americans brought there by your program to teach you? That might be just what you want, but if it isn't, you should know about it in advance. Are the course offerings structured or wide ranging? Are they offered at Bulgaria U. with Bulgarian students, or do you have your own little school just for you and yours? Again, you may want that: a place where you can be in class with other Americans. But at least find out in advance. Don't be surprised.

B. Where will you be living in Bulgaria? For example, if you want to live with a Bulgarian family, a "homestay" as it's called, is that a guaranteed situation, or simply a possibility? What kind of family are we talking about? Sometimes, family is a codeword for elderly widow. And if it's a dorm they're promising, is it an international one, a residence, or one simply for the Americans in the program? Do you have a choice? Can you choose to find your own housing? These are questions you shouldn't be afraid to ask.

C. What about all the extras, the museum visits, the excursions, the meals out, etc? If your program cost is said to be inclusive, then it should cover all or at least most of these extras. If it doesn't, then you should be aware of what it does cover, and what you're getting for that amount. Otherwise, you might find that you're expected to go each day to the Bulgarian National Museum for class—and each day you'll have to pay admission to get in.

TRAVELING ABROAD

Okay, you've decided you want to go to Bulgaria. You've taken one unit of the language and found it learnable, if difficult. You also found the country appealing in lots of ways, not the least of which being the Bulgarians' fondness for Americans. Now you need to learn what you must do to get to Bulgaria: the paper paraphernalia (passports, visas, green cards, etc.); what you must take—in your head and on your back, and where you're going to live, study, or work when you get there.

(1) Paper paraphernalia: You already know you will need a passport. Keep in mind that it will cost you about $50 (including the cost of the

passport photos you will need to include—and have a few extra made; they're useful for other applications also), and that the earlier you apply the more quickly you'll have that little folder in hand. Most post offices will take your application. Call your local post office and inquire. And bring your birth certificate, the real one, not a photostat.

Next, call the Bulgarian embassy in Washington. Tell the information officer what you intend to do in Bulgaria and ask whether you need a visa, a green card, etc., and how to go about getting those things. Chances are they will send you a packet of information; chances also are that you won't need a visa for a short visit, but will for a longer one.

VISAS

What we didn't say earlier is that all we're talking about here is a stamp or marking on your passport. This "endorsement" probably will cost you money, but it should be funds well invested. What it means is "[y]ou are now cleared to visit the country for a specified purpose within a limited time frame: a two-month tourist visa to Bulgaria, for example, or a 90-day business visa to Thailand." As Albert Beerbower advises in *Transitions Abroad* (May/June 1986), make sure you (1) allow lots of time for application—weeks, not days; (2) order extra passport photos in case the visa-issuing authority requires them; (3) request a copy of *Visa Requirements of Foreign Governments* from Superintendent of Documents, U.S. Government Printing Office, Washington, DC 20402, or check your phone book under visa services for a local firm that would do your work for you.

(2) What you must take: Here's a list of things to think about: medical care, climate and its extremes, what the culture you're entering is like, what university life in Bulgaria is like. Do everything you can to understand and appreciate Bulgarian culture—and that of the other nations to which you expect to be traveling. Find out what are acceptable forms of address, hand gestures, body language, ways to be a guest (and ways not to be). As Alice Edwards has pointed out, "Learning foreign etiquette is actually a lifelong pursuit. Every country has its own rules of etiquette, which can seem confusing or even ridiculous by American standards." If you are a bit reserved and restrained in the beginning—and if you politely ask questions about customs you don't understand—"you'll begin to feel like a citizen of the world."

3. Working abroad. Although most of what appears above obviously applies to this category also, it's fair to say that if you want to work abroad you need to take a variety of other issues into account also. First and most important is whether you'll be allowed to work in your chosen country. In other words, can you get a work permit? Unfortunately, for most Americans in most countries, the answer is likely to be no, particularly if you want to

work for longer than a few months. The alternative is to work illegally, and even the pursuit of that alternative will lead you only toward domestic service or tutoring in English. Obviously, the latter possibility also demands fluency in the language of your adopted country. In any event, be sure to look into the issue of a work permit, so you're not caught unprepared.

MONEY

This is a big issue, because you never have as much as you need or want, and chances are you will never be quite sure what yours or theirs is worth, since every currency's value changes daily relative to other currencies. For that reason, among others, you want to do as little currency exchanging as possible. It will save you money. And what should you be exchanging? Probably traveler's checks. They're easily obtainable (if you belong to any of several domestic organizations, like AAA, obtaining traveler's checks will cost you nothing. Ask around); they're relatively theft-proof; and they are easily cashed. But there will be a fee involved, so cash the larger denominations first, once you've established a pattern of spending. Do the latter in local cash: it's cheaper for you and, if you keep the exchange rate firmly in mind or have an instrument that will tell you, it's a lot easier.

Academic Study Abroad
402 Main Street
Box 38
Armonk, NY
(914) 273-2250
Program length: summer
Cost: varies by program; summer programs average between $2,600 and $5,000
Financial aid: none
Housing: provided, except in case of St. Clare's College; homestays possible

Age range of participants: 16 and up
Number of participants: varies by program
Application process: preliminary application to ASA, with fee; usually transcript and/or essay; teacher's recommendation
Application due date: May 27 for summer
Program locations: United States, Italy, Spain, France, England, Germany

Academic Study Abroad actually is an umbrella agency that serves to direct students either to its own programs in the United States and Europe (see p. 62) or to place students in an independent international college, St. Clare's, located in Oxford, England (see p. 118). Descriptions of the individual programs follow, but it is possible to characterize ASA in the following terms: individual attention; a variety of programs with a bias toward humanities, contemporary studies, and the arts; a combination of academic instruction and acculturation via homestays in non–English-speaking countries. ASA's programs offer extended work in art and art history; the chance to study for a semester or a year in Britain, France, Germany or Spain; and opportunities for high school students to spend a year abroad or to experience college during the summer on the Amherst College campus. None of these programs are inexpensive but all have in common qualified instruction in favored surroundings.

Academic Year Abroad

17 Jansen Road
New Paltz, NY 12561
(914) 255-8103
Program length: semester; year
Cost: $2,000–$2,500 per semester; $3,100–3,500 per year for tuition and academic fees; all other costs are extra and vary by program locale.
Financial aid: arranged through parent college or university
Housing: assistance given in finding accommodations; homestays possible in most locations; otherwise dormitory or pensions; some locations also offer au pair or language instruction as ways to defer cost of room and board

Age range of participants: college sophomores and up; noncollege students may also be accepted
Number of participants: varies by program
Application process: preliminary application from ASA; transcript; letter of recommendation; fee deposit; all programs require either language fluency or significant investment in learning language before entrance into local universities or programs
Application due date: rolling admissions
Program location: Milan and Siena, Italy; Paris, France; Madrid, Spain

Organized twenty-eight years ago. AYA has managed to preserve its family image despite competition from other more bureaucratic and imposing study-abroad programs. It has a small population; it works with one or two universities in each of its sites; and it offers a great deal of flexibility in both curricular and extracurricular arrangements. Be aware that some of that flexibility and some of those arrangements will be left up to you, with help from the AYA representative on site. The key here is relative language fluency. AYA is designed to plug you into the mainstream of the country and city of your choice. Once engaged, AYA then expects to help you utilize your language skill plus whatever willingness, interests, and talents you possess. AYA is willing to accept the less fluent, but its requirement is that those students begin with an intensive language program.

All this makes more sense when AYA's program is understood. First of all, each applicant joins a university or school program built around expressed interests. Since European universities do not offer courses in applied or "technological" subjects, in the performing arts, or in practical subjects like cinematography or photography, American students studying abroad usually are denied these options. AYA tries to facilitate learning in any area of interest (there are additional charges for nonacademic or, more properly, nonuniversity, placements). AYA is able to do this in its various locations principally because it serves essentially as facilitator or funnel for its clientele. Even cooking and fashion design are not beyond its purview.

The other area of notable flexibility in AYA's program is their approach to accommodations. Yes, depending on the site, you will be partially responsible for whatever accommodations you secure. That has its good and bad sides. Frustration is probably the most obvious negative. And that's avoidable in some sites and for those who can afford to rent single rooms or dormitory space. For those watching their budgets, AYA's lack of structure—and the frustration factor—increases. In Paris, au pair situations are available, particularly for women; in Siena and Milan, English-language instruction may be the currency you exchange for some portion of the rent. Such options are less likely to exist in Spain, where legal restrictions hamper any kind of employment by foreigners.

The final aspect of AYA's role as facilitator focuses on their enhancement of your time abroad. For a fixed fee, either $350 for the semester or $650 for the year, you can be included in the range of cultural activities to which the AYA on-site director subscribes. "You can go to La Scala to hear *Aida*, and it's great even if you don't love opera," noted one ex-student. In fact, AYA makes available similar excursions to the Louvre, to the Uffizi; in short, to the vastness of culture available in the city of your choice. There are two distinct advantages apparent in the AYA program. Initially, the program is small enough to hear your voice distinctly. That capacity may be irrelevant if AYA's sites or programs are unattractive, but the ability to negotiate a program, and even influence your destined residence, can be a great advantage. Secondly, AYA offers opportunities beyond the traditional university pattern. For those fluent enough to take advantage of them, the opportunities may be unequaled.

Aegean Center for the Fine Arts

Paros, Cyclades, Greece
365C Silverside Road, Suite 155
Wilmington, DE 19810
(302) 478-7694
Fax (on Paros): 011-30-284-23287
Contact person: Chris Anderson
Program length: fall program from September 15 to December 8, spring from April 1 to June 23
Cost: tuition is $4,500 for 12 weeks, for both fall and spring semesters; $2,000 for summer; application fee is $25; lodging, $8–$25 per day; food about the same as lodging; travel about $800 round trip from eastern United States
Financial aid: two scholarships may be available.
Housing: available; from homestays to luxury hotels
Age range of participants: 18 and up

Number of participants: varies
Application process: application
with fee; essay
Application due date: rolling
admissions; space guaranteed
upon remission of full tuition

Program location: Tuscany, Italy,
and Greece in fall; Greece in
spring

If the opportunity to study the visual arts and creative writing on an island caressed by the sun is appealing to you, your interest should be piqued by the Aegean Center for the Fine Arts. Located on the island of Paros in the Cyclades archipelago, the Aegean Center makes what amounts to an experiential facility of visual splendor open to artists and writers of every skill level.

As one alum of the program noted, teaching at the center isn't really teaching; it's "kind of one-on-one tutoring. During the four months I spent there, there were never more than six students in residence." There are some requirements: an art history lecture, a regular weekly meeting. There are organized classes: a life drawing class that attracts its subjects from the community and even from neighboring islands. But most of all, there is someone to help if help is needed, and then time and your own space. "One great thing about it was my own studio space."

No matter how low the student-teacher ratio, a program is only as valuable as the level of teaching available. What qualifies the Aegean Center? "John [Pack, the director] is just fantastic. He makes the place really operate well—and he's an incredible photographer." In fact, as alumni will note, it is the professional skills of the teachers, their own artistic work, that keeps them going. Hence the exceptionally low ratio of students to teachers; and the very positive response of students to the program the Aegean Center offers.

One reason the Aegean Center's faculty must depend on the success of their own artistic endeavors—in addition to the issue of credibility—is the simple fact that the program is remarkably inexpensive. Tuition is quite reasonable, and as alumni have observed, it's very cheap to live on Paros. The Aegean Center's literature quotes a range of room expenses; in fact, for anyone who tries, "You can easily live on less than eight dollars a day, at least for your room. I rented a house with a friend. I mean, it was two rooms, rather sparse, and we had a gas-operated stove and a hose for a shower. But it was fine—and much cheaper than two hundred and forty dollars a month. And food was probably eight dollars a day or a little less."

In 1990, the Aegean Center added to its repertoire by creating a fall offering that combined the beauty of Paros with another kind of landscape: the hills of Tuscany. Now, each fall, you have the opportunity to spend the first month of your time at the Aegean Center at a sixteenth-century villa near Florence. After that month, with the visions it creates, you then travel to Paros to complete your time with the Aegean Center. And, lest this not be considered the bargain its predecessor was, your tuition includes travel and room and board in Italy.

What's the downside to this program? For one thing, self-motivation is crucial. You have to want to do photography, printmaking, painting, sculpture—or investigate art history with an inclination toward the classical and Byzantine periods. And you have to be willing to do work by yourself. This is not a program based on a classroom and group dynamic as might exist in a traditional school setting. Perhaps the best way to characterize the Aegean Center is that it is a program that expects its students to capitalize on its inspirational setting rather than be lulled by it.

American Field Studies Intercultural Programs

313 East 43d Street
New York, NY 10017
(212) 949-9379 or 1-800-AFS-INFO
Contact person: Kristin Duckett, program information coordinator
Program length: summer, semester, and full-year options
Cost: $2,300–$5,400; summer: $2,495–$3,295; semester: $3,995; full year: $4,900–$5,395
Financial aid: available
Housing: homestays
Age range of participants: high school, 9th–12th grades
Number of participants per program: students individually placed

Application process: must be between 15 and 18 years of age when departing from this country; minimum 2.6 GPA; interview; essay; an objective test; parent statement; medical exam
Application due dates: summer programs: April 1; fall semester: April 1; spring semester: November 15, or September 15 for January departure
Program locations: 70 countries worldwide

AFS has been arranging high school student exchanges worldwide since 1949. It places students from the United States in homestay situations in more than seventy countries around the world. No language requirement is necessary, only the desire to experience another culture completely. Students can expect to live with a family and attend the local school, and will learn the language faster than they would have thought possible. No generalizations can be made about AFS due to the individual nature of the experience, but the program guarantees that its participants will gain a deeper understanding of another culture while having the experience of a lifetime.

Alexander Muss High School in Israel

3950 Biscayne Boulevard
Miami, FL 33137
(305) 576-3286 or 1-800-327-5980
Contact person: admission staff
Program location: Israel

Program length: 8 weeks, offered throughout the year
Cost: $2,925–$5,000
Financial aid: available
Housing: dormitory

Age range of participants: high
school, 11th and 12th grades
Number of participants per
session: 216
Application process: application;
essay; interview

Application due date: rolling
admission until 6 weeks to
departure

This opportunity is designed specifically for Americans who want to do something a little different. At Alexander Muss you will take classes taught by American teachers who now make Israel their home. Your main course will be a survey of history, and you will study it with teachers four to five hours a day, three days a week. "The teachers were great. They become the characters in history you are studying. They're are kinda [sic] like tour guides."—"Great access to your teachers . . . warm, approachable, knowledge-able profs." You also will continue with those other subjects that you were studying at home; the rest of the academic day is reserved for work on them.

Perhaps the most valuable part of the Alexander Muss experience comes on the other days of the week, designated "field days." These days are spent traveling to points of historic interest, where teachers give classes based on the historical significance of the surroundings. "The kind of program that takes you one step at a time through history. You study history in class then go out and see it with your own eyes the next day. It really is proof that seeing is believing." Students also get an early taste of dormitory living, of sharing space and spending twenty-four hours a day with peers, and they learn a great deal at the same time. "You don't just go to class; you live with the people in your class." As for the experience? Not only is it the kind of "learning experience that will help you get through college," it also produces the "kind of friends you'll have forever." As one student remarked, "I had high expectations and they were totally fulfilled."

American Association of Overseas Studies (AAOS)

158 West 81st Street, #112
New York, NY 10024
(212) 724-0804 or 1-800-EDU-
BRIT
Contact person: Janet Kollek
Evans, director
Program length: year, semester,
summer
Cost: varies by program; semester
from $8,500
Financial aid: help in organizing
loans
Housing: dormitory or apartment
living
Age range of participants: high
school and college, 16–21

Number of participants: varies
according to program:
summer: 30; year and semester:
individual placement
Application process: application
form; 1 or 2 letters of
recommendation; transcript (for
fall and spring programs only)
Application due date: rolling
admissions
Program locations: England,
Israel, France, Germany, Italy,
or Spain

The American Academy of Overseas Studies offers a wide range of opportunities for high school and college students interested in studying and having an internship abroad. Founded by Janet Kollek Evans, the AAOS is a unique conglomerate of options, including summer classes and internships in film, semester-length or yearlong study programs, and yearlong or summer internships in a variety of fields in one of six countries. The primary goal of AAOS is to offer students an experiential view of a foreign culture via internships, such as those below.

FEATURE FILM PROJECT

The Feature Film Project presents a unique opportunity for students wishing to learn more about television and movie producing. This is a six-week summer program in which students receive training in the technical side of filmmaking—including lighting, camera work, and sound—by actually being involved in producing a forty-five-minute film. "We wrote the screenplay, did the casting, filmed and edited [the] . . . movie." Students will work in studios and on location with professional screenwriters, directors, actors, and crew. They will be faced with, and asked to help solve, the problems that regularly occur in moving a story from script to finished film.

Feature Film participants will be housed in dormitories at the Imperial Medical College at London University and will be supervised by Janet Kollek Evans and her staff. The group also takes several day trips around England and a three-day tour of Wales or Scotland. Students also are given tours of points of interest in London.

While the fee is high, $4,672 not including airfare, students on this project gain the opportunity to work on a film from beginning to end. When they're finished, their film will be "in the can." Whether the structure of the project itself carries the promise it seems to contain is a matter of opinion. One parent noted, "Iffy . . . disorganized, and kids didn't have enough to do. [My daughter] didn't learn what she thought she would." However, this from the daughter: "I loved it. . . . It was a great educational experience and a great social experience all in one. I worked on the film from nine to five, then had my evenings free."

INTERNATIONAL INTERNSHIP NETWORK

The International Internship Network is a chance for students interested in an internship—usually with no stipend included—to secure a placement in Spain, Germany, Italy, Israel, or France. AAOS will place postgraduate or college-age students in internships in fashion, film, finance, law, art, and winemaking. Students are placed on an individual basis according to their particular needs and time frame. It is important to note that housing is *not* provided by the AAOS. Students are responsible for securing their own housing and meals.

FALL, SPRING, OR YEARLONG STUDY IN LONDON

AAOS will place students in either London's City University or Middlesex Polytechnic, where they can experience the British tutorial system. Students will be housed in the dormitories of the college they attend. These placements are done on an individual basis. Therefore, AAOS will not be placing students in Americans-only programs, as is the case for many other year- and semester-abroad programs.

"It was fantastic, the best thing I've ever done."—"I took great courses, like the History of London and Theatre Criticism. Both were great, because you would have a lecture and then go there, either to the theater or the historical landmark and see what you had just studied."—"I really became humble—I went thinking that the U.S. was the greatest. I learned a lot about the American and European Economic Community. My experience changed my viewpoint for the better."—"I realized how arrogant the U.S. is about education. We need to learn other things, things that Europeans are already studying, like foreign languages, in order to compete."—"The teachers were excellent: small classes, and really got to speak in class and got to know the professors. I got a lot more out of class."

The American College of Greece: Deree College

Office of Admissions
6 Gravias Street
GR-153 42 Aghia Paraskevi
Athens, Greece
011-30-6393250-9
Program length: year
Cost: varies; approximately
  $10,000
Financial aid: available
Housing: none
Age range of participants: college

Number of participants: varies
Application process: application
  with fee; secondary school
  transcript and diploma; 3
  teachers' recommendations;
  medical certificate
Application due dates: fall, July
  10; winter, December 15;
  spring, January 10; summer
  May 15
Program location: Athens, Greece

The American College of Greece, or Deree College, poses an interesting option for an interim opportunity—or for a year of credit toward a degree in business administration, Hellenic studies, or liberal arts. The college is affiliated with the New England Association of Schools and Colleges, eliminating some of the concern about credit transfer. The school itself is a truly international place, with students in attendance from thirty-five countries. If Greece is appealing, and a postgraduate year or a year away from the sameness of American higher education is an attractive alternative, Deree might be a consideration for you. You will need a visa, and you must arrange your own accommodations, although the college is willing to help you.

American College of Switzerland

Leysin, Switzerland
c/o American College of
   Switzerland U.S. Admissions
   Office
Henderson Carriage Building
2067 Massachusetts Avenue
Cambridge, MA 02140
(617) 354-8048
Program length: year, semester,
   summer
Cost: approximately $9,000 per
   semester, including room and
   board; approximately $7,500 for
   tuition alone; a minimum of
   $3,800 for summer session of 6
   weeks

Financial aid: available
Housing: available
Age range of participants: college
Number of participants: 300 plus
Application process: application;
   fee; transcript(s);
   recommendation; test scores;
   autobiographical essay
Application due date: rolling
   admissions
Program location: Leysin,
   Switzerland

Yes, this is an "American College." It offers courses taught in English; it has an American clientele. Yes, this is an international college. It is located in Switzerland; it has a significant international population. In fact, Americans are in the minority, representing only 30 percent of the student population. "I have friends from all over the world now that I still keep in touch with." In other words, the American College of Switzerland offers an international environment with the course and academic structure of an American college superimposed upon it. It is also located in a spectacular setting outside Geneva, close to both French and Italian borders. One former student said it was "the most beautiful place I've ever seen." Finally, the American College is an accredited institution, therefore open to interchange with American colleges in the United States. Students acclaim the faculty: "Great professors"; and many note the advantage of school in the midst of history. "A lot of what you learn you can actually go and see. My art history class was incredible for that reason."

If all of this sounds attractive, it certainly is, for someone who wants to study abroad for a summer, a semester, a year or more, without some of the orientation and enrollment difficulties posed by some other study-abroad programs. Particularly if Switzerland and a truly international peer group are desirable options, the American College is worth considering. "The people were the neatest. . . . I met kids who had to leave Iran because of the war and could never go back. Their stories were incredible."

However, there are limitations here. The liberal arts program is traditional: languages include only French, German, and Spanish; the litany of social sciences and humanities is a brief one. But there is particular breadth (and degree offerings) in business administration and management; in art and art history; in international political studies. What is important here, really, is a "holistic" view. This is education infused by a truly international spirit: through interaction with an international faculty, surrounded by students from forty-eight countries, in a cosmopolitan setting. Finally, the school takes advantage of its location in politically neutral Switzerland and of its international flavor to import a series of notable visitors to speak to and mingle with the student body. The school also gives its students some unusual independence. "I learned a lot about myself here. Basically I was on my own. Unless I chose to call home, I was [in a new and different place]. . . . I really felt I had a lot of control [over me and my future]."

The application process compares with that of any American college. Its advantages over some of its competitors is that the American College of Switzerland accepts applicants purely on the basis of their applications, without preference to residence or affiliation with another educational institution.

The American Institute for Foreign Study

102 Greenwich Avenue
Greenwich, CT 06830
(203) 869-9090 or 1-800-727-AIFS
Program length: semester, year
Cost: varies by program
Financial aid: minimal
Housing: usually homestays or dormitory
Age range of participants: high school, PG, college

Number of participants: varies by program
Admission process: call AIFS for details of individual programs
Program locations: semester and year programs in England, China, Ireland, Austria, Spain, France, and Italy; travel tours worldwide

So you want to go abroad. But you're not sure where, and you're not sure for how long. Some days you think you want to go away for a full year and become fluent in a language, and other days a three-week travel tour to foreign points seems just right. You're in a quandary, all right. Who could possibly offer all these opportunities? Well, chances are you can stop your quest right here. AIFS has programs in all shapes and sizes in its portfolio. Students can go abroad for two weeks to a year on any number of programs and travel tours offered by the organization.

AIFS is one of the biggest names in exchanges and student travel in the United States, and it got that way by taking meticulous care of its students and by offering a wide range of opportunities. Since the specifics for each program are very detailed, it is best to call for their catalogue to find the program that best meets your needs. You can be guaranteed that AIFS has something for everyone.

Some general notes about AIFS programs: Students on AIFS's semester and full-year programs will be placed in existing courses at the host university. You will not be segregated into an Americans-only learning environment. In addition, AIFS does its best to provide you with a support system in your new environment. An AIFS course director will be present to help you with any issue or problem you might have. With AIFS you can be guaranteed cultural immersion, not just a trip visiting another country. In the words of one alum, "My time with AIFS in France gave me a fuller and richer understanding of French the language and France the country. I didn't just visit France, I lived it."

The American Institute of Musical Studies

3500 Maple Avenue, Suite 120
Lockbox 22
Dallas, TX 75219-3901
(214) 528-9234
Program length: summer: July 15 to August 21
Cost: varies; approximately $4,900–$5,400 plus airfare and evening meals
Financial aid: available
Housing: provided
Age range of participants: college; graduate students

Number of participants: varies by program
Application process: application with fee; audition with specified repertoire; audition/interview questionnaire with fee; knowledge of conversational German advisable
Application due date: rolling admissions until June 1
Program location: Graz, Austria

The American Institute of Musical studies is a vehicle for exposing fledgling vocalists and instrumentalists to a training program with professional standards. In Graz, a music center in Austria second only to Vienna, AIMS has put together an outstanding group of teachers dedicated to providing coursework and concert experience for young performers. If you want to sing professionally, if you want to perform in an orchestra, then AIMS might be right for you.

To find out, you must be accepted, and the process isn't an easy one. Hundreds audition each year for the opportunity. Financial aid is available, but first you have to qualify. However, given the fact that nineteen thousand Americans graduate each year from American universities with degrees in voice, the AIMS program might provide a signal advantage. It's worth investigating if you feel you're talented enough to compete and interested enough in attending such a program to apply.

American International Youth Student Exchange Program

200 Round Hill Road
Tiburon, CA 94920
(415) 499-7669 or 1-800-327-9187
Contact person: Francella T. Hall, director
Program length: year, semester, summer

Cost: $3,500–4,000 for year; $3,300 for semester; $1,400–$1,695 for summer—includes airfare
Financial aid: available
Housing: homestays

Age range of participants: high school, 14–19 years old; will take PG

Number of participants: 240 each year

Application procedure: 3.0 GPA, 2.5 for summer; 4 letters of recommendation; essay; transcript; certificate of health; 4 passport photos; medical and liability insurance

Application due dates: April 10 or by special arrangement

Program location: worldwide

AIYSEP is a nonprofit organization founded by Dr. Walter Hall, a professor at the University of the Pacific Dental School, during a sabbatical year in Spain. It was his intention to create a homestay exchange that would allow American kids to go to Europe as well as bring European children to the States. Students live with host families and go to local schools. The emphasis of this program is on the cultural information exchanged by immersion in a different society.

Students placed in countries where the first language is not English need to have at least three years of language study in the host country's language. The Halls, who still oversee the program, believe that proficiency in the language is necessary in order to gain the best possible experience and to assure that the credit earned in overseas schools will be accepted at the student's home school. Students live with families, and both the student and the family go through a lengthy application and selection process. AIYSEP tries to find host families who will be active in the community and provide students with a solid living arrangement. As a result, host families are required to submit a detailed application form and to supply at least four letters of recommendation, including one from an employer and one from their church. Furthermore, AIYSEP counselors visit the home and speak with the family in most cases. It is important to note here that host families are not paid, and take in students merely because they want to share their country with an American. The Halls attempt to prepare their students carefully for what life in a foreign country will be like. Each student and host family receive a AIYSEP manual that outlines what both parties can expect. It includes sections on culture shock, on the school exchange, on currency and costs, as well as basic information, such as what kind of clothes to bring. The guide also contains a set of rules that AIYSEP requires both host families and students to adhere to, such as their "no driving" rule: AIYSEP students are forbidden to drive cars while on the program. In addition to the written material supplied, AIYSEP makes every attempt to let students and host families know what life with AIYSEP will be like through an organized orientation program.

AIYSEP offers a high school exchange program in a foreign country at an exceptionally good price, since host families are not paid and students attend public schools. Thus, for the money, it is tough to get this sort of experience anywhere else.

TIME OUT

The American Scandinavian Foundation
Exchange Division
7127 East 73d Street
New York, NY 10021
(212) 879-9779
The American Scandinavian Foundation's Exchange Division acts
as a clearinghouse for programs in the Scandinavian countries:
Denmark, Finland, Norway, Iceland, and Sweden. They publish a
guide called *Study in Scandinavia*, which you can get for free by
writing to the above address. In this guide, they provide important
details about opportunities for studying in the Scandinavian countries. If you are interested in that region of the world, this is a
publication you shouldn't miss!

American University Study Abroad Program

Dunblane House
Tenley Campus
4400 Massachusetts Avenue, NW
Washington, DC 20016-8083
(202) 895-4900
Contact person: director of
international programs
Program length: semester
Cost: $6,753 (not including a
program fee of $2,000)
Financial aid: available
Housing: homestays or dormitory
Age range of participants: college
Number of participants: 500 per
semester

Application process: 2 letters of
recommendation if GPA below
2.7; transcript; application form
Application due date: spring:
October 15; fall: February 15;
but admissions policy is flexible
Program locations: London,
Brussels, Madrid, Buenos
Aries, Rome, Vienna, Beijing,
and Crakow

The American University Study Abroad Programs are best described as a
seminar in the life and culture of another country. AU programs get you
to explore the country you are studying through fascinating tours and lectures from resident experts. In the words of one AU Abroad alum: "Speakers were chosen from a wide variety of topics which helped us get a good
impression of the country ... they were experts in their fields and were
always open to questions from the class. I personally found them enriching."
On each program, students are required to take an intensive language
course. They also take two courses designed to give them an in-depth look
at the culture and history of the country they are visiting. For their fourth
course students are placed in an internship that is arranged by AU or design
their own independent study project, such as studying the foreign policy of
one national leader or the school system in one region of the host country
(study projects are used in countries where internships are not possible,

such as Beijing). The internship and study projects are designed to get students involved. One alum sums up the program in this way: "The overall program was an incredible learning experience . . . not just from books, but simply by being there—traveling and seeing the evolution of history through art and culture."

Arts of London and Florence

Associated Colleges of the Midwest
18 South Michigan Avenue, Suite 1010
Chicago, IL 60603
(312) 263-5000
Contact person: program associate
Program length: semester
Cost: approximately $2,100 for program plus a minimum based on semester tuitions at member colleges or own college, whichever is higher; participants must pay living expenses and transportation costs: $2,200–$2,500
Financial aid: if available from home institution
Housing: available

Age range of participants: advanced college sophomores; junior and seniors
Number of participants: 50 (25 begin in London; 25 begin in Florence)
Application process: application with fee; transcript; 3 recommendations, 2 from faculty in areas pertinent to the program's academic content; parental consent form
Application due dates: March 15 for early decision: October 15, final deadline
Program locations: England and Italy

How else to marry the richness of London's museums and galleries, theaters and architecture, with the constancy of the Italian Renaissance, as preserved in today's Florence, but to visit both? Through this program, you will spend eight weeks in each city, studying the culture of each with the assistance of resident faculty. The arts will be your focus: theater, film, literature, architecture, music, and the plastic and graphic arts. Certainly, these two cultures are rich in both; clearly, the issue of cross-cultural fertilization is a subtext.

In addition, you may arrive in Italy early and polish up your Italian, so the introduction to that language provided by the program will enhance rather than awaken you to its beauty. (Also available through Associated Colleges of the Midwest is a fall semester in Italy, their Florence program. This program provides a reasonable complement to London/Florence.)

An intriguing feature of this program is the homestay while in Florence. There, you will be housed with families, with whom you will take breakfast and supper. For this reason, ACM strongly advises you to have some exposure to Italian before undertaking this adventure. The program's emphasis also suggests a fluency in the subject matter, "the languages" of the arts. While previous coursework is not required, not only will its presence in your background enhance your rewards in the program, it also will strengthen your chances of of acceptance.

Academic Study Abroad Summer Programs

402 Main Street
Box 38
Armonk, NY 10504
(914) 273-2250
Contact person: program director
Program length: summer
Cost: varies by program; average summer fees from $2,400 to $4,500, exclusive of travel and incidental costs
Financial aid: none

Housing: provided
Age range of participants: high school, PG: 15–20; ages vary by program to some extent
Number of participants: 20 and up
Application process: preliminary application to ASA, with fee
Application due date: May 27
Program locations: Italy, Spain, France, England, Germany, United States

ASA's summer programs stretch from Amherst, Massachusetts, to Venice, Italy, and include everything from SAT preparation to professional internships in Great Britain. If there is a single bias about these programs, it is toward the academic. All contain some classroom time. Even the London Research Internship Program puts its interns in the classroom for the first twelve days of the seven-week program. At the same time, almost every program contains a significant hands-on element. Whether pointed at art history, at British culture and society, at learning a language (French, Spanish, or German), at a performing art, or at SAT preparation, each program endeavors to get its students out of the classroom and into family living, outdoor sports, or the life of the performing arts. It is this balance that seems to make ASA's programs successful. "Learning French from real French people in the chateau was so exciting."—"The dance and theater program teachers were fantastic. . . . The courses were amazing. I learned so much and I really liked the group of incredibly different people in the program."—"My internship this summer gave me the chance to see the way English actors perform and the way they view their art. . . . I highly recommend this internship to anyone interested in an acting career."—"A great learning experience and the opportunity to meet other interesting people. Prior to reaching Oxford, I feared the program would be too rigorous and too restrictive. However, the program was superb. It was well run, well organized, intellectually stimulating, and, most of all, thoroughly enjoyable."

Ben-Gurion University of the Negev Oveseas Study Program

c/o American Associates of Ben-Gurion University of the Negev
342 Madison Avenue, Suite 1924
New York, NY 10173
(212) 687-7721

Contact person: director of admissions
Program length: semester, year, summer

Cost: tuition for semester is
$1,700; for year, $3,000;
Ulpan (Hebrew Language
Training), $500 or $600;
dormitory is $550 for semester
or $1,000 for year
Financial aid: available
Housing: available
Age range of participants: PG and
up

Number of participants: varies by
program
Application process: application
with fee; transcript; teachers'
recommendations; medical
examination report
Application due dates: May 10 for
fall or year; November 30 for
spring; April 30 for summer
Program location: Israel

Whether one spends the summer or a semester or a year at Ben-Gurion University, the experience is likely to be different in several ways from anything that might be experienced on another university campus. First of all, the two campuses of the university exist in the Negev, in what was two decades ago a desert world worthy of Lawrence of Arabia. Secondly, especially for those students whose backgrounds might lead them to Israel, Ben-Gurion "offers more to the student who has 'seen' Israel and now wants to 'live' it."

Anyone interested in the Mideast, in life in the desert, in archeology, or in more traditional collegiate programs in an unusual setting could find Ben-Gurion a welcome place. Courses in the Overseas Study Program are offered in English. The summer field course in archeology makes use of the extraordinarily rich environment in which Ben-Gurion is located. The university utilizes a site known as Tel Nizzana, which dates from the third century B.C.

The British American Educational Foundation

351 East 65th Street
New York, NY 10021
(212) 772-3890
Contact person: Steve Bauer
Program length: full academic
year or two years
Cost: 9,000 pounds sterling,
approximately
$20,000–$25,000, including
transportation, at current rate
of exchange (excludes airfare
and two monthlong vacation
periods at Christmas and
Easter)
Financial aid: available
Housing: dormitory

Age range of participants: high
school PG year; must be no
older than 18 when starting
program; programs also
available for high school
sophomores and seniors
Number of participants: up to 65
placements per year
Application process: interview;
letters of recommendations;
transcript; essay; financial-aid
form if needed
Application due date: rolling
admissions
Program location: public schools
throughout Great Britain

The British American Educational Foundation (BAEF) offers American high school graduates the chance to spend one year between high school and college studying at a British public (which in England means private) secondary school. Students enter the English system in the final year of the five-year secondary-school program. Once abroad, students can expect to spend their classroom time specializing in two or three subjects as opposed to the broad overview of academics characteristic of American high schools. Much of the time in class will be spent listening to lectures. There's less emphasis in the British system on discussion. But there's a great deal of emphasis on individual thinking and analysis. So plan on writing a lot of papers. "I worked hard . . . it's very much what you want to make of it. There's not a strong support system as in American prep schools. The masters are there to get the best results possible on A levels and O levels. They aren't there for learning for the sake of education. It's very success oriented. . . . Masters weren't willing to stray from the syllabus to examine an issue more closely. Professors have a finite amount of time and needed to get the students to know the important facts."—"The experience is unique and individual and it depends what you want out of it. If you want to work hard then you will have to be prepared to grind it out. There will be a lot of writing. Their exams are all essay."

BAEF places Americans in over fifty different schools. The precise placement is determined by a mandatory interview with a BAEF alumnus, after which applicants are matched with schools. What BAEF tries to do is to select the right school for each successful applicant, based on fields of interest and personality.

Because of the placement issue, BAEF stresses the importance of the interview and has a network of alums to cover all areas of the country. Once abroad, students live in the same dorms as their English counterparts. It is unusual for more than three Americans to be placed at the same school during the same year. Therefore, each American can be guaranteed his or her own experience in the British system.

BAEF offers students looking for a leap year between high school and college a tremendous opportunity to broaden their horizons both academically and experientially. "I'm most certainly glad I did it. It was a tremendous growing experience and it really helped put the past seventeen years in perspective. It helped fill out my viewpoint." The experience won't be all tea and crumpets: One student noted that the British had lots of opinions about Americans, not all good ones. "It was expected that I would be flamboyant about money, loud, and obnoxious. Their values are different than ours. I unwittingly contributed to that notion because I arrived with my Macintosh computer, and the idea of high school students having personal computers still hasn't hit England. They took it as a show of wealth. I also arrived with a boom box, which they thought was unnecessary. You have to be constantly aware of their predispositions."—"It's best to be reserved and try to decipher what social duties and decorum is expected of you. . . . Do not be timid. No one will seek you out. You have to be willing to get involved." The program offers the chance for an independent venture in a structured surrounding. A rare find!

Butterfield & Robinson Academic Programs

70 Bond Street
Toronto, Ontario
Canada M5B 1X3
(416) 864-0541
Contact person: staff
Program length: summer, 4 1/2–5 weeks
Cost: $2,700–$3,100
Financial aid: none
Housing: dormitory or homestays, depending on the program
Age range of participants: high school, 10th–12th grades
Number of participants per program: 139, divided into groups of 10–12

Application process: application form; deposit; at least 2 years intensive French or Spanish, depending on language program, or in the case of the art program, one senior-level art class; teacher recommendation form.
Application due date: rolling admissions
Program locations: France, Spain, Italy, England

Butterfield & Robinson is famous for its travel tours, which combine athletics with travel. So it's not surprising that it has an academic travel program as well. B&R offers two French programs (a school-based program for students who have had two years of high school French, and a homestay program for students who have completed three years of French), a Spanish-language homestay program, an Italian art school program, and an academic study program in England. Ever careful of details, B&R goes to the source of a particular subject for the inspiration of the student. What could be more inspiring to a student than to study art surrounded by all the wealth of Italian art and history, or to study English literature in Cambridge, England? And just like B&R's travel tours, the academic programs provide terrific attention to detail. Students live in carefully scrutinized settings. Whether homestays or dormitories—you can be sure the accommodations will be more than comfortable. Regardless of the specific program, the classes you take will be small in size but intensive in focus and in length—about three to five hours per day. Students uniformly rave about the staff. In the words of one: "All of the teachers were fabulous . . . I learned more in those five weeks than in five years of high school!" And while academic work is a major part of the program, B&R students are also treated to exciting outings and trips in traditional B&R fashion. Students can expect to visit several cities, points of interest, and museums during their time with B&R.

Center for Arabic Study Abroad
CASA, DH-20
Near Eastern Languages and
   Civilization
University of Washington
Seattle, WA 98195
(206) 543-8982
Program length: summer, year
Cost: summer: $500; full year:
   $1,500
Financial aid: none
Housing: provided
Age range of participants: upper-
   division college
   undergraduates; graduate
   students; professors
Number of participants: varies by
   program
Application process: application
   with fee; 2 years of college
   Arabic; written proficiency test
   in literary Arabic; enrollment
   in an academic program or
   teaching one; a physical
   examination; transcript;
   teachers' recommendations
Application due date: May 15 for
   summer and year
Program location: Cairo, Egypt

CASA works with the American University in Cairo to provide a means for American scholars to pursue their studies abroad. Actual offerings at the American University stretch across the breadth of Near Eastern studies, with the common link, of course, being Arabic. Thus, students involved in Near Eastern studies can utilize this program to spend time in the region of their concentration without enormous expense. Funding includes airfare, a maintenance allowance for room and board, and tuition at the American University. Although this is a specialized opportunity, its appeal is self-evident to the qualified.

Centre for Medieval and Renaissance Studies
St. Michael's Hall
Shoe Lane
Oxford OX1 2DP, England
44 + 0865 + 241071
Program length: semester; summer
Cost: $6,500 per semester, board
   not included; $2,800 for
   summer, board not included
Financial aid: none
Housing: provided; board
   estimates are approximately
   $65 per week
Age range of participants: college
   and up
Number of participants: 50 per
   semester
Application process: application
   with fee; transcript; 2 letters
   of recommendation from faculty
   members
Application due date: rolling
   admissions
Program location: Oxford,
   England

The center provides overseas students with access to some of the facilities of Oxford University and to relevant courses and faculty. The strength of the center is that it offers either specialized study in medieval and Renaissance culture via small classes or the Oxford tutorial system. This latter method is little known in the United States. It consists of an independent course of reading with regular meetings with one's tutor to discuss those readings and assigned work done on the basis of them. Students are then free to attend the open lectures on relevant subjects that are a regular part of the Oxford system. Finally, the Centre also offers what are called integral courses; these courses, placed at the beginning of the fall and end of the spring semester, provide background information on the Middle Ages and conclusory information about the Renaissance. Each course has lectures and/or seminars as its focus, with reading, term papers, and examinations as methods of closure.

If all the above sounds weighty, it is meant to. The Centre's academic program is designed for thoughtful overseas students who want to complete part of their education at Oxford but without a more formal affiliation with the university. The other side of this picture is involvement with the social life of the university. Students at the Centre are free to enjoy the privileges of Keble College, including meals in Hall, use of the junior common room and the sporting facilities, and privileges in various undergraduate clubs and societies.

If Oxford University has tempted you, affiliation with the Centre for Medieval and Renaissance Studies is one avenue to satisfying that interest. If you have a fascination with the Middle Ages and Renaissance, particularly with the art, archeology, literature, history, philosophy, religion, and politics of the periods, this program may serve you well. Some training in the arts of the periods—work in calligraphy and stained glass particularly—is also available to students at the Centre.

The Centre also functions in the summer, when it offers a more focused program, designed to examine a particular aspect of medieval and Renaissance culture. For instance, in 1989 the summer program looked at Shakespeare and Elizabethan England. With the exception of topic, the program in the summer is the miniature counterpart of the Centre in winter term. Both programs offer a different kind of educational experience.

College Consortium for International Studies

301 Oxford Valley Road
Suite 203
Yardley, PA 19087
(215) 493-4224
Contact person: Dr. Richard
  Greenfield
Program length: semester, full
  academic year
Cost: $3,000–$8,000 per
  semester including airfare;
  cost varies due to location
Financial aid: available
Housing: provided, primarily
  homestay

Age range of participants:
  college sophomore and
  up; graduates welcome
Number of participants per
  program: average size,
  40–50, though in some
  countries there can be as
  few as 2 or as many as 300.
Application process: varies
  from program to program
Application due date: varies
  from program to program
Program location: worldwide

The College Consortium for International Studies is a clearinghouse for the international programs sponsored by a variety of community colleges. The consortium allows its member schools to offer foreign exchanges and be assured of filling the spaces; thus, students can be guaranteed overseas studies at a reasonable cost.

Students in the CCIS programs can take courses in the host language while having their principal instruction in English; if they are proficient, all their coursework can be in the host language.

American students are not segregated from the rest of the university, except where they choose to take courses in English. All classes are taught by the faculty at the host university. Students take four days of classes and are at liberty to travel during the long weekends. As a rule, students live with local families, although they are free to find and fund other arrangements. While CCIS caters to its own member schools, any student at any college is welcome in its programs. It offers a semester in the following countries: China, Colombia, Denmark, Ecuador, England, France, Germany, Ireland, Italy, Mexico, Portugal, Scotland, Spain, and Sweden.

College Europa Study Abroad Program

St. Vincent's College Office
St. John's University
Grand Central and Utopia
  Parkways
Jamaica, NY 11439
(718) 990-6070, extension 6415
Program length: semester
Cost: $8,500; does not include
  airfare
Financial aid: if available from
  home institution
Housing: provided
Age range of participants: college
  sophomore and up

Number of participants: varies
Application process: application
  with fee; transcript; 2 letters
  of recommendation; possible
  interview; brief statement of
  purpose
Application due dates: July 1 for
  fall; December 1 for spring
Program location: Budapest,
  Hungary; with excursions to
  Austria, Italy, and Greece

"[If] what . . . you think of when . . . an Eastern European . . . country is mentioned . . . is that it is cold and bleak, and absolutely no one is happy nor do they have any fun, well, may I be the first to inform you that this is certainly not the case in Budapest, Hungary." With this comment, an alumna of the College Europa program begins a paean to her experience in Hungary. She goes on to laud the accommodations—"very comfortable chalets all in a row"—and the environment—"friendly, peaceful, picturesque." Indeed, this program offers you a chance to study for a semester in an area infamous in legend but increasingly accessible in fact. And not only is Hungary a desirable location but Budapest is one of Europe's most civilized cities. What St. John's has done is to provide a program of study that allows you to pursue courses of study not widely divergent from those at home—courses offered range from art to mathematics to the sciences, social and physical—but to do so in a different place. Thus, you are afforded the advantage of a new experience while gaining as many as eighteen semester hours.

St. John's quarters are located atop a hill overlooking the city, with separate living quarters for every two or three students. Coursework is done on the campus of the Technical University, with library and study facilities available at the Hotel Panorama, the center of student living quarters. Finally, the experience of Hungary is embellished by three weeks traveling through Austria, Italy, and Greece. This segment of the program is integrated into the academic experience by the host professors, some of whom travel with you on this expedition.

College Year in Athens

Catalogues and admissions forms available from: Cornelia Mayer Herzfeld
College Year in Athens, Inc.
1910 East 1st Street
Bloomington, IN 47401-6746
812-336-2841
Applications sent to: Director, College Year in Athens
Box 17176
GR-100 24 Athens, Greece
Program length: year; semester; summer (June 14–August 1)
Cost: year: $13,200; semester $7,700; summer: $2,200

Financial aid: available
Housing: student apartments
Age range of participants: PG, college; summer: anyone 18 or older
Number of participants: varies
Application process: application with fee; transcript; 2 recommendations; certificate of physical and mental health; certification of leave of absence
Application due date: rolling admissions
Program location: Athens, Greece

To study Greek civilization, to live in another culture but with one's peers, to be given credit at home for the whole experience: What better way to spend a year? All of the above are available from the College Year in Athens program—with some qualifications. Clearly, the program does offer Greek civilization in Greece, with a broad range of courses from ancient Greek history to literature and the arts, archeology, and philosophy, to modern Greek and modern Greece, and even the culture and politics of the Middle East. As one young woman remarked, "I was a classics major in college, and this was the combination of everything I'd been studying for three years." But you do not need to be a Greek scholar, ancient or modern, to understand the faculty. Courses are taught in English. In fact, you live in "English," because when your day ends, you return to an apartment shared with other students in the program. "We lived in apartments, which was good because we got to do all our own shopping and really had to interact with the local people." But one alumnus has cautioned: "I would recommend taking modern Greek before going over. It really helps if you know at least some of the language." The program has a well-qualified faculty— "Great academics," says one graduate—an impressive series of excursions to other parts of Greece, all covered by your set fee. "The best part was the field trips. We went everywhere and they really made history come alive. There was just so much to do and see and learn; it was great."

Like most proprietary programs abroad, College Year in Athens cannot guarantee that your work with them will be accepted by your home institution. That's something you need to work out with your college or university before you leave it. But be reassured that College Year in Athens has not only an impressive set of credentials but also a working relationship with DePauw University. However, don't get the idea that you must be in college to attend this program. College Year will accept students who have not yet matriculated, although you may expect your application to receive careful scrutiny, and if you've graduated from college and discover belatedly a fervent interest in ancient culture, you, too, can attend the College Year program. In fact, occasionally, a teacher of Greek or ancient Greece will turn up at the program. The obvious reason: The program offers an excellent course of study in unparalleled setting.

Council on International Educational Exchange
205 East 42d Street
New York, NY 10017
(212) 661-1414
Contact person: staff

The council offers a wide range of opportunities for students interested in work and study abroad. Founded in 1947, CIEE is one of the oldest organizations dedicated to the cause of student exchange and travel. CIEE is an nonprofit organization, and its members must be nonprofit organizations and institutions that conduct, or assist in the conduction of, educational exchange programs. The best way to describe the council and its activities is to say that it is a conduit to opportunities abroad. It is involved in both student and professional exchanges, and it has something for everyone. CIEE acts as a clearinghouse for member undergraduate and graduate university programs in China, the Dominican Republic, France, Indonesia, Japan, Spain, and the USSR. The council also arranges temporary work opportunities abroad and manages a high school exchange program called School Partners Abroad. It arranges professional exchanges and will aid in obtaining internships abroad for interested students. It also provides opportunities for U.S. and foreign youth to take part in International Work Camps. Furthermore, the council publishes several handbooks dedicated to studying and working abroad. These include *The*

Teenager's Guide to Study, Travel, and Adventure Abroad and *Work, Study, Travel Abroad: The Whole World Handbook*. Now, the specifics:

TEMPORARY WORKING ABROAD

Age range: 18–21; must have been a full-time student within the last six months before departure abroad
Cost: $82 registration fee
Application process: application form; reference; proof of student status

HOW IT WORKS:

The council provides the paperwork that enables American students to work in Great Britain, Ireland, France, West Germany, New Zealand, Costa Rica, and Jamaica. Students travel on their own and with the help of the council find jobs and housing in the host country. While the council offers guidance in the search for employment and housing, it is up to the student to secure her/his own placement. The jobs are usually typical American summer jobs, such as waiting tables or working in shops. But the experience of being self-sufficient in a foreign country is a valuable one, and one that few people have known.

Students may work in the following countries during the following times:
Great Britain: any time of year up to three months
Ireland: any time of year up to four months
France: any time of year up to three months
West Germany: June 1 to October 1
Costa Rica: June 1 to October 1
New Zealand: June 1 to October 31
Jamaica: June 1 to October 1

STUDY ABROAD FOR COLLEGE UNDERGRADUATES AND GRADUATES

The council offers twelve different study-abroad options in seven countries. The programs are run by a member institution and often have other member institutions affiliated with them. They are open to any student, and applications and information can be obtained directly from the council. Each program requires a separate application. The member school in charge of the program is responsible for the selection of student participants. Programs are available for semester, summer, and full-year periods of study in China, France, the Dominican Republic, Indonesia, Japan, Spain, and the USSR.

SCHOOL PARTNERS ABROAD

School Partners Abroad is an exchange program that allows high schools in the States to exchange with counterpart schools in South America, Europe, Asia, and the Middle East. A group of ten to fifteen students and a faculty member travel to the foreign counterpart school for a three-week exchange. Students live with families and attend the classes of the counterpart school. The exchange is reversed later in the year. Interested schools should contact the CIEE for more details.

INTERNATIONAL WORK CAMPS

CIEE is involved in placing American and foreign youth in international volunteer work camps in the following countries: Great Britain, Canada, Czechoslovakia, Denmark, France, Germany, Ireland, the Netherlands, Poland, Portugal, Spain, Turkey, and Yugoslavia. For the most part, these work camps take place during the summer months. Participants are housed together and provided with board in exchange for their services on a project that will benefit the host community. Projects have included working with handicapped children in Denmark or organizing a local fiesta in Spain. The projects vary in length but are generally a six- to eight-week commitment.

OTHER SERVICES

Perhaps the greatest service that CIEE provides is information. CIEE publishes several invaluable guides including the *Whole World Handbook* and the *Teenager's Guide to Work, Study and Travel Abroad*. A listing of the entire selection can be obtained by writing to the publications division at the above address. While CIEE does sell many of its guides, it also publishes several free pamphlets that supply important information in a quick way. These, too, are available through the above address.

CIEE provides travel tips and will assist students in "getting the best deals" through their regional offices and publications. Interested students should contact the New York office to find the closest branch.

Finally, CIEE issues the International Student Identity Card, which will allow students to receive special rates on travel, accommodations, restaurants, museums, etc. The ID costs $10 and is well worth the investment. An application for the ID can be obtained by contacting CIEE's student ID division.

Davidson College Junior Year Abroad

Box 1719
Davidson, NC 28036
(704) 892-2250
Program length: semester, year
Cost: varies by program
Financial aid: available through
   home institution
Housing: available
Age range of participants: college
   junior
Number of participants: varies by
   program

Application process: application
   with fee; transcript and essays;
   several recommendations,
   including dean of students
   and relevant faculty (language,
   if applicable, and other subject
   area)
Application due date: February 1
Program locations: India, Mexico,
   Spain, France, Germany

Davidson College is a fine representative of the kind of junior-year-abroad program that gives its participants a chance to live in another culture. The year-abroad programs in Würzburg, Germany, and Montpellier, France, offer you a chance to go to school with your German and French peers, while a resident Davidson faculty member is available for that sometimes necessary contact with home. In contrast, Davidson's Spanish, Mexican, and Indian programs offer introductions to those cultures, with a large portion of language training. However, rather than leave it at that, the Davidson programs in these countries also give you a taste and feel for the culture you're learning about. "When I told people I was going to India, they always said, 'India? Why don't you go someplace fun?' But India proved a thousand times more threatening and more beautiful than 'fun.' I have slept on the beach at Goa, wrestled over scarves with shopkeepers in Jaipur, watched a full moon rise behind the Taj Mahal, and escaped a marriage proposal from a carpet dealer in Kashmir. So when those same people ask me if I would go back, would I do it again, now I say, 'in a heartbeat.' "

These programs are selective; to go to India you must have at least a 2.75 GPA on a 4.0 scale, in addition to lots of recommendations and essays. But it seems to be worth it, from the comments of those who have gone: "It's the best opportunity Davidson offers, the ultimate in a liberal education."—"I gained self-confidence, maturity, perspective. . . . Now I appreciate what a liberal arts education is."

Duke Study in China Program

Asian/Pacific Studies Institute
Duke University
2111 Campus Drive
Durham, NC 27706
(919) 684-2604
Program length: semester (actually
six months; the program
begins in June)
Cost: $10,200
Financial aid: available

Housing: provided
Age range of participants: college
Number of participants: 20–25
Application process: application
with fee; transcript; 2 letters
of recommendation
Application due date: March 1
Program locations: Beijing and
Nanjing, China

If you have had at least one year of college-level Chinese (but not more than three), this program is open to you, and the opportunities of Duke's program—run in association with Washington University of St. Louis and Wesleyan—are significant. Not only can you avail yourself of two separate environments for study, Beijing and Nanjing, you also will finish the semester with a vastly increased proficiency in Chinese. Moreover, at Nanda (the familiar name of Nanjing University), you can take coursework from the resident director, a Duke University faculty member who travels with you. Or, if your Chinese is good enough, you may attend courses offered at Nanda for foreign students. Finally, the semester includes approximately four weeks of educational travel within China.

Educational Academic Year Abroad

1 Memorial Drive
Cambridge, MA 02142
(617) 252-6100 or 1-800-992-9479;
fax: (617) 494-1389
Contact person: Jane Fischbein,
Director of Admissions
Length; semester, year
Cost: approximately $4,500–
$6,500 for semester, $8,350–
$10,000 for year
Financial aid: none
Housing: homestays
Age range of participants: 16–22
Number of participants: 500 per
year

Application process: essay;
transcript with GPA of 2.7 or
better, interview; 2
recommendations; letter to host
family
Application due dates: rolling
admissions until April 15;
must apply by February 15 to be
guaranteed placement in first-
choice country.
Program locations: Australia,
Great Britain, Canada, France,
Germany, Spain, and Sweden

Would you like to spend a year in another country and perhaps learn another language? Yes, but you don't want to lose a year of school, right? Well, you can travel, live abroad, and graduate on time. Educational Foundation provides semester and yearlong homestay study programs in all of the above countries. You can spend up to ten months abroad living with a family and going to a local school. You will learn the language and the culture of your host country and get the chance to meet some wonderful people as well. An alum of the EF program in England said that "the best part was getting to know all the English people who were my own age. I was very shy when I left and after my year with EF I came back much more my own person, much more independent."

While abroad, your day will not be unlike your school day now. You will spend the day in school and spend the afternoon either involved in sports or extracurriculars or doing homework. After dinner with your host family you will spend evenings with homework, TV, or books. While this all seems familiar, remember, you'll be doing it in an unfamiliar place. In fact, you might be surprised by the differences you encounter. One EF alum says: "I went because I was bored with my high school. The courses [abroad] were a lot harder. I took a course called home economics, which surprised me. It had an awful lot more biology and chemistry than I would have thought."

While on EF, you will be placed independently in a town or school. Other Americans are not likely to be nearby, at least not in your school. However, EF does get its other participants together for weekend outings or occasional visits. It is also good to know that EF has an excellent network of area representatives who serve as your guidance counselors away from home. They will be near you in case of emergency or if you just want to talk. And they often plan group activities for EF kids in their area.

EF offers a wonderful way to spend a year abroad. You will continue your high school studies and gain a year that, as one alum says, "is something everyone should do if they have the chance."

European Term in Comparative Urban Studies

Antioch Education Abroad
GLCA Urban Term
Yellow Springs, OH 45387
(513) 767-6366
1-800-445-6743 extension 366
Program length: semester
Cost: $7,500
Financial aid: if available from
  home institution
Housing: provided
Age range of participants: college
  junior

Number of participants: varies
Application process: application
  with fee; transcript; 2
  references; statement discussing
  your background in urban
  studies and your intentions for
  the program, including an
  independent study proposal
Application due date: March 1
Program locations: various cities in
  Yugoslavia, the Netherlands,
  and England

If you're an urban being, this program should be on your agenda. If you believe that the cities of the future must learn from the cities of the present to survive, how better to gain that knowledge than by residing in three major cities in three months? Add to that the requirement that you must come to this program having completed "required readings during the

spring and summer prior to departure, and . . . [having spent] some time
in field observations of American cities, using guidelines and bibliographies
developed for the program." And conclude by noting the requirement that
you complete an individual field research project: How can you leave this
program without a sense of several cultures and the cities within them?

It also is worth noting that you must be prepared for a good deal of
independent work. The Urban Term program is based on the assumption
that you will be able to work on your own for several weeks, developing
your independent project. So, beyond the advantage of exposure, this program also places a premium on maturity and self-motivation.

Exchange Program in China

Office of International Programs,
 LI 84
University at Albany
State University of New York
Albany, NY 12222
(518) 442-3525
Program length: year
Cost: $7,000 in state; $9,600 out
 of state
Financial aid: if available from
 home institution
Housing: provided
Age range of participants: college
 sophomore and up

Number of participants: varies
Application process: application
 with fee; transcript; 3
 recommendations; interview on
 home campus or at Albany;
 admission to SUNY-Albany as
 nondegree student required
Application due date: February 15
Program locations: China:
 Shanghai, Tianjin, Nanjing,
 Beijing; Taiwan: Taipei

You can pass muster for this program if you've had a year of Mandarin
Chinese. However, your chances of enrollment increase markedly if you've
had at least two years of Mandarin "and . . . a course in Chinese civilization
or a survey course in Chinese literature." What makes this program attractive is its breadth of offerings. Dozens of courses at the several universities
accessed by the program are open to you. Obviously, you will have the
chance to perfect your Chinese. In addition, ancient or modern Chinese
literature, ancient or modern Chinese history, and philosophy are available.
Depending on your proficiency in Chinese, the regular curriculum of each
of the member universities is open to you. Perhaps one of the most interesting aspects of this program is the variety of university education itself. You
may consider applying for a space in Beijing, or you may choose among
the variations in city size and style offered by Tianjin, Shanghai, Nanjing,
or even Taipei, Taiwan. In each of these cities, the local university has a
potential space for you. Because you can attend any of these institutions
and can earn twenty-four to thirty credits for the academic year, Albany's
program has some real advantages.

Fall Term in Australia

International Programs Office
Box 2759
Rollins College
Winter Park, FL 32789
Program length: semester, fall
term
Cost: $7,200 ($6,800 for Sydney)
Financial aid: none
Housing: homestays
Age range of participants: college

Number of participants: varies
Applications process: application
with fee; transcript;
professor's recommendation;
dean's statement of
permission; parent consent
form; housing questionnaire
Application due date: March 1
Program locations: Melbourne or
Sydney, Australia

If your head is being turned by the allure of Australia, Rollins's connection with Melbourne and Sydney should be of immediate interest. But if your interest focuses on environmental studies, by all means pay special attention to the Melbourne part of this offering. Built into the Rollins program in Melbourne is a concentrated look at the Australian environment, particularly along the Murray River, running in northern Victoria and southwestern New South Wales. This course features a ten-day excursion to these sites. A similar focus, but without the grandeur of the Murray, is taken by courses in Sydney. Courses, taught by resident faculty, are held at the respective universities, but you will not be in classes with Australian students.

Experiment in International Living
Kipling Road
Brattleboro, VT 05301
(802) 257-7751

The Experiment in International Living has been sending Americans abroad and hosting foreigners in the States since its founding in 1932. This long history of arranging exchanges has provided the Experiment with resources virtually no other exchange organization possesses. The Experiment is most widely known for its high school–and college-age summer and school-year exchanges, in which homestays and language study play an active role. However, the Experiment does much more than that. It has evolved into an organization that counts among its holdings two graduate programs in international studies, college-semester programs in virtually every region of the globe, homestay/language programs in more than twenty countries, grant work throughout the less-privileged portions of the world, and a two- and four-year college program in international studies at its campus in Vermont. As a result of the growth of the Experiment, the offerings available to one interested in foreign exchange or study have increased dramatically. Those opportunities are detailed below. All inquiries may be directed to the address and phone number above.

THE COLLEGE SEMESTER ABROAD

School for International
   Training
Contact person: college
   semester admissions
Program length: semester
Cost: $6,400–$10,500,
   including airfare, full
   room and board; variation
   due to program location
Financial aid: available
Age range of participants:
   college, 19–22
Number of participants: 6–25
   per group

Admissions process: must
   have a 2.5 GPA or better;
   transcript; essays;
   references; $400 deposit
Application due dates: fall
   semester: preliminary
   application due May 15;
   spring semester:
   preliminary application due
   November 15
Program locations: worldwide
   in locations throughout
   Africa, East Asia, Australia,
   South Asia, Europe, and
   Latin America

The College Semester Abroad program is one of the most complete
study-abroad programs offered anywhere. The Experiment combines studying at a local university with homestay opportunities
while allowing the student to identity with a group of Americans.
In fact, the Experiment has evolved a fascinating way of fitting you
into another culture. As one alumna noted: "I loved the way they
structured it. They took you from being totally dependent and
gradually made you totally independent through small, graduated
steps. In the beginning, you spend your time with just Americans
and slowly you move away from that and end up spending the
last month alone on an independent field study. It was a natural
progression to self-sufficiency in another culture."

   The Experiment combines the best of both worlds in its semester
program. There is no segregation of American students in the
programs, and a participant in the semester program can expect
to study at a foreign university in the regular courses offered.
However, this may be the worst part of your experience. It's possible that the academics may be less than challenging. You need to
decide whether that really matters to you. Some reactions from
students: "Academics were not a strong point but it hardly mat-
tered. You are learning so much all the time just by being there.
In fact, it was great to go to school because that was time I could
spend with just other Americans. It was a little bit of a breather in
my day and a really important part."—"The rest of the program
was both wonderful and stressful." Best part of the program: "I
got to go somewhere different and find out how totally enriching
it is to become part of a culture that isn't your own. I know that
sounds like a cliché, but it really was wonderfully neat!" A partici-

pant can also expect to take part in at least one homestay during the semester. "Homestays are great, though it honestly depends on whether or not you get a good family."

Yet, while participants may spend a great part of the program living away from other Americans, they have the comfort of seeing a few familiar faces on campus. An important part of the College Semester Abroad is the intensive language training that takes place during a participant's time abroad. While some of the programs do require a degree of proficiency in the host country's language, one does not have to be fluent in the language of the country one wishes to travel to in order to take part in the wonderful programs offered. In fact, in most cases, the Experiment will take care of teaching the host language by offering intensive classroom and practical language study for all levels of proficiency during the time a student spends abroad. And since the classroom time is reinforced with language use in the homestay (and pretty much everywhere else, too), a participant learns tremendous amounts; and even the worst language student finds him/herself gaining proficiency in the language. It is the sink-or-swim philosophy at its best! "The most amazing thing is the personal growth that happens without your even knowing it. Your eyes get opened to so many things, and the process is so unacademic as we know it. But you are learning so much, and that's what's great."

The academic focus of each program varies according to the specifics of the country, but all include a Life and Culture Seminar; this course is an interdisciplinary look at the basic features of the host country's culture. Students also take part in a seminar entitled Methods and Techniques of Field Study. Here, students examine how to learn more effectively from the broad field setting and prepare for their independent field study. The Independent Field Study is the final component to the academic side of the semester. The Experiment allots four weeks at the end of the semester for students independently to pursue an aspect of the host country that fascinates them. This project can take almost any form. For example, one recent alumna studied the school system in the African country in which she had been living. Another alum investigated role of development organizations in developing countries, using present surroundings as a sample case. Finally, a third alumnus looked at the effects of the resort industry on Thailand's coast.

The College Semester Abroad program offered by the Experiment is a valuable way to experience another country. The program takes care of all the major areas of worry and provides students with a truly enriching experience. If you're interested in a semester abroad, look into this program's offerings. They are impressive.

AU PAIR HOMESTAY ABROAD

Program length: 6, 9, or 12
   months
Cost: $590–$805;
   administrative fees, excluding
   international transportation
Financial aid: none
Housing: homestays
Stipend: available
Age range of participants: 18–
   25
Application process: form;
   interview
Program locations: France,
   Germany, Denmark,
   Great Britain

Au Pair Homestay Abroad is a brand-new Experiment program that takes participants, male or female, and places them with families abroad in exchange for child care. Participants must be willing to deal with children, and in return will have the opportunity to live in a foreign country and experience the language and culture. Participants are paid a salary, and the Experiment has taken great care to make sure that the working situation is monitored and carefully structured. The Experiment does its best to create a good match between au pair and family. If you are interested in an economical and interesting way to experience a different culture, this is an unusual alternative. However, keep in mind the fundamental requirement: You must enjoy children and be prepared for some serious child care. You also should be committed to the idea of homestay and cultural exchange in order to make this work.

Fall Term in Dublin
International Programs Office
Box 2759
Rollins College
Winter Park, FL 32789
Program length: semester, fall
   term
Cost: $6,100
Financial aid: if available from
   home institution
Housing: homestays
Age range of participants: college
   sophomore and up

Number of participants: 20
Application process: application
   with fee; transcript;
   professor's recommendation;
   dean's statement of
   permission; parent consent
   form; housing questionnaire
Application due date: April 1
Program location: Dublin, Ireland

This program is tied to the Irish National Institute of Higher Education (NIHE), although it also incorporates faculty from Trinity College, Dublin, and from the Abbey Theatre. Therefore, not only is this program strong in the areas stressed by NIHE—business, computers, accounting, politics, math—it also offers you a window on the worlds of Irish art, literature, and theater.

Foreign Study/Lacoste

Information and applications from either:

Cleveland Institute of Art
11141 East Boulevard
Cleveland, OH 44106
(216) 421-7338 or (216) 421-7333 (fax)

or:

School of the Arts in France
84710 Lacoste
Vauclose, France
Contact person (at Cleveland Institute): Lisa Goss
Program length: fall semester; summer; spring semester

Cost: varies by program; $6,900 for semester; $3,900 for summer
Financial aid: available
Housing: provided
Age range of participants: 18 and up
Number of participants: varies by program
Application process: application with fee: usually transcript and/or essay; teacher's recommendation
Application due date: rolling admissions
Program location: Lacoste, France

Great art and Provence seem to have something in common. You can appreciate this special ambience if you attend the Cleveland Institute's program in Lacoste, France, a medieval village in the heart of Provence, where students are encouraged to make artistic use of the countryside. Some reactions: "Lacoste is an ideal setting for an art program. For six weeks I was totally immersed in painting and sculpting."—"The Provençal landscape is really Lacoste's painting teacher: its colors, its volumes, the insights it offers to one's perception of the great French landscape painters . . ."—"The school provides a unique place in which to grow tremendously—artistic growth being only the tip of the iceberg. I have made lasting friendships with the people of the village, gone truffle hunting, sculpted stone in a stone quarry . . . I know I will continue to discover little gifts given me this fall, when I fell into stone and came up smiling." What veterans of Lacoste call *la maladie des pierres*, or stone fever, the love of stone, is the effect of living in and working with stone. Students and instructors live in the stone houses of Lacoste and they work in and around them. As you might imagine, this is an intense experience, with classes taught in English but with French language instruction available and encouraged. At Lacoste you will find instruction in drawing, painting, photography, printmaking, and sculpture, along with various humanities offerings. Students may also receive instruction in art history and in poetry, as well as in an intriguing course entitled Self in Art and Nature, a course closely tied to the environs of Lacoste and Provence.

Lest the above suggest otherwise, the experiences of students suggest that Lacoste is a program for fledgling artists as well as for the more expert. "Speaking as someone who had little experience with art before I went to Lacoste, I came away with a whole perspective on the art world—what it is to do art and what it is that other artists have done in the past and why. . . . I'm inspired!"

Friends World College

Plover Lane
Huntington, NY 11743
(516) 549-1102
Program length: semester or year
Cost: varies by location; range
    from $10,000 to $13,500
Financial aid: none
Housing: provided
Age range of participants: high
    school senior; PG; college
Number of participants: varies by
    program

Application process: application
    with fee; usually transcript
    and/or essay; teacher's
    recommendation; personal
    interview
Application due date: rolling
    admissions
Program locations: United States,
    Costa Rica, England, Israel,
    Kenya, India, Japan, China

Unquestionably, this is an unusual college. Friends World College seems devoted to two ideas: personal responsibility for one's education, and an investment in the notion of a truly international community. In order to forward the first notion, FWC has put together a most unusual learning plan. Students split their year or years with FWC. (It is a degree-granting institution, and you can spend your college career there.) Half the time is spent preparing through study to go abroad; half the time is spent in London, England; Jerusalem, Israel; San Jose, Costa Rica; Bangalore, India; Machakos, Kenya; or at the East Asian Center, where the choices include Kyoto, Japan; or Kowloon, Hong Kong; and Jilin. In the latter locations, study—which means not only language but culture—is combined with experiential work. For instance, students might work as English-language teachers; as researchers on scientific problems; as archeologists, farmers, or interns to sophisticated industries in Japan or a European nation. Or students could stay in North America and find themselves doing everything from yoga to following dolphins off the California coast.

The consensus of alumni opinion seems to be that it is the fact of field experience, not its specific location, that creates the chemistry necessary for an unusually productive result. As one visiting student remarked: "I found that Friends World College was the most appropriate vehicle for me to pursue my academic interest in primate research . . . [it] has the freedom and flexibility." This quotation was taken from a student journal—not inappropriately, because the journal is the primary documentation of your experience with FWC and the means by which you are evaluated. This journal is also the manifestation of your grasp on the issue of responsibility for your education. Faculty members serve as resources, to help, to guide, to develop. But it is the student—you—who creates an academic curriculum, travels to a self-selected region of the world to actuate that curriculum, learns a new language, and, through subsequent experiences, gains new perspective on your culture and on the one being visited.

It's possible to take part in FWC for a semester or a year. "Last spring I went on leave from [college] and enrolled for a semester as a visiting student at Friends World College. I spent nine months in Kenya . . . where I was teaching secondary school. I found this to be a tremendously valuable experience. . . . My formal introduction to FWC began with a monthlong orientation program. . . . One of [its] strength[s] . . . was that the other students involved came from a much wider cross section of social, racial, and economic backgrounds than I had found at [my college]. There was a process of mutual consciousness-raising going on in an informal way, and while I didn't always find this easy to handle, it left a deep impression on me. . . . For me another value was that my FWC experience helped me to clarify my career goals . . . through work experience. I think this is an education that concentrates on growing as much as learning."

Global Semester; Semesters in Far or Middle East

Office of International Studies
St. Olaf College
Northfield, MN 55057
(507) 663-3069
Program length: semester
Cost: varies by program
Financial aid: none
Housing: provided
Age range of participants: college
  sophomore and up
Number of participants: 30
Application process: application
  with fee; transcript; essay
  dealing with a personal or
  academic project; essays on
  program you are applying to; 3
  faculty recommendations

Application due date: March 1
Program locations: Middle and
  Far East, including Egypt,
  China (Taiwan), Japan, India,
  Morocco, Turkey, Israel,
  Thailand (specific sites depend
  on program)

St. Olaf's programs take you to several locations in the course of a single semester. For example, in their Global Semester, you will be in residence in Egypt, China, India, and Japan. In each country, you will spend a month studying and working with local experts while a St. Olaf faculty member travels with you. Your focus will vary: art, history, economics, religion, and an investigation into the interconnectedness of these nations with your own.

Or you might choose the Term in the Far East. Here, you will divide your time between Chiang Mai University in Thailand and Soochow University in Taipei, Taiwan. A major emphasis of this program is on cross-cultural studies. Because of the time spent in Thailand, language instruction in Thai and a homestay situation will be available there.

The final choice is the Term in the Middle East. This program takes you to Turkey, Egypt, Israel, and Morocco. In all locations, you will have university affiliation. Here again, the emphasis is cross-cultural, but with a distinctly social and political edge. In addition to the time abroad, you will receive a week's orientation in Washington, D.C., to acquaint you with the current Middle Eastern situation.

These programs are offered in the fall. You must apply directly and have no other requirements concerning admission. Taken together or singly, here are some unusual chances to investigate several cultures from a unique perspective.

Graeco-Roman Program

Office of International Studies
College of St. Benedict—St. John's
  University
Collegeville, MN 56321
(612) 363-3612
Program length: fall semester
Cost: $6,800, including airfare
  from Minneapolis/St. Paul
Financial aid: none
Housing: provided
Age range of participants: college

Number of participants: varies
Application process: application
  with fee of $85; transcript;
  recommendations from
  academic adviser, faculty/staff
  resident, and 1 faculty member;
  interview; 2.5 GPA required
Application due date: February 28
Program locations: Athens,
  Greece, and Rome, Italy

The Graeco-Roman Program is designed to be a multidisciplinary and cross-cultural experience. If that sounds like a mouthful, remember that it simply means the blending of disciplines in such a way that you come away with a true sense of the wholeness of each culture. The classroom portion of this program underscores that goal by providing instruction in art, history, and literature. There is also a lively discussion of the theological underpinnings of Western and Eastern religions.

What makes this instruction particularly valuable is its environment: first the meld of classical past and metropolitan present in Athens; then the Eternal City, Rome, with its classical and Christian past. You will visit both locales, plus make excursions to Istanbul, Turkey, and Florence, Italy. The program permits you to maximize your time in Europe by providing you with a Eurail pass.

The requirement of an interview and attendance at orientation meetings held in the semester previous to departure may make the program difficult to manage for anyone not particularly committed. The orientation meetings are intended to focus interest on the program, with assigned readings and written reports included.

Great Lakes College Association Latin-American Program

Kenyon College
Gambier, OH 43022
(614) 427-4733
Program length: summer,
  semester, year
Cost: $2,100 summer; $4,500
  semester; $8,900 year
Financial aid: available
Housing: provided

Age range of participants: college
Number of participants: 18–50
Application process: application;
  transcript; 2 recommendations
Application due date: rolling
  admissions
Program location: Bogotá,
  Colombia

The GLCA Latin-American program is a working example of another commonplace in education abroad: the branch institution. CEUCA, GLCA's "branch" in Bogotá, has its own resident faculty and staff and acts as a school away from school for GLCA students. In addition, the program makes provision for CEUCA students to take classes at several of the universities in Bogotá. CEUCA offers internships each semester in business, social science, education, journalism, and government service. Recently, those internships included work with *El Tiempo*, a major newspaper, and with a customs agency dealing with exports and imports.

There are many opportunities here, which are further enriched by the fact that students live in homestay situations while in Colombia, taking meals with their host families. CEUCA takes advantage of the cosmopolitan nature of Bogotá by featuring several guest lecturers per semester.

One of the virtues of study in Latin America is the cost, considerably below a comparable term or year in the United States. To qualify for CEUCA you must have had at least two years of college-level Spanish or the equivalent. The summer program will accept beginning Spanish speakers.

Gustavus at Melbourne

Office of International Education
Gustavus Adolphus College
St. Peter, MN 56082
(507) 931-7545
Program length: semester
Cost: $8,000
Financial aid: available from home
  institution
Housing: homestays
Age range of participants: college
  junior or senior

Number of participants: varies
Application process: application
  with fee; transcript; 3 letters
  of recommendation; overall
  GPA of 2.75, and a 3.0 in
  major
Application due dates: March 1
  for fall; October 1 for spring
Program location: Melbourne,
  Australia

Gustavus Adolphus College offers an Australian program with two distinct features: first, the program operates at and with Melbourne University, located at the southeastern tip of Australia. That's almost as far from America as you can get, and a part of Australia with which you might be less familiar than, for instance, Sydney or Perth. The second advantage of this program is its level of integration with the local community—not only do you take courses with students at the university, you also live in homestay situations. So, if the Antipodes are of interest; if a semester studying about Australia strikes your fancy, here's one possibility. See Fall Term in Australia for another (p. 77).

The Hansard Scholars Program

The Hansard Society for
    Parliamentary Government
16 Gower Street
London WC1E 6DP, England
011-01-323-1131
Program length: semester
Cost: $7,000
Financial aid: none
Housing: provided
Age range of participants: college
    and graduate students

Number of participants: varies
Application process: application
    with fee; transcript and essay;
    2 recommendations
Application due date: rolling
    admissions
Program location: London,
    England

The Hansard Society was founded to study and explain parliamentary democracy. Hansard scholars are placed with key members of government and business while simultaneously carrying on academic work through three courses at Birkbeck College of the University of London.

This program becomes doubly relevant on the eve of greater European unification. So, if you're a student of politics, of economics, of any international field, you might be a perfect Hansard scholar. The program is not without cost. In addition to the fee, which covers the program itself and housing, you are responsible for your food and travel. But because of Birkbeck College's association with the University of London, you have access to the facilities of the university, and you can gain full credit for your semester with the Hansard Society. So find out about the woolsack, learn about cabinet government, by sending a semester in London with the Hansard Society.

Institute for Central American Development Studies

Department 826
P.O. Box 025216
Miami, FL 33012-5216

or:

Apartado 32070 Sabañilla
San José, Costa Rica
506-25 05 08

Fax: 506341357
Contact Person: Dr. Sandra
    Kinghorn, director
Program length: semester,
    summer
Cost: $4,000 semester; $2,900
    summer
Financial aid: through parent
    institution

Housing: provided
Age range of participants: college
juniors, seniors, and graduate
students
Number of participants: 10–12 in
each program
Application process: application
with fee; transcript and essay;
3 teachers' recommendations;
parent waiver
Application due dates: April 1 for
summer; June 1 for fall;
November 1 for spring
Program locations: Costa Rica and
Nicaragua

Have you wanted to visit Central America? Do you want to know more than
the newspaper accounts about life in Central America? Are you interested
in furthering your study of the environment, of multinational corporations,
of women's issues, of economic development, of agricultural science?

If you answered yes to any of the above questions, you should look into
ICADS. This nonprofit foundation was set up to make Americans more aware
of the Central American region by focusing on research, study, and analysis
of Central American social and environmental issues. Each semester a variety
of internships in Nicaragua and Costa Rica are offered to ten to twelve students. Those opportunities might include work with family planning, comput-
erizing a banking operation, studying the use of pesticides, working in a rural
health post, organizing workshops to raise women's consciousness by cross-
cultural comparisons, helping to promote ecotourism in a sea turtle nesting
site. Interns work with "highly qualified U.S. and Latin-American academicians
and international professionals." All internships are accompanied by coursework and conclusory research papers, and interns are given intensive training
in Spanish and Hispanic culture before beginning fieldwork. During their
internships, students are housed in homestays; they then return to the institute
for the final two weeks of the semester for completion of their written work.

If this sounds somewhat daunting, it's meant to. ICADS is not a walk on
the beach. The internships are rigorous and very focused. This a program
for students who are interested in the opportunity to "do meaningful academic and practical work." By "meaningful," ICADS seems to be suggesting
that it aims to create in its students a "critical approach with a view to
identifying and overcoming inherent 'first-world' biases." In keeping with
this rigor, the application process is demanding.

Institute for Study Abroad Programs

The University of Wisconsin-
Platteville
1 University Plaza
Platteville, Wisconsin 53818-3099
(608) 342-1726
Program length: semester, year
Cost: varies by program;
approximately $4,800 for a
London semester and $4,000 for
a term in Spain.
Financial aid: where applicable
from home institution
Housing: provided
Age range of participants: college
sophomore and up
Number of participants: varies by
program

Application process: application
with fee; transcript and essay;
teacher's recommendations;
minimum grade point of 2.5
on 4.0 system

Application due dates: April 30
for fall; November 1 for
spring
Program locations: London,
England; Seville, Spain

Wisconsin-Platteville offers two interesting opportunities abroad: a program
in Seville, Spain, and one in London, England. Each possesses its own peculiar advantages. If you choose to go to Spain, you need not be fluent in
Spanish. Most of your coursework will be in English, although you will be
expected to be learning Spanish through the term of your stay. But your
instruction is at the Spanish-American Institute in Seville, not at a Spanish
university. Moreover, although you are placed in a homestay situation by
the program, it, too, is unusual because you will live with a family and
another student. The advantage of this approach is that it reduces your
isolation while encouraging you to speak Spanish.

Meanwhile, the London program also has some unusual characteristics.
Unlike the program described above, it offers a variety of living situations.
And Wisconsin-Platteville's program in England places you in a British college, specifically, Ealing College of Higher Education, where your courses
and curriculum will be those of your British colleagues.

These programs possess one other real advantage: cost. Both offer inexpensive passage to their respective destinations (airfare from Chicago is
included in the London price) and a prepaid package once there that
includes tuition and room and board. You should note that course offerings
at both sites are biased toward literature, contemporary culture, and
business.

Interdisciplinary European Cultural History Program
Office of International Studies
Eastern Michigan University
Ypsilanti, MI 48197
(313) 487-2424
Program length: semester,
summer
Cost: semester $6,450; summer:
$3,000
Financial aid: through student's
home institution

Housing: provided
Age range of participants: college
Number of participants: 40
Application process: application
with fee; transcript and essays;
2 teachers' recommendations
Application due date: rolling
admissions
Program locations: Western and
Eastern Europe

"I truly believe that the European Cultural History Program is the best
European program available anywhere. I have been associated with various
programs, and nowhere else do you learn as much about music, art, history,
and culture, and nowhere else do you learn such independence. The program and its staff inspire the student to travel, to learn languages, and to
appreciate music and art."

The European Cultural History Program offers you a chance to travel throughout Eastern and Western Europe and the Mideast in either a semester of the academic year or during the summer. All trips have a student-faculty ratio of about 10:1, with accredited faculty from various universities, all of whom have experience traveling and teaching in Europe. You probably will begin each day with a lecture, supplemented by less-organized commentary throughout the day as you visit museums, galleries, historic sites, monuments, and other important buildings. As one alum of the program has noted: "Each day offered [so many] enriching activities; I am still astounded by how much was accomplished."

As the director of the program has noted, IECHP takes the "blue-jeans and backpack approach" to the trip. While your mind is nurtured through exposure to the cultural resources of Europe, you will not be faced with the necessity of spending great amounts of money for accommodations and food. Occasionally, you may camp out, and most of your layovers will be in inexpensive hostels and international student centers.

The program's only drawback is the difficulty you might have qualifying for a spot, which requires good academic standing and two faculty recommendations plus a real interest in learning experientially rather than passively.

International Christian Youth Exchange

134 West 26th Street
New York, NY 10001
(212) 206-7307
Contact person: director for
  outbound programs
Program length: 12 months
Cost: approximately $5,000
Financial aid: available
Housing: homestays
Age range of participants: 16–24
  (programs in boldface type
  [see below] will take students
  under 18)
Number of participants per
  program: 120

Application process: application;
  transcript; interview
Application due date: rolling
  admission until March 15;
  college credit available
Program locations: **Australia**,
  Austria, Belgium, Bolivia,
  Brazil, China, **Colombia**, **Costa
  Rica**, **Denmark**, **Finland**, France,
  Germany, **Ghana**, Honduras,
  Iceland, India, **Italy**, **Japan**,
  Kenya, **Korea**, Liberia, **Mexico**,
  New Zealand, Nigeria,
  Norway, Poland, Sierra Leone,
  Sweden, **Switzerland**, Turkey

ICYE was founded at the end of World War II in an effort to close the gulf of hatred created by the war by bringing American and German children together. Protestants and Catholics were among the original founders of ICYE; hence, the "Christian" in the name. Over the years, ICYE has evolved into a nonsectarian organization dedicated to "global peace and understanding." This evolutionary process also has meant an expansion from ICYE's German roots to an organization that moderates exchanges among twenty-eight countries.

ICYE is one of the few programs that takes students at a variety of ages. It is not just a high school exchange; it is not just a thirteenth-year option; it is not just a college program. ICYE is all of those and a placement service for those just out of school as well. ICYE does have an important requirement—that you agree to go for the full twelve-month period. ICYE believes strongly that the best part about going abroad is the opportunity to become totally immersed in another culture. That means living in your destination country a full year, seeing every part of your host family's life: school, vacation, all the seasons, all the holidays. While this may seem stringent, it makes a lot of sense. Because you are there for a full year, you stop being a guest and really get comfortable.

It is important to note that not all countries are available for students under eighteen. In the list above, those countries in boldface type are available to you if you're under eighteen. Another important note is that language proficiency is preferred but not required. ICYE will teach you what you need to know. But the deadlines mentioned above are real ones, so don't miss them. This is a program that requires planning: planning from ICYE in order to make it work and planning from you if you're going to take advantage of it.

What do you do when you get over there? If you are in high school, ICYE will place you in a corresponding school in another country. You will live with a family and spend your days at school. If you are a thirteenth-year student or older, you will spend your year volunteering in an area that interests you. ICYE works closely with Partnership for Service-Learning (see p. 106) to place you in a volunteer position that will be rewarding and challenging. You will live with a family, or in some cases within your service project. This is a great way to experience the culture of another country and help people at the same time.

ICYE offers individuals of all ages a chance to experience life in another country. And the alums rave about this opportunity to learn about themselves and the culture and language of another country. One alum wrote during her trip to Sweden:

> Obviously I've learned a lot of practical things about working with disabled people (something I've never done before), not to mention 100 percent more Swedish than I knew five months ago, but what I value most . . . is the new appreciation of laughter and humor. I was amazed at the quickness laughter came to the students where I work. Faced with some of their difficulties, I'd more readily cry. It's been with groups of Swedish friends, when I was unable to participate in the banter and the teasing, that I missed my friends at home (and English) the most. I was delighted when I recently understood my first pun in Swedish. I didn't quite realize before how much of a cultural, but more importantly, linguistic base humor has.

What does this tell you? First, that ICYE will provide you with an unforgettable year. Second, this organization offers an unusual number of opportunities. If you're looking for a way to broaden your horizons and gain a little insight into yourself and another part of the world, ICYE is worth the effort.

The International Honors Program

The International Honors
  Program
19 Braddock Park
Boston, MA 02116
(617) 267-8612
Contact person: Joan Tiffany,
  director
Program length: year, semester
Cost: year: $18,950 (covers tuition,
  travel, room and board);
  semester option approx.
  $10,000

Financial aid: if available from
  home institution
Housing: provided
Age range of participants: college
Number of participants: 30
Application process: application
  with fee; transcript; two
  essays; two references; parental
  permissions; medical form
Application due date: April 30;
  November 15 for spring
Program location: worldwide

Imagine the opportunity to study in many countries around the globe. Imagine studying a topic you have found compelling but difficult to pursue. Imagine being taught by—and traveling with—world-famous scholars. All of this is possible with the International Honors Program. If accepted, you will become one of the few who have experienced this intensive year of coursework. "So much in the way of new information, new ideas about culture, came my way during the year that it will be a long time before I assimilate all of it." For instance, in 1991–92, IHP will offer Global Ecology—Integrating Nature and Society. This eight-month program will investigate the survival of the ecosphere, beginning with study in England and traveling on to places like Malaysia, New Zealand, and the United States. Since 1990, the program also has been offered to students who wish to begin their studies in the second semester.

The program was designed twenty years ago to provide an education that would match the then brand-new bargain of global air travel. The founders of IHP discovered that a combination of homestays in several local cultures and exposure to individuals and ideas in each of those cultures, with a coherent connection provided by a program theme and core faculty, generated an ideal product. The result? "The year I spent with IHP was the single most important educational experience of the eighteen years I spent in educational institutions."—"On a philosophical and interpersonal level, the year was a Copernican revolution."

Ithaka—Collegiate, Mentor, and Cultural Studies Programs

1692 Massachusetts Avenue
Cambridge, MA 02138
(617) 868-4547
Contact person: director of
  admissions

Program length: semester;
  summer
Cost: $7,500–$9,000 semester;
  $3,000 summer, excluding
  airfare

Financial aid: available
Housing: dormitory
Age range of participants: high
school, PG, and college
Number of participants: 13–17
per program

Application process: transcript;
essay; 1 to 2
recommendations; medical form
Application due date: rolling
admissions
Program location: Crete, Greece

What do you get when you combine intensive academic instruction, small-group learning, a foreign country, and working with locals? The answer is Ithaka, a program that offers a full term of cultural study. Located on the island of Crete, the Ithaka program combines a rigorous academic experience with total immersion in Greek village life. Students on the Ithaka program receive classroom instruction in courses that range from modern Greek—which they need for daily life—to archeology, history, and literature. The program emphasizes applying the knowledge learned in the classroom to day-to-day life in Greece. The student-teacher ratio is an exceptional three students to every faculty member, and the faculty also lives with the students. This constant companionship is essential to creating the sort of atmosphere Ithaka needs in order to make the program work: a close-knit community devoted to constant learning.

There are three programs within the Ithaka structure, each of which varies slightly from the others in its academic focus. The Collegiate Program was designed for college study. High school and PG-year students may choose between the Mentor Program, which focuses more intensely on the archeological wealth of Greece, and the Cultural Studies Program, which provides a broad overview of the culture of Greece. All three options operate from the same philosophical foundation.

An important element to Ithaka is the interaction one enjoys with the Greek community. In this regard, students can expect to spend several mornings a week as apprentices to local families or businesses. Students work side by side with the locals, becoming participants rather than observers in the daily life of the island. This interaction also provides students with an opportunity to sharpen and improve their language and cultural skills. At Ithaka, the classroom extends far beyond the desk and blackboard.

Sundays at Ithaka are reserved for daylong excursions to other islands. Students also take part in a four- to six-day archeological expedition and a six-day trip to Athens to visit points of interest.

Ithaka focuses on the essence of experiential learning. Its location makes it possible for students to interact with a rich academic life and with the cultural surroundings that would make any student understand and "live in Greek."

Kibbutz Aliya Desk
27 West 20th Street
New York, NY 10011
(212) 255-1338 or 1-800-444-
7007
Contact person: director of
outgoing programs
Cost: varies by program, see
below
Age range of participants: 18–
27
Number of participants:
depends on program

Application process: see below
Application due date: see
below
Financial aid: available in all
programs
Housing: provided in all cases
Program locations: various
locations throughout
Israel

The Kibbutz Aliya Desk is a clearinghouse for programs in Israel that combine language training with time spent working on a kibbutz. The Desk offers you several choices for experiencing this unique lifestyle. The kibbutz's distinctiveness has to do with its sense of community. In simplest terms, it is a commune, a place in which every resident has a task or series of tasks, which together allow the community to function. On the kibbutzim spread across Israel, this communitarian approach has worked extremely well. And through the years, years of struggling with often infertile soil and with hazardous conditions, the policy of the kibbutzim has evolved a simple tenet: work to live. As a consequence, whether you visit for a night or a lifetime, you will be given responsibilities. You can expect those responsibilities to continue for six out of every seven days you reside at the kibbutz. You also will be given a place to sleep. The accommodations might be a bit Spartan, but they will not lack the necessities.

THE PROGRAMS:

Kibbutz Ulpan
Program length: 3–6 months
Cost: $145 registration fee;
airfare; an additional $50
at the outset for university
credit
Age range of participants: 18–
35; must be a high school
graduate

Number of participants: 25
Application process:
interview; medical and
psychological exam;
application form
Application due date: rolling
admissions

The Kibbutz Ulpan is a work-study program that allows those interested in learning Hebrew the opportunity to study the language intensely, with half of each workday devoted to studying and the other half working on the kibbutz. This program demands your immersion in the culture of the kibbutz. Needless to say, it also is an effective way to study Hebrew. This isn't a bad trade-off; in return for work, and at minimal cost, you will have an invaluable experience and learn Hebrew.

Short Summer Ulpan on Kibbutz
Program length: 10 weeks during summer
Cost: $145 registration fee; $1,560 (airfare included)
Age range of participants: 18–27
Number of participants: 25
Application process: interview; medical exam; application forms
Application due date: rolling admissions, but before May 1

The Short Summer Ulpan on Kibbutz provides those interested in learning Hebrew with a unique summer opportunity. Participants on this program can spend eight weeks living and working on a kibbutz while they study Hebrew two hours a day. This program then gives its participants the possibility of touring Israel and a week free to travel on their own.

Temporary Workers on Kibbutz
Program length: minimum 1-month commitment required
Cost: $90, plus airfare and insurance
Age range of participants: 18–32
Number of participants per program: varies
Application process: interview; medical exam; application form
Application due date: none

The Temporary Workers program gives interested persons the chance to experience life on a kibbutz. Participants work alongside kibbutz members, and, if the kibbutz agrees, they are free to stay for as long as they like. This is a marvelously inexpensive way to experience life on a kibbutz.

Tel Aviv University Kibbutz Program
Program length: semester or full year
Cost: approximately $4,500 per semester (airfare included)
Age range of participants: 18–27
Number of participants per program: 25
Application process: transcript; interview; medical exam; application forms
Application due dates: May 30 for fall; December 15 for spring
Academic credit: 12–15 credits available

The Tel Aviv University Kibbutz program offers students the chance to live and work on a kibbutz while taking classes at the university two days a week. Participants can expect to work twenty-eight hours a week on the kibbutz and to take part in intensive Hebrew language courses two evenings a week. This program allows its students to live on a kibbutz and to study at the university, an unusual combination of opportunities.

Kibbutz University Semester with Haifa University
Program length: semester, with a full-year option
Cost: $3,290 per semester, airfare included
Age range of participants: must be a full-time undergraduate student
Number of participants per program: 25
Application process: interview; medical exam; application forms; transcript
Application due dates: May 30 for fall; December 15 for spring
Academic credit: up to 23 credit hours available

The Haifa University program differs from the Tel Aviv program; students at Haifa spend the first eight to ten weeks of their stay in Israel working full time on a kibbutz. After the kibbutz, participants go on to Haifa University, where they can choose from any of its course offerings. Once in the university setting, participants live in a dormitory and take part in the university activities, similar in many respects to college life in the United States.

La Sabranenque
Centre International
St. Victor-la-Coste
30290 Laudun
France
011-33 + 66-50-05-05
Contact person: Jacqueline C. Simon
217 High Park Boulevard
Buffalo, NY 14226
(716) 836-8698
Program length: semester, 3 months: September–December; February–May

Cost: $3,700
Financial aid: none
Housing: provided
Age range of participants: 18 and up
Number of participants: 12 per session
Application process: application with fee; transcript and essay; application
Application due date: rolling admissions
Program location: southern France near Avignon

What La Sabranenque represents is total immersion in another culture. While you will be surrounded by other Americans, at La Sabranenque the language of choice, *de rigueur*, is French. So is the atmosphere; so is the environment. By living, studying, and working in the small village of St.-Victor-la-Coste, students of La Sabranenque not only work through intensive courses in French, they also "mix it with [their] . . . lives." Beyond language training, you will also be able to study French history, politics, and culture. And all this training will be in French, a struggle for understanding that you will share with your eleven or twelve classmates.

Undeniably, all this could be done in a classroom in Pittsburgh. The difference here is that once you step outside, you find yourself standing in an eleventh-century hamlet, enclosed in turn by the modern village of St.-Victor-la-Coste, with a population of 1,200. The village's locale, in the winemaking region around Avignon, is medieval in character and timeless in style. This sense of "localness" is at one with La Sabranenque. You not only study but live with your classmates; the staff prepares your meals, and, if you choose, you may also add your labor to those helping to do restoration work. There has been an enormous amount of restoration work connected to but not synonymous with Le Sabranenque. The attempt is to re-create an eleventh-century village, with the modern town located on the plain and the restoring village on the hillside. You may spend two afternoons a week so engaged—but nothing is required. Finally, there are periodic excursions to the sights and sites of southern France. "As remarkable as these two- or three-day van trips were the incredible meals that accompanied them—and, of course, the constancy of our French instruction." One alumnus described La Sabranenque as "a genuine and stimulating immersion in to French, and a broad discovery of life in southern France."

What's more, the price is right. This program is inexpensive, providing all aspects—from room and board to excursions—for the total price of $3,700 for three months. La Sabranenque's value is enhanced further by the personalized attention of the staff and the commitment they foster. "I've never been in a place before in which no one complained about work," said one alum. "Here, people did more homework than was required. I've never heard so many people use the term 'life-changing.' Have you ever been anywhere where people kept a common refrigerator clean—and didn't 'borrow' from others? Well, that was symptomatic of the attitude here." During the summer, the emphasis is on restoration work, although French instruction is available as an option. Vans are available to take you on wine and cheese excursions, to the coast, on unbelievable picnics. Incredible hospitality continues to be the motif of La Sabranenque, but make no mistake about its purpose. If you can tolerate the intensity and focus of this program and the isolation of this rural village, La Sabranenque has unusual promise as an opportunity to absorb another culture. And what more beautiful place to do it than in this setting?

Le College Cevenol

Le Chambon sur Lignon
France
Contact: c/o Moses Brown School
250 Lloyd Avenue
Providence RI 02906
(401) 272-5158
Program length: year, summer
Cost: varies by program
Financial aid: some available
Housing: provided
Age range of participants: 14–20
in school year and summer
school; 17–24 in work camp
Number of participants: 300 in
school year, about 20 percent
of whom are non-French;
summer school of 150; 20
percent non-French; work camp
of 20–30, with 5–8 Americans

Application process: application
with fee; transcript and essay
giving reasons for choosing
College Cevenol; teachers'
recommendations (1
can be from a nonteacher; 1
should be from a French
teacher)
Application due date: May 15
Program location: south-central
France

Located in the mountains of the eastern massif Central, Le College Cevenol hearkens to a tradition that began with its founder during World War II. Through the efforts of Pastor André Trocme and his fellow villagers of Le Chambon, thousands of refugees from Nazism were saved. The college carries on that tradition, noted through its institutional description as an organization aiming "to work for world peace by bringing together people of many origins. Fifteen or twenty countries are usually represented."

This lofty purpose is carried out amid surroundings reminiscent of the woods of Maine or of the northwestern United States. Even as the school was erected in the forest in 1938, its buildings captured that rustic atmosphere. Nor has that been lost in the ensuing fifty years. This is not a campus of the twenty-first century. However, its facilities are adequate to the task: the college has a full sports program, computer terminals, and arts facilities; dormitories are arranged around two or three to a room, and the rooms themselves are equipped with the essentials of bed, chair, chest, and desk for each resident. Don't expect luxuries, despite the fact that the French see the school as relatively privileged. And the environment can be isolating. Le Chambon is a small village, and the area is without a major city. Lyon is the closest city, about two hours away.

Le College Cevenol authorities recommend that non-French entrants take at least two years of French before considering application. Once admitted, students may pursue the international baccalaureate degree, recognized by many institutions of higher learning around the world.

In addition to its school-year program, Le College Cevenol also offers a summer school, with two three-week sessions, and a work camp in which about thirty college-age youth spend their weekends working for the college. Americans are eligible for both programs, with the stipulation that students have at least two years of French preparation before attending either program. "I feel it is the best-integrated school of its kind . . . incredible diversity. Students do come from all over the world. And the college is really good at building a community out of this diversity—that's the legacy of building an international pacifist community . . . without any particular religious or political leanings. Roget Hollard is a particularly charismatic figure who has a real vision of the mission of the school. It's unique in the French system for helping students find out who they are. In each dormitory there is someone who is 'responsible' (and they are called the Responsibles) for the students in that dorm."

The work camp is located on the campus. Its duties might be described as the summer work camp of Le College Cevenol. This population can vary, but it tends be skewed toward a majority of Americans. So it might be fun, but not necessarily great language training.

Le Cordon Bleu, Ecole de Cuisine et de Pâtisserie (School of Cooking and Pastry)

8, rue Leon Delhomme
75015 Paris, France
011-1-48-56-06-06

or:

114 Marylebone Lane
London W1M 6HH, England
011-01-935-3505
Contact person: admissions staff
Program length: 3–15 months; 4–5-day workshops also available
Cost: varies by program; approximately $800 per month

Financial aid: none
Housing: none
Age range of participants: 18 and up
Number of participants per program: class size of 6–8
Application process: application with fee
Application due date: rolling admissions
Program locations: schools in Paris, London

Le Cordon Bleu, for anyone who knows or cares about cooking, is the Harvard of cooking schools. Its chefs' creations are gastronomic delicacies designed to put pounds on the eater. Students here work with the best in the trade (all teachers are renowned for their skill in their field) as they learn the techniques of puff pastry, cream sauces, and perfectly cooked main courses. For the perspective student Le Cordon Bleu offers several course options:
1. The diploma course: three terms of twelve weeks. In the words of Le Cordon Bleu catalogue, "This course is recommended for the student who wishes to become a professional and [the course] provides the best basis for a career in the culinary world." The diploma course consists exclusively of

hands-on learning. Four days out of the week, students work in pairs preparing three-course menus. The final day of the week is reserved for practical work on specialized subjects, such as cream sauces. Students in the course can expect to learn the basics of cooking during the first term, and as the year progresses, graduate into complex preparation and presentation. Clearly, this course is designed for the student who wishes to become an expert chef. Examinations both on paper and in the kitchen are required at the end of each term. Diplomas are awarded only to those who pass. Offered once a year, in September.

2. Intensive diploma course: two terms of twelve weeks. The intensive diploma course is just what it says it is. It takes the diploma course and fits it into two terms. Le Cordon Bleu cautions that this course is very intense and should be attempted only by the most serious students. Offered once a year, in January.

3. Certificate course: one term of twelve weeks. The certificate course is a little bit like a wonderful sampler of cooking and techniques. It is designed "for those who wish to gain recognized qualification in a limited period of time" and is an excellent stepping-stone into the world of culinary arts. As in the diploma course, in the certificate course students spend four days a week preparing three-course menus, while the fifth day is reserved for practical work on specified subjects, such as pâtisserie. This course takes place in January, May, and September and is a wonderful way to hone your skill. By beginning here, you also can see if you might like to cook professionally.

4. Intermediate certificate: one term of twelve weeks. This is for students who are already competent cooks but wish to brush up on certain techniques and "advance their skills." It is important that applicants have a sound knowledge of the basics. Here the day is divided into two sections. The morning is filled with the practical preparation "of three or more dishes" followed by demonstrations and lectures in the afternoon. This course is offered in the spring and fall of each year.

5. Advanced certificate: one term of twelve weeks. This course is designed for individuals with a strong working knowledge of cooking and practical experience as well. This course assumes the basics; you must be prepared. Students can expect the same format as the intermediate certificate course, but with more advanced techniques. This course is almost completely practical in its nature and is offered once a year only, in May.

6. Introductory and advanced courses: four-week terms throughout the year. These courses are for students who want to cook, and cook well, but probably never cook professionally. The introductory course is for students with interest, but not necessarily practice, in the field. This program is intensive and will provide students with a strong working knowledge of the kitchen and food by month's end. The advanced course was designed for individuals who are strong cooks. The emphasis within this course is on seasoning and presentation. Both courses are scheduled so that a menu is prepared each morning, followed by an afternoon of demonstrations and

further practical work. These courses are offered at numerous times throughout the year.

Le Cordon Bleu has something for everyone. No matter what your skill level or time frame, Le Cordon Bleu can meet your needs. It also offers several one-week courses in specific areas throughout the year. And there is no question that at Le Cordon Bleu you'll learn to cook. One graduate of a summer four-week session told us: "I arrived barely knowing how to beat an egg, by the time I left there was little I feared in the kitchen. I spent four weeks cooking and creating every day. I certainly eat better now then before! And while it wasn't always a piece of cake, it was fun." And another graduate that we spoke with, now a professional caterer, speaks highly of the knowledge one gains about food, kitchen chemistry, and how to make it all come together. To her Le Cordon Bleu was "an education in and about food" that continues to serve her well.

The Leo Marchutz School of Painting and Drawing

6, rue Mazarine
13100 Aix-en Provence, France
Program length: semester
Cost: varies by program
Financial aid: none
Housing: available
Age range of participants: PG,
 college
Number of participants: varies

Application process: application
 with fee; usually transcript
 and/or essay; teacher's
 recommendation (see Institute
 for American Universities [p.
 208] for more details on
 admissions procedures)
Application due date: rolling
 admissions
Program location: Aix-en-
 Provence, France

This school is operated by former students of the expressionist artist Leo Marchutz. Following the master, the school is dedicated to teaching in terms of "organic" wholeness—common elements and relationships—in nature, landscape, and architecture rather than technique. "We are more interested in Guardi than Caneletto." One studio, an old caisson factory—"the funkiest place you've even seen"—is the retreat in bad weather. Overall, the Marchutz School looks for students "open to inquiry into the fundamental nature of painting" in the tradition of Marchutz's idol, Cézanne.

Application should be done through the American Institute of Universities. No specific prerequisites exist, other than an interest in exploring and developing one's talent.

Leysin American School in Switzerland

Director of Admissions
1854 Leysin, Switzerland
41-25-34-1361

or:

U.S. Director of Admissions
Leysin American School
Box 4016
Portmouth, NH 03801
(603) 431-7654

Information and applications accepted at either address
Program length: year, summer
Cost: $16,500 year; $1,925 summer
Financial aid: available
Housing: provided
Age range of participants: high school, PG
Number of participants: varies by program

Application process: application with fee; transcript and essay; teachers' recommendations
Application due date: rolling admissions
Program location: Leysin, Switzerland

In addition to its regular high school curriculum, Leysin American School offers a postgraduate year that combines exposure to further preparation for college work with extensive travel and cultural opportunities. "It was a year of total excitement and success for me in the postgraduate program. I had never realized before what a wonderful opportunity schooling is, and after this one year at Leysin, I am ready to take on the challenges of college. I can't say enough about the PG program. With the studies and the travel, it is outstanding."

Leysin's Alpine location also makes it possible for students interested in outdoor sports, and particularly in skiing, to participate with unusual ease. Ski lifts are located only a hundred yards from the front door of the school. The school's location makes learning French a matter of visiting the locale: "Every day I am using the French I am learning in my classes."

The Leysin American School offers a clear alternative to domestic postgraduate programs. Relative advantages of each should be investigated. Leysin also offers a complete summer school program, including two tours, one in France and one in Italy. The school also operates as a four-year high school, with a full curriculum and apparatus for interchange with American college preparation.

Lock Haven International Studies

Office of International Education
Raub Hall Lobby
Lock Haven University
Lock Haven, PA 17745
(717) 893-2140
Contact: Dean Johnston
Program length: semester, year
Cost: varies by program; all tuitions based on in-state rates
Financial aid: none
Housing: provided
Age range of participants: college; sophomore year recommended

Number of participants: varies by program
Application process: application with fee; transcript; 2.5 GPA; 3 recommendations; medical report; interview
Application due date: rolling admissions
Program locations: Australia, England, Germany, Japan, Taiwan, People's Republic of China, Poland, Yugoslavia, Ecuador, Mexico

Lock Haven's programs offer distinct advantages if you're able to meet the requirements of the one that interests you. Several of these programs have language options; few require you to be fluent in the language before you go (the programs in Paderborn, Germany, and some of the options in China—Nanjing and Changsha—advise previous language options; few require you to be fluent in the language before you go (the programs in Paderborn, Germany, and some of the options in China–Nanjing and Changsha—advise previous language training). These programs are designed for sophomores, and their cost basis is in-state tuition for Pennsylvania residents. However, Lock Haven does require you to apply to the Office of International Education as a Lock Haven student, and you will have to make whatever arrangements are necessary with your home institution.

Also interesting are the Lock Haven student-teacher opportunities. For more information about these possibilities, contact the Student Teaching Office, Lock Haven University, Lock Haven, PA 17745, (717) 893-2140

The London Semester

Drew University
Madison, NJ 07940
(201) 408-3438
Contact person: Catherine T.
  Messmer, director of off-
  campus programs
Program length: semester
Cost: approximately $9,000;
  includes a weekly food stipend
Financial aid: available
Housing: provided

Age range of participants: college junior and senior
Number of participants: varies by program
Application process: application; transcript; 1 faculty recommendation
Application due dates: April 15 for fall; November 15 for spring
Program location: London

The Drew University London semester exposes you to the breadth of British literary and/or political culture—and then makes you translate and analyze your impressions through a major research project. If you do the Semester in Modern British Theatre and Literature, you will spend time not only in the theatre but also dealing with the people who represent culture and the arts in Britain.

If your interests lead you toward politics, the London Semester takes you right into British political life. Your faculty include members of Parliament; your work might include hands-on political investigations. For instance, students in this program in 1988 complied data that helped some politicians make strategic decisions in the 1988 general election.

Throughout, you will live in a flat in London. For those used to dormitory living, this is an unforgettable experience.

The London Theatre Program

Department of Theatre
Roger Williams College

Bristol, RI 02809
(401) 253-1040, ext. 3026

Program length: fall semester only
Cost: approximately $6,500
Financial aid: available
Housing: provided
Age range of participants: college and up
Number of participants: 24–36

Application process: application with fee; teachers' recommendations
Application due date: before June 1
Program location: London, England

A quick glance at the number of theatrical performances attended in a typical fall for the London Theatre Program will wake you right up. Would you believe fifty-four? Not to mention numerous trips to a variety of architectural and scenic locales in greater England! The program does all that in addition to a regular schedule of classes and workshops. Thus, you end up with not only a rich experience born of nights at London theatres but also a healthy dose of academia and the credits that go with it. "And we did go to that many and more," declares a former student. "In fact, if you consider the whole program, with all the lecturers from British theatre, our exposure was about ten hours a day." But, as the brochure notes, the program's primary goal is not solely academic. Rather, it is based on the "premise that a student cannot have a complete introduction to the theatre without a balance of studying theatre seriously, doing a great deal of theatre, and seeing fine professional theatre."

To facilitate this purpose, the program secures a small hotel in central London, where you and the program reside. Hence, breakfast *and* classes are at your doorstep, and the theatre district but a few blocks away. Most teaching is done by a permanent staff, but London actors, directors, playwrights, and teachers from the world of British theatre supplement their work.

To attend this program, you need to be intellectually curious, anxious to learn about and experience the theatre in London (where it is more accessible than anywhere else in the world), and be prepared to apply in the spring. This program operates only in the fall. "But it's worth every effort. This is the best thing I've done in four years of college. The people who run it really care about having you experience the theatre—and learn from that experience."

Mediterranean Studies Program

DePauw University
Greencastle, IN 46135-0037
(317) 658-4800; (317) 658-4373
Program length: semester
Cost: approximately $9,000
Financial aid: available
Housing: provided
Age range of participants: college
Number of participants: 20

Application process: application with fee; transcript; 3 faculty recommendations; personal essay; 1 semester of modern Greek preferred; $400 deposit for non-DePauw students.
Application due date: rolling admissions
Program locations: Athens, Greece, and Near East

DePauw sponsors a semester in Greece—with a twist: an opportunity to visit Turkey and Egypt before the conclusion of the semester. The program is operated in conjunction with the College Year in Athens and so makes available to you the various facilities used by CYA (see p. 69). The semester's work is of particular value to those interested in archeological study, classical civilization, and modern Greece and Near Eastern cultures.

Eastern European Program; Vienna Music Program
DePauw also sponsors two programs centered in Austria. The first will take you from Vienna, where for ten weeks you will be studying with faculty from the Austrian Institute of East and South-East European Studies and the Austrian Institute of Education, to Hungary. There you will have four weeks of instruction in the form of a comprehensive seminar conducted by Hungarian faculty. In Austria, you will live in a homestay; in Hungary, in rooms obtained by the university. Coursework will be in English, and a resident director travels from Vienna to Budapest with the group.

If your passion is music, the Vienna program might be perfect for you. It includes instruction with professionals in one of the world's music centers; the opportunity to attend many music performances, including the Viennese State Opera; instruction in German; and participation in other aspects of the musical heritage of Vienna. If you attend this program, you will spend your entire semester in Vienna and you will reside with a Viennese family.

National Registration Center for Study Abroad
823 North 2d Street
Box 1393
Milwaukee, WI 53201
(414) 278-0631
Contact person: admission staff

NRCSA is a wonderful source if you want to learn a language and study abroad. NCRSA offers programs in Austria, Great Britain, Canada, Costa Rica, Ecuador, Germany, France, Italy, Mexico, Portugal, Spain, and Switzerland. Basically the organization acts as a clearinghouse. You apply to it directly; it places you in one of its affiliated universities or language schools, after working out which is best suited to your needs. The great thing about NRCSA is that its programs include opportunities ranging from a few weeks to three years. Because of this variety, however, it's difficult to describe exactly a typical program offering. What you can expect is breadth of choice. Your best option with NRCSA—as with any of the several clearinghouses described in this book—is to ask for references. In this case, just ask NRCSA for the names of several people who went to the school to which you've been assigned. Conversation with them should help clarify the situation for you. Keep in mind that, in most cases, you're likely to be living in a homestay situation, although you can choose to live in an apartment or a hotel. If you need credit for your stay abroad, make sure your home institution accepts NRCSA credit before signing on the dotted line. Don't be caught short.

Open Door Student Exchange

250 Fulton Avenue
Box 71
Hempstead, NY 11551
(516) 486-7330
Contact person: admission staff
Program length: summer, semester, or academic year
Cost: $2,000–$4,000
Financial aid: available
Housing: homestays
Age range of participants: high school, 15–18; PG year
Number of participants per program: varies by location
Application process: written application, including essay; school recommendation; interview; medical report

Application due date: April 15
Program locations: The Americas: Argentina, Bolivia, Brazil, Chile, Colombia, Costa Rica, Ecuador, El Salvador, Guatemala, Honduras, Mexico, Paraguay, Peru, Uruguay. Europe: Czechoslovakia, Denmark, France, Germany, Great Britain, Hungary, Italy, Poland, Romania, Spain, Sweden, Yugoslavia. Middle East: Egypt, Israel. Asia: Australia, Hong Kong, Japan, Philippines, Singapore, Thailand

Open Door Student Exchange has been in the exchange business for twenty-five years. What this means is that you will be connected with a placement chosen by experts. Moreover, the exchange will be what the term was meant to imply. You will not simply visit in another country. Rather, you will be placed in a home as a member of the family, not a guest; you will go to school and learn the language. Open Door believes that the most valuable benefit of living in another country is learning to communicate in the host language. So you can be assured that part of your exchange will be intensive language study. In most cases, Open Door does not require previous language study in the host country's language (French-, German-, and Spanish-speaking countries are the exception), but you are required to have had two years of some foreign language study.

Open Door stresses that your exchange will be about growth and new experiences: from food to entertainment to lifestyle and to a whole new set of cultural rules. Therefore, the most important prerequisite for a successful exchange is your willingness to roll with the punches and respect your host family and its culture. The gains you make during your stay will hold you in good stead for the rest of your life.

The Partnership for Service Learning

815 Second Avenue, Suite 315
New York, NY 10017
(212) 986-0989
Contact person: Linda Chisholm
Program length: semester, year, or
summer
Cost: approximately $3,400 per
semester; $2,900 per summer
Financial aid: available
Housing: dormitory, homestays,
or agency quarters

Age range of participants: college
sophomore and up
Number of participants: 5–15 per
country
Application process: application;
deposit; 2 recommendations
Application due date: 8 weeks
before program begins
Locations: England, Jamaica,
Ecuador, the Philippines,
Liberia

The recipe followed by the Partnership for Service Learning is so brilliant, yet so simple, that you wonder why you haven't heard it before. The Partnership combines academics and volunteer work to provide you with a multidimensional view of whatever society you might end up traveling to. Students on the Partnership program study in local universities while they are assigned simultaneously to a human service agency for twenty hours a week of service work. Placement opportunities include working in an orphanage, working with battered children or wives, or working in a local hospital. The work is not glamorous, but the accomplishment is real. Coursework in the Partnership program is taught by professors at the local universities, not by a house staff maintained by the program. Moreover, your courses are designed to work in tandem with your experiential learning. The questions you bring home from work about your adopted culture should be answered by what you are learning in the classroom, and vice versa. For example, in your history course, you might be asked to write a paper on the background of migration to the city, how that problem had been answered in the past, and how that problem might be addressed in the future. Since housing—or its absence—is an endemic problem in many of the societies you might journey to, it's likely that your sense of this problem would be rather more acute than it might have been at home.

The key to this program is the service element. As Linda Chisholm, the director of the Partnership, says: "The twenty hours a week of service really thrusts students into the society and culture. As a result students discover things they had to give an inner resources they never knew they had." According to one Partnership alum, the service side of the program was an invaluable experience. He says of his experience in Africa with the program: "It made me brave."

Students will likely be housed in dorms during their stay, although a few do get housed with an agency or in a homestay. The Partnership likes its students to have some free time together, because by the very nature of the program they spend so much time involved in the culture. The Partnership for Service Learning is an outstanding opportunity for any student interested in studying abroad and in having a chance to understand another culture. This is a program that directly benefits the host community and simultaneously provides its students with a real appreciation for that community's culture and an understanding of the issues that face that culture. If you want to study and get involved as well, this is a terrific way to do it.

Program for Cultural Growth

Goddard College
Plainfield, VT 05667
(802) 454-7835 or (802) 454-8311
Contact person: program director
Program length: as long as you wish
Cost: $75 per semester credit hour (see below)
Financial aid: none
Age range of participants: 18 and up

Number of participants per year: 700
Application procedure: must send in a detailed study plan and $70 per each credit unit (see below)
Application due date: none
Program locations: worldwide

So you're going away. You're traveling to Asia, to England, to Arizona or to one of a hundred other destinations. And you would like to get some academic credit for that travel. But how? This is a pleasure trip, not a course; you can't get credit for that. That's where you're wrong. If you are willing to do a little pretrip preparation, the Goddard travel program is a terrific way for you to gain credit as you travel. Goddard believes that travel by its very nature is educational. If structured properly, that trip can teach you more than any class and text could. As a result of this belief, the college has set up a program that allows undergraduate and graduate students to receive credit for their travels. The program works like this: You send in your study plan, which consists of a detailed itinerary and the purpose and professional objectives for each locale you plan to visit. You establish learning objectives for your journey, plus a bibliography of the books you are reading to prepare for your travel. Then you detail how this travel will be applied to your academic or professional life: your "back-home application." Once Goddard has received your plan, James Galloway, the director of the program, works with you to refine your submission into a working plan. You receive one semester of academic credit for each full academic week (five days) you travel. You are required to keep a travel log, and upon returning you are expected to turn your log into an essay that will expand on your back-home application.

What may be the best part of the Goddard experience is the attention to detail forced on the prospective traveler. One alum states of the planning stages: "The planning was indispensable; the experience, incomparable." Furthermore, Goddard's travel-study program gives its participants a mission while away. And as the words of a past participant will attest, that mission translates into a deeper investigation of the area of travel because the course "makes traveling a professional activity and not a mere pursuit of pleasurable experiences abroad. It encouraged me to explore the educational system of China away from the tour, and those explorations yielded some of my most unforgettable moments."

The Goddard travel-study option is a great way to delve deeply into your journey as a result of better planning and a sense of purpose. And don't forget about the credit you can earn. So turn that trip into an investment in your future. As one well-prepared traveler remarked: "My journey is richer every time I recall it."

Program in the South Pacific

International Programs
208 Old Main Building
University of Wisconsin
at Stevens Point
Stevens Point, WI 54481
(715) 346-2717
Program length: fall semester
Cost: $5,800 plus $1,950 for out-
of-state admission to UW-SP
Financial aid: if available from
home institution
Housing: provided
Age range of participants: college
sophomore and up
Number of participants: 25

Application process: application
with fee; transcript; 4
recommendations, including an
adviser, faculty member,
employer, and someone who can
attest to your group-living
record (residence director, camp
counselor, family friend, etc);
snapshot; personal essay on
goals for overseas study;
interview
Application due date: rolling
admissions
Program locations: Fiji, New
Zealand, Australia

If the South Pacific has special allure, this semester-long program might be your way of reaching that tropical paradise you've dreamed about. You will go to Fiji and stay in a village, spend nine weeks at an Australian university, and five weeks at Waikato University in New Zealand. Not only is the experience a stunner geographically, its value is enhanced by the marked contrasts in culture you will observe.

UW-SP requires you to enroll there in to order to gain admission to the program. In addition, the university requires attendance at orientation sessions unless the travel is prohibitive.

UW-SP also offers a spring semester at Soochow University on the outskirts of Taipei, Taiwan, which includes trips to mainland China and to Hong Kong. Not language facility is required. Moreover, students can earn small amounts of money by tutoring Chinese college students in conversational English. The program begins on January 4 and ends on April 30. The cost is approximately $5,500, and that includes a homestay situation in Taipei during the Chinese New Year in February.

Quarter Abroad

Director, Study Abroad Programs
324 Fine Arts Building

University of Wisconsin—River
Falls

River Falls, WI 54022
(715) 425-3992
Program length: 14 weeks
Cost: $5,800
Financial aid: if available from
   home institution
Housing: provided
Age range of participants: college
Number of participants: varies

Application process: application
   with fee; transcript;
   recommendations; research
   project approved by academic
   adviser and department
   chairman, home institution
Application due date: March 15
Program location: Europe

This program offers an unusual opportunity: the chance to come up with a research project that fascinates you and then go abroad for a term and do it. In addition, you will stay in Paris; you will travel for four weeks and pursue your research in the European setting of your choice. You also will be given the opportunity to have a homestay situation. If all these pieces taken together boggle your mind, let's try to sort them out. Essentially, this program, begun in 1963, gives you the opportunity to go to Europe and research that question you've puzzled about. What is the cultural affinity of bargemen on Seine? How are multinationals dealing with the imminent reality of the European Community? Project topics range from art to sociology, from agriculture to speech.

Lest you get too excited, the program also has some restrictions: Participants must attend the foreign study seminar held during the spring quarter at Wisconsin-River Falls. The program is offered only during the fall quarter.

Royal Holloway and Bedford New College: University of London

Egham Hill
Egham, Surrey TW20 0EX
England
011-44 + 0784-34455
Program length: year, semester
Cost: varies by program
Financial aid: none
Housing: provided
Age range of participants: college
   junior

Number of participants: varies by
   program
Application process: application
   with fee; transcript; teachers'
   recommendations; minimum
   GPA of 3.0 on 4.0 system
Application due date: February 1
Program location: Surrey,
   England

What makes this program stand out are its location—in rural Surrey but within striking distance of London—and the attractive mix of elegant Victoriana and modernism in its physical plant. The former conveys a sense of permanence; the latter promises the advantages of the latest in technology as well as a lure to faculty as well as students. It is not unreasonable, therefore, to find that the Royal College divides its strengths into arts and music, European languages and literature, and science, including management studies and geography.

There is one other advantage. The Royal College guarantees you a single room and your own tutor, which means the ability to experience British university education at its fullest. The program is highly selective and expensive, but its advantages make it worth your examination.

Royal Scottish Academy of Music and Drama

100 Renfrew Street
 Glasgow G2 3DB, Scotland
011-44 +041-332-4101
Program length: year
Cost: varies by program
Financial aid: none
Housing: some available
Age range of participants: high
 school; PG, college
Number of participants: varies by
 program

Application process: application,
 audition if possible; usually
 transcript and/or essay; teacher's
 recommendation
Application due date: rolling
 admissions
Program location: Glasgow,
 Scotland

The Royal Scottish Academy is a degree-granting institution with affiliations to the University of Glasgow. Here you may further your studies in music or theater—or gain a B.A. in either area. This program gives you the chance to work in the arts in arenas very different from those in the United States, thereby exposing you to new ideas and techniques.

Scandinavian Seminar

24 Dickinson Street
Amherst, MA 01002
1-800-828-3343 (outside MA);
 (413) 253-9736 (in MA)
Program length: semester, year,
 summer
Cost: varies by program; $14,000
 per year; $6,400 per semester;
Financial aid: available
Housing: provided
Age range of participants: PG,
 college
Number of participants: varies by
 program; 16 in Icelandic
 summer program

Application process: application
 with fee; transcript; 3
 recommendations, 2 from
 teachers; 2 passport-type
 photos; health form, filled out
 by physician
Application due dates: May 1, for
 year and fall semester;
 October 15 for spring; April 28
 for summer
Program locations: Finland,
 Denmark, Sweden, Norway

At the heart of Scandinavian Seminar is its alliance to the invention of a nineteenth-century Danish educator named Nikolai Grundtvig. His creation, the folk college, or "school for life," has proliferated in Scandinavia. There are more than six hundred of them in the five countries served by the seminar. It is to one of these schools that you will go if you enter the program. The experience is entirely acculturating, which is to say it puts you in position to absorb as much of your chosen country's culture as possible in a year. "It is impossible to become completely Danish; but, as I discovered, one can learn to think like a Dane, acquire a Dane's relationship to government, education, social values, and family structure."—"Being in Norway for a year gave me the time to just become a part of living, everyday culture—indeed, of being an immigrant of sorts."

Through its connection with the folk college, the seminar is able to introduce its students to their chosen countries as no other program can. Perhaps the best description of the colleges themselves comes from students: "This year placed responsibility for my education entirely on me." The folk college is in many ways "a commune: students and teachers not only attend classes and social functions together; we pick vegetables, rake leaves and do dishes together as well, and the school itself seeks to develop its students intellectually, physically, and socially."—"A teacher was included in each group, but the teacher acted as the students' equal." Sound strange? Well, keep in mind the fact that the folk colleges range in size from fifty to two hundred, and that while they include standard humanities courses, many are focused on particular nontraditional areas, with both kinds of program being equally available to students. The key phrase is "training for life."

But there is more to this program than simply attending a foreign institution. If you don't speak one of the Scandinavian languages—Norwegian, Danish, Swedish, or Finnish—and very few Americans do, you'll have to learn. Those are the languages in which you'll be going to school. The seminar has considered this problem, however, and its solution is to provide you with an intensive course upon your arrival in your chosen country. At the same time, you begin a homestay that lasts until your college starts up in the fall. "[Unfortunately], language acquisition isn't instantaneous. Because I refused to speak English, however, I was forced to accept as reality my ignorance and the fraction of myself I could express. . . . As a result, I became a stronger person because my listening, observing, and 'detective' skills in general increased exponentially." In a similar way, the homestays program requires you adjust to your new culture (there is usually more than one homestay, although the homestay situation is governed by the starting time of the folk college). "In general, my family stays gave me two different examples of Danish culture and a firm base for learning Danish."

Finally, you enter your folk college, where you remain for the school year. The one exception is the seminar's semester program on Nordic and Global Issues. In this program, classes are held at certain folk colleges in English, although students must take the language of their chosen country during the term. Otherwise, coursework and extracurricular life are about the same as in the yearlong program. The disadvantage in the semester opportunity lies in its failure to provide you with the vital language tool before you begin living full-time in your chosen country.

The seminar is not an inexpensive program. Its yearlong program fee does not include airfare or incidental costs. However, credit exchange is available through the University of Massachusetts, and the seminar's credit recommendations have been accepted widely since the program's inception in 1949. Ultimately, however, the question of credit is one you need to raise with your own institution—before you leave for Scandinavia.

Is this program worthwhile? Beyond the life-changing statements one always finds in program literature, it's clear that the seminar does possess a unique quality. Because its programs are built around yearlong involvement in an institution unique to Scandinavia, attendance has to result in acculturation to an unusual degree.

The School for Field Studies

16 Broadway
Beverly, MA 01915
(508) 927-7777
Contact person: admissions
  department
Program length: semester,
  summer, and January option
Cost: $6,300–$7,360 per semester;
  $1,600–$2,290 per summer
Financial aid: available
Housing: provided
Age range of participants: 18 and
  up, PG

Number of participants: 14–24
  per program
Application process: must have
  completed college-level
  biology course; application
  form; essay; transcript (for
  semester only); reference form
Application due date: rolling
  admissions
Program locations: (semester)
  Mexico, Australia, Kenya,
  Virgin Islands, Vermont

The School for Field Studies is a training ground for those interested in studying and working with the environment—and much more. It's also a place where you can find out about your own interests and intentions by taking part in extensive field research. For example, you can choose to study marine biology and management in the Virgin Islands or wildlife ecology and management in Kenya. In the process, you can learn about potential careers, discover information about other cultures, and, incidentally, gain a little college credit.

Students can expect to work very hard while in the School for Field Studies. Each day is made up of approximately two to three hours of classroom time and then four to five hours of related fieldwork. The main goal of every program and the philosophy that drives SFFS are the essence of the scientific method. SFFS teaches theory and then asks you to apply it in the field. As a result of this mixture of traditional and experiential learning, students gain a much stronger sense of the material and its relevance to their lives and the world. SFFS makes your textbooks come alive.

It is important to realize that SFFS is a very academic and intense place. Students carry five courses and an independent field research project during their term. They are tested in each course; however, since much of their homework is fieldwork, the experience is very different from that of the classroom. Students also gain from the commitment of their teachers, most of them professors carrying out their own research projects. Watching these experts work gives students an additional view into the world of field research.

Living arrangements on all SFFS sites are rustic at best, and students are required to cook their own meals and work together to make their camp home. But the rewards are great. SFFS gives students the opportunity to work on real world problems and issues. The result is often meaningful on levels beyond that of the discipline involved.

School of International Education

National Institute for Higher Education
Plassey Technological Park
Limerick, Ireland
011-353 + 35361 333644, ext. 2270
Program length: semester; year; summer
Cost: varies by program
Financial aid: none
Housing: various options available
Age range of participants: college
Number of participants: varies by program
Application process: application with fee; transcript and statement of financial independence; adviser's recommendation; parental consent; 2 passport photos
Application due date: July 1
Program location: Limerick, Ireland

This unusual institution is based on the modular system of education. Each module, or course, is self-contained, lasting about eleven weeks. You will be asked to take five or six "mods" in each term, of which there are three in the year. Particular emphasis within the university is given to courses in engineering and the sciences, business and international affairs.

If this system appeals to you—it's quite different from four courses a semester—so might the National Institute for Higher Education (NIHE). Extracurricular aspects of life at NIHE are similar to those at universities elsewhere. Students may live in a student village, in a homestay situation, or find their own accommodations. Within the village, each room is equipped with a computer work station. In addition, NIHE offers a wide range of activities beyond the classroom. All the standard extracurriculars are available, including a variety of sports, ranging from golf to tae kwan do. Then there are the societies, which meet both passions—the Society against apartheid—and interests—Campus Television. These are but a few of the more than forty clubs and societies open to the student population.

Semester at Sea

Institute for Shipboard Education
University of Pittsburgh
811 William Pitt Union
Pittsburgh, PA 15260
1-800-854-0195
Contact person: Paul Watson, director of admissions
Program length: semester
Cost: $8,975–$12,375 depending on accommodations choice

Financial aid: available

Age range of participants: college undergraduates

Number of participants per program: 450–500

Application process: transcript; essay; 2 recommendations

Application due date: rolling admissions

Program locations: worldwide, departing from Nassau, Bahamas, or Vancouver, British Columbia

Even before the *Love Boat* made cruise ship a familiar phrase, the idea of sailing in luxury to exotic ports of call was an incredibly attractive one. But to cruise around the world—even partway—and earn academic credit for it? Now, that is unbelievable. At least, it was once. But for the last twenty years or so, students enrolled in college have been able to take advantage of Semester at Sea. Yes, if you go, you will do everything academic you do at home: attend classes, study with talented professors, write papers, take exams. But in the process, you'll visit many different countries and earn a full semester of credit. That is exactly what happens aboard the *Universe*, Semester at Sea's cruise ship. Students on Semester at Sea spend a full semester traveling to different countries aboard a floating college. "The best thing I've ever done . . . gives the advantage of the classroom and the added input of the outside world. The things you learned about in lectures you went out and did the next day. It really was experiential learning."

Courses are offered in almost every discipline from anthropology to theater arts. Every student is required to take the core course, an interdisciplinary look at the global environment. Students then enroll in three or four other courses. Classes meet every day while at sea, and the average class size is twenty to thirty.

What these statistics on Semester at Sea don't tell you is the incredible experience you will have while in port. Fifty percent of the program is spent at sea, and 50 percent in various ports. While in port, your stay will last from three to seven days, plenty of time to explore the city. Furthermore, Semester at Sea has developed a series of trips they call practia. These trips provide a focus for your visit and relate directly to your studies. There's also plenty of time for browsing through museums, shops, and national monuments. Semester at Sea strikes a good balance between academic involvement and experiential travel.

Because the SS *Universe* was once a cruise ship, it is divided into various levels of accommodations. Your price for the semester will reflect the kind of accommodations you choose. For example, the price for a single with a window on the ocean in first class and the charge for a triple in third class will vary dramatically. In other words, it's just like most college living situations. "I never felt claustrophobic aboard the ship."—"Shipboard community is great!" Some rooms are terrific, some just livable. The difference here is that you pay for what you get.

Otherwise, all facilities are shared. There is one central dining facility, and all meals are taken there. Beyond eating and sleeping, the SS *Universe* offers the normal collegiate amenities. There is a closed-circuit television system, a gym complete with aerobic classes, basketball, weightlifting, a medical facility with a resident doctor, and a fully functional student government.

Semester at Sea provides students with a floating campus. They are able to draw on the culture and history of many exciting areas of port. And because their time in port is complemented by academics, they have a greater understanding of and appreciation for the many cultures they experience. "You may have all the money in the world to travel, but you'll never do it the way they coordinate it for you. Semester at Sea was the best learning experience I ever had."

Shanghai International Studies University Exchange

Office of International Studies
110 Eisenberg Classroom Building
Slippery Rock University
Slippery Rock, PA 16057
(412) 794-7425
Program length: semester or year
Cost: Slippery Rock tuition, room and board, and fees
Financial aid: if available from home institution
Housing: provided
Age range of participants: college

Number of participants: varies
Application process: application with fee; transcript; 2.5 GPA; approval of academic adviser: minimum 1 semester of Chinese language (1 year highly recommended); approval by dean of International Studies, Slippery Rock
Application due dates: April 1 for fall; October 1 for spring
Program location: Shanghai, China

The bottom line on this program is quite simple: For the cost of a year at Slippery Rock University, you can spend a year at Shanghai International Studies University. The advantages are equally straightforward. By going on this program, you can return to the United States with a measurable command of Chinese. Shanghai International was founded as a language institute, and one of the strengths of the university continues to be the teaching of Chinese as a foreign language. Moreover, you will live as Chinese students do, residing in a student residence hall and dining in university-owned "canteens." You should take note of the academic calendar: Shanghai's school year in September; the year ends at the end of July.

Sotheby's Educational Studies—Three Months and Year in London

1334 York Avenue
New York, NY 10021
(212) 606-7822
Program length: 3 months or full year
Cost: 5,950 pounds sterling for year (approximately $10,000);

2,000 pounds sterling for 3-month course (approximately $4,000)
Financial aid: available
Housing: none
Age range of participants: college graduate and up

Number of participants per
  program: 60
Application process: essay;
  transcript; letters of
  recommendation; interview

Application due date: January 1
  for full year, and rolling
  admission for 3-month courses
Program location: London

If you're interested in learning as much as you can about art history from a group of unusually qualified experts, you should think about a year in London with Sotheby's, one of the two premier art auction houses in the world (Christie's is the other). Your year, or three months if you prefer, will be jam-packed with lectures and seminars, field trips to museums, and trips through the auction house under the guidance of some of the world's greatest art historians. The structure of the yearlong course is thematic and designed to give students interested in a career in visual or decorative arts a solid base in their art history. The three monthlong courses focus on particular artistic periods. Classes run from 10:00 A.M. to 5:00 P.M. Monday through Friday. Commitment is an important prerequisite.

Studio Arts Center International in Florence

c/o Cleveland Institute of Art
11141 East Boulevard
Cleveland, OH 44106
(216) 229-0938
Program length: semester,
  summer
Cost: varies by program;
  approximately $5,000 per
  term
Financial aid: none
Housing: available
Age range of participants: 18 and
  up

Number of participants: varies by
  program
Application process: application
  with fee; usually transcript
  and/or essay; teacher's
  recommendation (preferably
  in art); health certificate
Application due date: rolling
  admissions
Program location: Florence, Italy;
  Oxford, England

This program exposes students interested in art and in the culture of Italy to the beauties of that country's most famous artistic center: Florence. Students work in the studio with the help and advice of working artists; in addition, they learn Italian and are exposed to the history of Italian culture. But the program is primarily designed for the active practice of art. As one enrollee quickly discovered, "I found myself in the midst of an artists' colony rather than an art school. The school caters to the needs of its students and their specific interests. As a result, no two students follow the same course of study. . . . In a class of six, it was possible to have present a jewelry maker, a weaver, a photographer, a sculptor, a painter, and a printmaker." Students are also likely to be palette to palette with counterparts from six different countries: "In that same class of six, the students were from Australia, Portugal, Sweden, Switzerland, Germany, and America." It's easy to infer that the common language here is as likely to be Italian as English, hence the encouragement to learn Italian as soon as possible. Students live around the school in apartments. Florence is a welcoming city, and the student's experience is likely to be a most comfortable one.

As artist-to-be, however, that experience is likely to test the depths of the student's talent. SACI is a school for artists. There, students stretch their talents dozens of hours each week, building on the knowledge they are gaining simultaneously from the sights they see around them and from the words of their instructors. Perhaps the most remarkable characteristic of the school is its institutional encouragement to experiment artistically. If the arts are in your future, SACI may prove it to you.

In the spring of 1990, SACI added a second location, at Oxford Polytechnic. Students who attend the Oxford version of SACI will be able to get college credit while being taught by SACI staff. In addition to the regular program at SACI Oxford, a seminar course in the fine arts is a requirement of attendance.

SACI Florence has added a graduate program through affiliation with Virginia Commonwealth University. If this interests you, apply directly to SACI Florence, with your aim in this case a masters in fine arts. This degree will be offered to qualified students in the areas of painting, printmaking, sculpture, and ceramics.

St. Andrews University

The American Enrollment Adviser
Old Union Building
79 North Street
St. Andrews, Fife
Scotland KY 169AJ
011-44 +0334 76161
Program length: year
Cost: $10,000–$12,000
Financial aid: available
Housing: provided
Number of participants: varies by
program

Age range of participants: PG,
college
Application process: application
with fee; transcript and
personal statement; at least 1
faculty recommendation
Application due date: May 1
Program location: St. Andrews,
Scotland

If you're interested in golf, the name St. Andrews needs no introduction. Likely, that name conjures up a picture of wind-swept heather, the North Sea nearby, and one of the world's most famous golf courses. Well, you may or may not know that St. Andrews also is home to one of the English-speaking world's oldest universities. St. Andrews University arrived several centuries before the Old Courses, but it shares its picturesque locale and a well-deserved reputation. Most important to you—whether a golfer or not—is that St. Andrews University welcomes overseas students. The university believes that its curriculum is ideal for the visiting student. Because students are admitted "to a faculty—of arts or science," they are free to make their own course selections (unlike English universities, where students are admitted to a department and forced to specialize). "This method offers more breadth and more flexibility, and makes it easier to deal with Americans coming over to study for one year from liberal arts colleges. St. Andrews lies between the American breadth and the English narrowness of education."

Moreover, St. Andrews does not confine its interest to overseas students in their junior year. In fact, the university welcomes applications from any overseas student who has completed high school.

St. Clare's Liberal Arts Program

St. Clare's College
139 Banbury Road
Oxford OX2 7AL, England
011-44 + 865-52031
Program length: semester, year, summer (including St. Clare's Art School in Italy)
Cost: varies by program; semester fee is $3,500, exclusive of travel, housing, and incidental costs; inclusive summer program is $3,150–$3,250, not including airfare to England and incidentals
Financial aid: 3 scholarships per year
Housing: assistance is provided in finding accommodations in Oxford during the regular term

Age range of participants: high school, PG, 15–18 (summer), 17 and up
Number of participants: St. Clare's population numbers 280
Application process: preliminary application to Academic Study Abroad, with fee; application with transcript and teacher recommendation
Application due date: rolling admissions
Program locations: England, Italy (summer art school)

St. Clare's College is an independent international college located in Oxford. Here the word "independent" is the giveaway. Although St. Clare's has allied itself with a variety of extracurricular activities at Oxford University, it is in no way associated with that institution. What must be determined is what independent purpose St. Clare's itself serves. First of all, it is a center for the teaching of English as a second language. Like other schools of its ilk around the world, it has broadened that purpose to include a second and, for Americans, more interesting function: St. Clare's grants the international baccalaureate (IB), the only product of a preuniversity course recognized internationally, in fact, by sixty-six countries around the world. The degree has a variety of prerequisites, including two languages, science and mathematics, English literature, and history, as well as other options that cover a two-year program. St. Clare's has created enough upper-level options to make its program attractive to American university students seeking alternatives for the junior year abroad—or any year abroad, since St. Clare's does not restrict its program to juniors. Participants seem to agree that what is most important about these programs is the level of instruction. "This is the best teaching I've ever had."—"My history teacher . . . spit out information like a computer does when you press the right key." Perhaps the issue here is approachability. Beyond all else, St. Clare's offers education you can't escape. "My largest class was six, counting me."—"This was the first time in my life I sought out teachers—and they were always there for me."

In addition to these regular winter, or term-time, programs, St. Clare's also offers a summer program for high school age students focused on coursework in British history and culture and on SAT preparation. St. Clare's Art School in Italy, utilizing a university dormitory in Venice, provides summer instruction in art history, in studio art, and in Italian for high school students. These programs last about six weeks.

St. Olaf Interims Abroad

Office of International Studies
Manitou Cottage
St. Olaf College
Northfield, MN 55057
(507) 663-3069
Contact person: staff
Program length: January term, approximately 3 1/2 weeks
Cost: approximately $2,500 (will vary according to location); includes round-trip airfare from Minneapolis
Financial aid: available if enrolled at St. Olaf

Age range of participants: college
Number of participants per program: 14–30
Application process: application form; $50 registration fee
Application deadline: October 1
Academic credit available
Program locations: vary according to course offerings. In 1991, the locations include: Japan, China, Italy, Spain, Greece, Ireland, France, Germany, England, Hawaii, Brazil, Costa Rica, USSR

If you're a college student, you are probably familiar with the following: "WOW! I've got six weeks off at Christmas!" Sounds great, but truthfully, six weeks is a long time to be on vacation without doing something. Chances are your college offers some sort of short term during January (most do), but this is your vacation—you want to be away from campus. So you are stuck with a period of time that's too long to be a vacation but not long enough to allow you to do something productive . . . or so you think. St. Olaf College has solved your dilemma. Through their Interims Abroad program, St. Olaf offers students January courses that go abroad on the ultimate field trip. Students can choose from over seventeen course offerings that encompass a variety of disciplines: art history, language, religion, political science, to name just a few. While abroad, you receive instruction from your group leader, a St. Olaf professor—and you experience the coursework. In an art class you don't see slides, you see actual works of art. The courses are approximately 3 1/2 weeks long, which allows you plenty of time to become involved with the subject and with the country you're visiting. You will stay in hotels, unless otherwise noted; for example, some of the language-oriented courses have homestays, with breakfast and one other meal a day included in the tuition. While you are there for a course, there is plenty of time provided to explore on your own. St. Olaf Interim Abroad offers a great way to spend a long Christmas break. This is a vacation with a difference!

Study in Britain

Beaver College
Center for Education Abroad
Glenside PA 19038
(215) 572-2901
Program length: semester, year
Cost: varies by program; approximately $6,000–$9,000 per term; includes travel to Britain, tuition, housing in session
Financial aid: available, principally through home institution
Housing: provided; homestays possible
Age range of participants: college junior and above

Number of participants: varies
Application process: application and fee; transcript; photographs; 1 faculty recommendation; signed approval by home college official; minimum GPA varies, approximately 3.0
Application due dates: depends on site to which you apply, usually October 5 for spring; March 10–April 10 for fall
Program locations: United Kingdom, Ireland (also Vienna, Austria)

CEA offers the advantage of placements throughout Great Britain and Ireland. In London you may enroll in one of the University of London's complex of colleges (as a municipal university, the University of London oversees several faculties; it is to one of these that you will go to study) or in either the City of London Polytechnic or Middlesex Polytechnic. (Polytechnics are the "closest thing[s] to an American liberal arts college. [They] . . . offer courses in all the major disciplines, and unlike the university, [they] operate . . . on a semester basis for those who want to stay abroad for only one term. But classes, students, and faculties are distinctly British.") In addition, CEA has direct affiliation with eleven universities around the British Isles, as well as with five universities in Ireland. In short, CEA offers an incredible breadth of possibilities for junior year study in Britain, Wales, Scotland, and Ireland. Moreover, Beaver's programs are designed to put you in the classroom with British, Welsch, Scottish, and Irish students—and then make sure you get credit for your work when you return home. With CEA you have the advantage of an experienced resident facility in London to plan and coordinate each program.

Perhaps the single drawback to the CEA program is that curricular contact is likely to be the most you will have with the native population. In the CEA program, you live with other Americans, and that means fewer opportunities to get to know your British classmates. But as one alum notes:

"For Americans living abroad, many great and lasting friendships are formed."

Also worth noting is the relative value of education at a polytechnic or a college of higher education versus a university in the British system. Standards are likely to be lower in the former categories, although the curricular framework—the structure of the course on a daily and weekly basis—is much more likely to be what you are used to. So, as usual, keep in mind the tradeoffs you have to make. This is a program that can give you access to a wide variety of institutions.

CEA also offers the opportunity to participate in several hybrid programs specially designed for American students. Among these are the London Humanities Semesters, the Oxford Semesters, and the Vienna semester and year program. Each has distinct advantages. The London Humanities Semesters, offered in conjunction with the City of London Polytechnic but for Americans only, provides not only focused instruction but several extended trips to Berlin and Paris. The Oxford Semester allows American participants to share in the vaunted facilities of Oxford University, while taking courses in history, politics, and economics. The Vienna program offers instruction in German as well as coursework in the rapidly changing political culture of Central and Eastern Europe.

SUNY Semester in India

Office of International Education
State University College
Oneonta, NY 13820
(607) 431-3320 or (607) 431-3369
Program length: fall semester
Cost: $3,750
Financial aid: if available from
   home institution
Housing: provided
Age range of participants: college
Number of participants: varies

Application process: application with fee; transcript; a statement discussing your reasons for this program of study; 3 references, including 2 letters of recommendation from faculty
Application due date: December 15
Program location: India

It would be inaccurate to describe this program as a semester in residence at an Indian university. Instead, it is a program designed to introduce you to India. By trips and excursions, by lectures and conversation, you will meet this land, about which Mark Twain rhapsodized. You do attend classes with Indian students, as well as have the benefit of seminars taught by the program director, a native Indian, who is also a veteran teacher in the United States. This program does require you to attend an orientation session at Oneonta in August, immediately before departure (on India, see also Davidson College Junior Year Abroad, p. 73).

Syracuse University Abroad

Division of International Programs
  Abroad
Syracuse University
119 Euclid Avenue
Syracuse, NY 13244-4170
(315) 443-3471
Program length: semester, year,
  summer
Cost: varies by program
Financial aid: available
Housing: provided
Age range of participants: college
  sophomore and up; grads

Number of participants: varies
Application process: application
  with fee; transcript; 2
  recommendations (1
  nonacademic); dean's statement
Application due dates: March 15
  for fall and academic year;
  October 15 for spring; February
  1 for British university
Program locations: Germany,
  Spain, Italy, England, France,
  Austria, Israel

Certainly one of the largest and arguably one of the best-known study-abroad programs is that sponsored by Syracuse University. As their literature proclaims, more than seventeen hundred students annually make use of their programs. This well-traveled and tested quality is clearly a virtue to many. If you apply to Syracuse, you are virtually assured of credit transfers, of liberal course offerings, and of the facilities of a Syracuse University center, one of which is located in each program city. In these centers, perhaps the most important advantage of the Syracuse programs, are a variety of facilities, including well-stocked libraries. You might note also that Syracuse provides a core of its own faculty, supplemented by local professors. In both cases, you can expect to find trained professionals teaching you.

Given the opportunities of the program and its advantageous facilities, why shouldn't you choose Syracuse? In addition to those outlined above, you can add the advantage of a number of fellow Americans, out of which group you're almost assured of finding a friend or two. However, it is the very nature of this group that leads to one of the disadvantages of this program. It is big. Indeed, it is so big that unless you are lucky enough to land in an exceptional homestay situation, you may well spend your semester or year abroad living with the very culture you left. Again, the issue of acculturation is one you must decide on. But if you decide to plunge into the culture of the country you're visiting, the Syracuse program may prove an impediment instead of a facilitator. This problem is made worse by the absence of insistence on speaking the host language. If you want to speak Italian in Italy, you may. Syracuse will make instruction available. But if you want to get by without Italian in Italy, that's certainly possible. Classes are taught in English, but you are expected to take Italian (or French or Spanish or German or Hebrew).

Syracuse is anxious to accommodate you, so the program has made space for both full-year and semester applicants. The university is careful to recommend that you remain in your chosen country for a full year. Their argument is a good one. As the program literature points out: "A semester is just too short to see and do everything." It goes on to note that preference is given to full-year applicants. And rightly so.

TASIS Postgraduate Program

TASIS
CH 6926 Montagnola
Switzerland
011-41 + 081-54-64-71
Program length: full year
Cost: depends on exchange rate:
approximately $16,000
Financial aid: available
Housing: provided
Age range of participants: 16–19,
high school, and PG

Number of participants: 24
Application process: application
with fee; usually transcript
and essay; teachers'
recommendations
Application due date: rolling
admissions
Program location: Lugano,
Switzerland

Like its companion programs mentioned below, the American School in Switzerland has maintained a postgraduate program for some years. This program repays its rather startling cost by offering some particular advantages. First, TASIS is located in a spectacular setting, overlooking the lake and city of Lugano in southern Switzerland. This environment is made even more appealing by the fact that TASIS offers its PGs separate living quarters in their own house. Add to this a specially designed curriculum and a faculty-to-student ratio of 1:5, and you can realize quickly how this program compensates for the additional costs of going to school in Switzerland. Of course, the setting also works to the advantage of education by putting you smack in the middle of two cultures, Lugano being in an Italian Swiss canton, and quite close to the art treasures of Milan, Venice, and Florence. TASIS furthers this advantage by offering a homestay program with an Italian family in the fall and a winterim (a two-week winter term) at St. Moritz in January. Of course, there is further academic work in European literature and history, plus opportunities for Achievement and AP work.

As a student, you will be able to avail yourself of a residence with your peers, where you will dine twice a week and "occasionally give dinners, dances, or hold parties for invited guests." There also are opportunities to continue with sports you'd played in school—or to begin something new, like water polo or serious hiking in the Swiss countryside. You also may expect to travel to Rome, to Paris, and perhaps, as recent classes have done, to the Soviet Union or elsewhere in Europe. If a PG year is a consideration, TASIS offers an alluring possibility.

University Studies Abroad Consortium

University of Nevada at Reno
University of Nevada Library
Reno, NV 89557-0093
(702) 784-6569

Program length: semester, year
Cost: varies by program
Financial aid: none
Housing: provided

Age range of participants: college
  sophomore and above
Number of participants: varies
Application process: application
  with fee; transcription

Application due date: rolling
  admissions
Program locations: Spain, France

This program's unique feature? The opportunity to study a subculture. By placing you for a semester in Basque country, the Reno program offers you the opportunity to experience a culture far removed even from the mainstream of either French or Spanish society.

Vienna with Central College

International Studies Office
Central College
Pella, IA 50219
1-800-458-5503
Program length: semester or year
Cost: $7,900 for semester; $11,000
  for year (does not include air
  travel, meals, etc.)
Financial aid: if available from
  home institution
Housing: provided
Number of participants: varies

Age range: college
Application process: application
  with fee; transcript; 2 faculty
  recommendations; 2.5 GPA; at
  least 2 years of college level
  German with a B average;
  personal essay; medical report
Application due date: April 15 for
  fall or year; November 1 for
  spring
Program locations: Germany and
  Austria

As one alumna of this program remarked: "You can't learn German by speaking in English." You want to place a bet on your learning German? This program is a good place to put your money. You begin at the end of July in residence in Rudesheim, Germany. After a few days of orientation there, you go on to Prien, a spa and lakeside town in Bavaria, southern Germany, where you will spend almost two months polishing up those umlauts at a Goethe Institute. From there it's into the fray at the University of Vienna. The semester usually begins at Vienna around October 2. If you're only in residence for the fall, you will not finish until February 1. Accordingly, spring semester students will begin in Murnau, Germany, on January 6, not to conclude the entire program until June 30. So make no mistake. This is an investment in learning. Its advantages are obvious. You will learn enough German to become fluent; otherwise, the classes you will be attending at the university will be a waste of time. You also will have the opportunity to take a variety of other courses offered by Austrian professors exclusively for you. And there's another distinct opportunity here: internships. If you spend the year in Vienna, and if your performance in the fall warrants it, you may be eligible for a program of internships offered in the spring semester. These opportunities range from positions in business to politics, communications to education.

Throughout this program, you will be housed with other students. In

Vienna, however, those students will be Austrian, since you will be living in university dormitories. A feature of this lifestyle is the provision for kitchen facilities in your rooms, since meals are not provided by the university. Where better to learn about food than in Vienna? The program also has a director on site, an advantage when so many options exist.

Postgraduate Programs at Secondary Schools (PG Years)

◇ ◇ ◇

A principal source of postgraduate (PG) opportunities, although more mainstream than many that appear in this volume, are the openings that exist at many independent secondary schools for a single year of "transitional education" after high school. These opportunities exist both here and abroad. However, this section will describe only American opportunities, with an eye to the advantages and disadvantages of this form of PG opportunity.

As one of the publications of the National Association of Independent Schools notes: "PG programs offer students an extra year of high school in which to improve their study habits, strengthen their academic records, and enrich their personal maturity. Most PG programs are designed to prepare students for both the academic and social aspects of college life."

Given the fact that there are over eighty schools in the United States and Canada that accept PGs, this statement is largely accurate. However, the specifics of each program vary widely from school to school, as do more obvious differences. For example, there are institutions that accept PGs that have fewer than seventy-five students in the entire student body. Other institutions number more than a thousand in grades 9–PG, with significant numbers of PGs (occasionally more than two hundred). Most PGs are suburban or decidedly rural; very few are urban. In the former category are several institutions in mountainous areas from Maine to California, some of which stress outdoor activities as a principal aspect of their programs. But let's examine the statement quoted above in more detail, because it's important for you to understand what a PG year holds in store for you; what its opportunities are.

First of all, the PG year is definitely another year of high school. Don't be misled by the phrase "prepare students for ... the ... social aspects of college life" used above. For anyone coming from a public school or from an independent day school, life in a boarding school as a postgraduate means living with others of the same sex in a boarding situation. That may be like college. But don't expect the social freedoms you've read or perhaps dreamed about existing in college. You won't find them during a PG year. The important word above is "prepare." That is exactly what this year should be about.

And that's number two. PG years are extra years of high school. That extra year is intended to polish your skills and give you some extra time. Because the year is likely to take you out of your accustomed environment, you will benefit from it in ways analogous to other PG opportunities described in this book. But, of all the programs for PGs mentioned in this volume, PG school years are the least likely to be something entirely different. You are going to be in school; you are going to be taught; and you are going to be expected to do homework, write papers, and take lots of tests. The difference is that PG programs are designed especially for you; they're not just the tail end of high school. Recall what the National Association of Independent Schools says: "improve study habits and strengthen academic records." That translates into a real investment in learning. PG programs in independent boarding schools will give you all the work you can handle, no matter what high school program you finished the previous year. That's true because the deciding force here is yours. You chose a PG year, and therefore you are likely to get that "improvement and strengthening" in ways that even your twelve years at Most Excellent Academy couldn't transmit.

What the statement quoted above does not state explicitly may be among the most important aspects of this category of opportunities. You will be able to enrich your personal maturity by enjoying a somewhat privileged status outside the classroom in whatever activity you choose to concentrate on. If you're an athlete, chances are your skills will be called upon in ways that polish the expertise you learned in high school without having to endure the demands of a collegiate program. If your extracurricular interests lie elsewhere, the same conditions hold: more exposure, a peculiar enjoyment of a special "top-of-the-heap" status, without the heightened competition and stress of college programs. Are you good enough to play collegiate soccer, to dance on a more professional level, to play the oboe or throw a college curveball? It's likely a PG year may give you a chance to find out.

Notwithstanding all of the above, which we might characterize as "what this PG year is going to do for you on the outside," realize also what it enables you to do for yourself from the inside. As an admissions director at a prestigious school recently put it: "Boarding schools are places to live as well as places to learn." A postgraduate entering a PG program also enters a residential community, a small town, in all likelihood very different in some fundamental ways from the place that student lived in before. This new community offers "a range of associations more various than those previously known," a situation enhanced by the necessary closeness of contact created by a residential community. Additionally, the PG "starts from scratch." Coming into a PG program gives you the chance to re-create yourself, to define yourself in new ways away from your old associations. Since growing up is in many ways the process of trying on new identities, here is an unusual opportunity to do so in an already delimited situation.

The following includes an arbitrary selection of a few PG programs noted because of some unusual characteristic. Beyond that point of interest, none of the schools mentioned should be assumed to be qualitatively better or worse than its several dozen associates. A complete list of PG programs begins on p. 131. More information about all the schools listed can be obtained from them individually or from the National Association of Independent Schools. The latter organization publishes an informative volume entitled *Boarding Schools*. It may be obtained by writing to Boarding Schools; 18 Tremont Street; Boston, MA 02186.

The Walnut Hill School

Director of Admissions
Walnut Hill School
12 Highland Street
Natick, MA 01760
(508) 653–4312
Program length: year
Cost: $14,520
Financial aid: available
Housing: provided
Number of participants: varies
Age range of participants: PG
Application process: application
   with fee; transcript; writing
   sample; standardized test

results; audition (If distance prohibits a personal interview, "applicants in music and theatre should send a high quality audio- or video-taped audition.... For dancers, clear black and white photographs or a recent video.... Visual artists should send samples of their work")
Application due date: February 15
Program location: Natick, Massachusetts

Walnut Hill is, in the words of one student, "a place where people understand what I want to do and value it ... Here I am the mainstream." In that comment is much of the intent of this school. Under the leadership of its current head, Stephanie Perrin, Walnut Hill has shaped itself into a school that commends and enriches young artists of every variety. Here "creative and artistic talent" is shaped, while equal attention is paid to the ideas that shaped the arts these students have chosen. "I'll never forget the day science and music came together," was one music major's comment. Beyond Walnut Hill's core program of academics are the opportunities in the arts. Here dancers, musicians, actors, designers, painters, sculptors, and writers are instructed, given ample practice and rehearsal time—and perform. A recent visitor to the campus came away startled by the quality of one of those performances. "I'm a veteran of student performances, high school and college. But what I saw here fit neither category. The musical performance I witnessed was of concert quality. I've heard worse from visiting professionals. And the musical I attended? The dancing, the acting, the singing especially: *Pal Joey* was never better, even with Sinatra and Hayworth."

A distinct plus of the Walnut Hill program is its accessibility to Boston. Because of its location, Walnut Hill dancers can take advantage of the school's affiliation with the Boston Ballet, musicians of the school's connection with the New England Conservatory and the Youth Philharmonic Orchestra. Visual artists are able to attend classes at Boston University's School of Fine and Applied Arts. Walnut Hill also offers a competitive gymnastics program in cooperation with Woodland Gymnastics.

Clearly, the Walnut Hill School is worth your consideration if you have a sincere interest in fine arts. It is worth noting, however, that your interest should be accompanied by commitment. Not only will you need to audition for a place at the school, you also must be willing to invest yourself in the program if admitted. As the dean for the arts notes: "All schools strive to develop competence and self-worth in their students; at Walnut Hill, we help each student use his or her artistic abilities as means to that end."

A Postgraduate Year at Putney

The Putney School
Elm Lea Farm
Putney, VT 05346
(802) 387–5566
Program length: year
Cost: $15,000
Financial aid: available
Housing: provided
Age range of participants: PG

Number of participants: varies
Application process: application with fee; transcript; personal essay; teachers' recommendations
Application due date: rolling admissions
Program location: Putney, Vermont

The distinct advantage of this postgraduate program is that Putney is located on a working farm. Therefore students may avail themselves of that experience, as well as the larger interests encompassed by the concept of rural ecology. The latter is but one of the several courses offered by Putney for postgraduate students. Other areas of specialty include art history and molecular biology. But the key to the entire program is the issue of learning by doing, a phrase that echoes throughout life at Putney, both curricular and extracurricular. One of the ways that this concept is carried out in the daily life of the school is through Putney's efforts to be self-sufficient. Students regularly perform farm chores, especially working with the school's herd of forty Jersey cows. As many members of the community note: "This is one place where you'll surely get your hands dirty."

You'll also get a workout: fall, winter, and spring, both recreational and interscholastic sports exist, including an extensive riding program and all types of winter sports. Putney has been distinguished by providing at least one Olympian for the last several winter Olympics. Putney provides an unusual opportunity for transitions from secondary school in two respects.

First, Putney offers a "work term," which allows you to shape your own project, perhaps the first truly independent research and work you may have done in an academic context. Second, Putney offers small dormitory situations, including a few self-managed cabins for older students.

Deerfield Academy

Deerfield, MA 01342
(413) 772–0241
Program length: year
Cost: $15,000
Financial aid: available
Housing: provided
Age range of participants: PG
Number of participants: varies

Application process: application with fee; transcript; personal essay; teachers' recommendations
Application due date: March 1
Program location: Deerfield, Massachusetts

What better time to see old traditions upheld and new ones made than during these formative years at Deerfield Academy, to which young women have come as students after almost two hundred years of single-sex education? Regardless of your gender, this day is yours to seize, if you're open to the challenge. And that's the right word, because, as one alumnus has commented: "[Deerfield is] always challenging. . . . [It] has exposed my true potential while raising my commitment and goal setting toward education. Even after the first term I noticed a significant improvement in my reasoning, academic perspective, and overall ability."

And where better to experience that growth than amid the gloriously beautiful hills of western Massachusetts, among which Deerfield is nestled. The campus is an adroit combination of old and new, incorporating the seventeenth-century buildings of historic Deerfield, site of the famous Indian Massacre, with the modern facilities of an innovative school. Deerfield's PG's are meant to "add to excellence." It is the school's task to provide the materials and atmosphere; it is your job to use these tools to, in the words of Deerfield's director of admissions, "strengthen academic skills and broaden college choices." Deerfield further facilitates your transition to college by housing you with your peers in senior dormitories and integrating you into the school's extensive athletic and extracurricular program.

The Orme School

H.C. 63, Box 3040
Mayer, AZ 86333–9990
(602) 632–7601
Program length: year
Cost: $13,500
Financial aid: available
Housing: provided
Age range of participants: PG

Number of participants: varies
Application process: application with fee; transcript; personal essay; teachers' recommendations
Application due date: March 1
Program location: Mayer, Arizona

Orme offers the prospective PG an unusual opportunity. If you participate in a postgraduate year at Orme, you will not be joining a large group of your peers. Rather, you'll become part of a small, tightly knit community. Students thrive at Orme because they respond to what Orme represents: an identifiable community, "set apart, in its open country location [Orme is located on a 40,000-acre ranch] and [therefore] . . . easily understood and appreciated by youth." Students agree. "What I like about Orme is the small size of the school and the homey, relaxed atmosphere. I think the unassuming, friendly attitude of the people at Orme really helps the students to feel at ease, enabling them to concentrate on schoolwork and other activities." In addition, what Orme offers outside the classroom is noteworthy. You will find opportunities for riding and rodeo work, as well as extensive survival training and extended trips into the countryside.

Phillips Exeter Academy

60 Front Street
Exeter, NH 03833
(603) 772–4311
Program length: year
Cost: $15,000
Financial aid: available
Housing: provided
Age range of participants: PG

Number of participants: varies
Application process: application
    with fee; transcript; personal
    essay; teachers'
    recommendations
Application due date: March 1
Program location: Exeter, New
    Hampshire

There is one problem with attending Phillips Exeter Academy as a postgraduate student: You may wish afterward that you'd simply stayed there rather than moved on to college. Even as you go beyond the daunting tradition of the school and its over two hundred years of distinguished graduates (many of whom were PGs), you can't help but be taken struck by the grandeur of the facilities—for instance, there are two swimming pools—the stature of the faculty, and the impressive countenances of your peers-to-be. Nor are these simply first impressions. The place really does live up to its press notices. It is also a testing experience. Exeter believes in making students take responsibility for their own learning. The faculty is there to help but not to carry students along. Consequently, you will have an experience that you can liken to that promised by college. However, you will still be in secondary school, and on that score, Exeter is equally clear. You must obey the rules and meet the academy's expectations socially and athletically. On the athletic field, the demands will be contained within the school program, but the competition is often from the college level.

PG PROGRAMS AT SECONDARY SCHOOLS

Note: Remember to ask for the director of admissions, as the specific personnel may have changed.

Admiral Farragut Academy (boys only)
Pine Beach, NJ 08741
Cdr. Anthony A. D'Elia, Jr.
(201) 349–1121

American School in Switzerland
CH 6926 Montagnola-Lugano,
Switzerland
Caroline Cox
(212) 570–1066

Asheville School
Asheville, NC 28806
Everett E. Gourley, Jr.
(704) 254–6345

Avon Old Farms School (boys only)
500 Old Farms Road
Avon, CT 06001
Frank G. Leavitt
(203) 673–3201

Berkshire School
Sheffield, MA 01257
Jackman Stewart
(413) 229–8511

Brewster Academy
Main Street
Wolfeboro, NH 03894
Stewart M. Dunlop
(603) 569–1604

Cambridge School (features fine arts option)
Georgian Road
Weston, MA 02193
Lee S. Coffin
(617) 642–8600

Chapel Hill–Chauncy Hall School
785 Beaver Street
Waltham, MA 02254
Henry S. Russell, Jr.
(617) 894–2644

Cheshire Academy
10 Main Street
Cheshire, CT 06410
Patricia Monahan
(203) 272–5396

Choate Rosemary Hall
Box 788
Wallingford, CT 06492
Andrew F. Wooden
(203) 269–7722

Christchurch School (boys only)
Christchurch, VA 23031
Donald W. Smith
(804) 758–2306

Cushing Academy
School Street
Ashburnham, MA 01430
Judith S. Beams
(617) 827–5911

Darlington School
Cave Spring Road
Rome, GA 30161
Robert E. Dobson
(404) 235–6051

Deerfield Academy (boys only)
Deerfield, MA 01342
Beth Moore
(413) 772–0241

Elliott-Pope Preparatory School
Box 338
Idyllwild, CA 92349
Herta Melas
(714) 659–2191

Fork Union Military Academy (boys only)
Box 278–B
Fork Union, VA 23055
Lt. Col. Evan H. Lacy, Jr.
(804) 842–3216

Forman School
Norfolk Road
Litchfield, CT 06759
Karen A. Lambert
(203) 567–8712

Gould Academy
Box 860
Bethel, ME 04217
Robert S. Stuart, Jr.
(207) 824–2161

Gow School (boys only)
South Wales, NY 14139
David W. Gow
(716) 652–3450

Grand River Academy (boys only)
3042 College Street
Austinburg, OH 44010
Edmund Field
(216) 275–2811

Grier School (girls only)
Tyrone, PA 16686
Lynne Smith Feyk
(814) 684–3000

Gunnery
Washington, CT 06793
Andrew McNeill
(203) 868–7334

Hawaii Preparatory School
Kamuela, HI 96743
Bernard B. Nogues
(808) 885–7321

Hebron Academy
Hebron, ME 04238
Mitchell B. Overbye
(207) 966–2100

Hill School (boys only)
Pottstown, PA 19464
Carter P. Reese
(215) 326–1000

Hotchkiss School
Lakeville, CT 06039
Parnell P. Hagerman
(203) 435–2591

Hun School of Princeton
Box 271, Edgerstoune Road
Princeton, NJ 08542
P. Terrence Beach
(609) 921–7600

Hyde School
616 High Street
Bath, ME 04530
Laurie G. Hurd
(207) 443–5584

Interlochen Arts Academy
Interlochen, MI 49643
Chad Atkins
(616) 276–9221

John Woolman School
12585 Jones Bar Road
Nevada City, CA 95959
Brian Fry
(916) 273–3183

Judson School
Box 1569
Scottsdale, AZ 85252
Allan Hilton
(602) 948–7731

Kent School
Box 2006
Kent, CT 06757
J.S. Kerr and M.W. Lampe
(203) 927–3501

Kents Hill School
Kents Hill, ME 04349
Mary E. Marble
(207) 685–4914

Kimball Union Academy
Main Street
Meriden, NH 03770
James M. Sheehan
(603) 469–3211

Kiskiminetas School (boys only)
1888 Brett Lane
Saltsburg, PA 15681
J. Kristian Pueschel
(412) 639–3586

Lawrenceville School
Box 6008
Lawrenceville, NJ 08648
Philip G. Pratt
(609) 896–0400

Leelanau School
Glen Arbor, MI 49636
H. Michael Buhler
(616) 334–3072

Linden Hall School (girls only)
212 East Main Street
Lititz, PA 17543
Pat R. Sullivan
(717) 626–8512

Loomis Chaffee School
Batcheldor Road
Windsor, CT 06095
Drew J. Casertano
(203) 688–4934

MacDuffie School
Ames Hill Drive
Springfield, MA 01105
Ed Hinkley
(413) 734–4971

Mercersburg Academy
Mercersburg, PA 17236
Mark Fish
(717) 328–2151

Missouri Military Academy (boys only)
886 Grand Avenue
Mexico, MO 65265
Capt. Roger L. Hill
(314) 581–1776

Moravian Academy
4313 Green Pond
Bethlehem, PA 18017
Douglas D. Trotter, Jr.
(215) 691–1600

New Hampton School
New Hampton, NH 03256
Robert W. Spear, Jr.
(603) 744–5401

New York Miltary Academy
Cornwall-on-Hudson, NY 12520
Peter C. Wicker
(914) 534–3710

Northfield Mount Hermon
East Northfield, MA 01360
Virginia M. DeVeer
(413) 498–5311

Northwood School
Lake Placid, NY 12946
W. John Friedlander
(518) 523–3357

Oak Grove—Coburn School
Vassalboro, ME 04989
Kathleen Hanson
(207) 872–2741

Oak Ridge Military Academy
Oak Ridge, NC 27310
Lt. Pam Henry
(919) 643–4131

Oakwood School
515 South Road
Poughkeepsie, NY 12601
Thomas B. Huff
(914) 462–4200

Orme School
Mayer, AZ 86333
Barbara Barrick
(602) 632–7601

Oxford Academy (boys only)
Box P
Westbrook, CT 06498
Ruth H. Fagerstrom
(203) 399–6247

Peddie School
South Main Street
Hightstown, NJ 08520
John D. Martin
(609) 448–0155

Perkiomen School
Box 130
Pennsburg, PA 18073
Susan Thomas
(215) 679–9511

Phelps School (boys only)
Sugartown Road & Paoli Pike
Malvern, PA 19355
George Naron
(215) 644–1754

Phillips Academy
Andover, MA 01810
Jeannie Dissette
(617) 475–3400

Phillips Exeter Academy
Exeter, NH 03833
John D. Herney
(603) 772–4311

Pickering College (boys only)
Box 206
Newmarket, Ontario
Canada L3Y4X2
Sheldon H. Clark
(416) 895–1700

Ridley College
Box 3013
St. Catharines, Ontario
Canada L2R7C3
Don Rickers
(416) 684–8193

Riverview
551 Route 6A
East Sandwich, MA 02537
Carol Curtin
(617) 888–0489

Sandy Spring Friends School
Sandy Spring, MD 20860
Ruthann Fagan
(301) 774–7455

Solebury School
Box 429, Philips Mill Road
New Hope, PA 18938
Susan Klein
(215) 862–5261

St. John's Preparatory School (boys only)
Collegeville, MN 56321
Jerald L. Howard
(612) 363–3317

St. Johnsbury Academy
7 Main Street
St. Johnsbury, VT 05819
John Cummings
(802) 748–8171

Stanstead College
Stanstead, Quebec
Canada JOB 3EO
Andrew Elliot
(819) 876–2702

Stoneleigh-Burnham School (girls only)
Bernardston Road
Greenfield, MA 01301
Carrie Cadwell
(413) 774–2711

Storm King School
314 Mountain Road
Cornwall-on-Hudson, NY 12420
Austin C. Stern
(914) 534–7892

Suffield Academy
Suffield, CT 06078
William DeSalvo
(203) 668–7315

Taft School
110 Woodbury Road
Watertown, CT 06795
Frederick H. Wandelt III
(203) 274–2516

Thomas Jefferson School
4100 South Lindbergh
St. Louis, MO 63127
William C. Rowe
(314) 843–4151

Tilton School
Tilton, NY 03276
Bruce Watson
(603) 286–4342

Trinity College School (boys only)
Port Hope, Ontario
Canada L1A3W2
Brian D. Proctor
(416) 885–4565

Valley Forge Military Academy
(boys only)
Radnor and Eagle Roads
Wayne, PA 19087
Col. Frank M. Schoendorfer
(215) 688–1800

Verde Valley School
3511 Verde Valley School Road
Sedona, AZ 86336
(602) 282–7148

Vermont Academy
Saxtons River, VT 05154
William J. Neman
(802) 869–2121

**Walnut Hill School of Performing
Arts**
12 Highland Street
Natick, MA 01760
Tony Blackman
(617) 643–4312

Webb School
Box 488
Bell Buckle, TN 37020
Zachary James
(615) 389–9322

West Nottingham Academy
Firetower Road
Colora, MD 21917
Lori A. Daniele
(301) 658–5556

Westminster School
995 Hopmeadow Street
Simsbury, CT 06070
Tuck Ganzemuller
(203) 658–4444

Wilbraham and Monson Academy
Main Street
Wilbraham, MA 01095
Francis M. Casey
(413) 596–6811

Williston Northampton School
19 Payson Avenue
Easthampton, MA 01027
Lisa A. Connelly
(413) 527–1520

Winchendon School
Ash Street
Winchendon, MA 01475
Stephen V. A. Samborski
(617) 297–1223

Woodall School (boys only)
Main Street, Box 550
Bethlehem, CT 06751
Sally C. Woodhall
(203) 266–7788

**Woodlands Academy of the Sacred
  Heart** (girls only)
760 East Westleigh Road
Lake Forest, IL 60045
Juliette Wallace Taylor
(312) 234–4300

Worcester Academy
81 Providence Street
Worcester, MA 01604
Todd Holt
(617) 754–5302

Wykeham Rise School (girls only)
Wykeham Road
Washington, CT 06793
Ruth Boerger
(203) 868–7347

Wyoming Seminary
North Sprague Avenue
Kingston, PA 18704
John R. Eidam
(717) 283–6060

Work Opportunities in the United States

◇ ◇ ◇

The focus of this book is learning, and while you learn on the job, this book is not intended to be a guide to employment at your local Burger King. That kind of mainstream job is for you to search out on your own, which you should by all means do. Indeed, working and living at home is often a necessary part of any "break" package. Taking part of your break to live at home has several salutary effects. First of all, it's likely to be the first time you have ever lived in the world some call "real." You may discover in the process that not only is school much more attractive than you might have thought but the complexity of life outside the educational world demands planning and preparation on your part. That's really the second reason more jobs are not listed here. Most meaningful work requires skills. If you have those skills—and by all means think carefully about what skills you do have before looking for a job—your chances of gaining employment increase significantly. So don't sell yourself short. You might examine the introduction to the chapter below on internships because the same advice given there holds true for job applications. You should pursue every job possibility by letter and phone—and in person, if that's appropriate. Winning a job is a process in which the persistent triumph.

That same advice holds for the opportunities listed below. These opportunities appear in this book because they are not likely to occur to the average job seeker. Each is aimed at giving you an unusual experience, one that may yield some money but is also truly alternative.

DUDE RANCHES

There is no better working vacation than working on a dude ranch. As one ex-waitress/wrangler says: "This is the best life I know. What's better than spending your days riding, sunning, and playing the way cowboys used to—at least in our fantasies." Dude ranches are basically resorts that cater to people who want a dose of living out that cowboy fantasy. Guests spend their days riding, fishing, and enjoying the scenery, the magnificence of Colorado, Wyoming, and Montana, for the most part. Each ranch has its own character, and that character defines the collective personality of the clientele. Most have a strong stream of guests who have been staying at that ranch every summer since . . . well, one rancher says: "Some guests seem to have been coming since the world began." That's the sort of place these ranches are. Ranches vary in size, but the average "spread" accommodates about forty guests at a time.

There's hard work here: jobs range from wrangler—the cowboy or cow-girl who takes the guests out on a morning, afternoon, or all-day ride—to kitchen help, cabin maids, and handymen. All ranches need help. But don't be fooled; this is a very old-fashioned part of the country when it comes to gender stereotypes. Girls work in the kitchen, helping to prepare meals, and in the cabins. They can be wranglers (and are preferred for children), though men are more likely to get these spots. The handyman is *always* a man. Equal rights haven't reached this part of the world yet. But if you can live with that condition, you'll never find a nicer way to spend a summer. One wrangler calls this life "camp for grownups." And the best part is that you get to go all summer long and earn money too! You will live on the ranch in a cabin, probably with roommates. The other workers primarily will be in their college years to mid-twenties (you must be eighteen to apply). Apply early, certainly by January 1. Remember that to be a wrangler a great deal of experience riding and working with horses is required. Here are some places to look:

RANCHES

WYOMING
ALBANY COUNTY

Flying X Ranch
799 Halleck Canyon Road
Wheatland, WY 82201
(307) 322–9626
(307) 322–5351

Rawah Guest Ranch
Jelm, WY 82063
(303) 435–5715

Two Bars Seven Ranch
Box 67–W
Tie Siding, WY 82084
(307) 742–6072

V-Bar Ranch
Rex Route, Box 2091
Laramie, WY 82070
(307) 745–7036
(307) 745–5966

Mountain Meadow Cabins
summer:
Centennial, WY 82055
(307) 742–6042
winter:
Harold A. Kissel
11241 Yellowstone Road
Cheyenne, WY 82009
(307) 634–1706

BIG HORN COUNTY

TX Ranch
Abbie Tillett
Box 453
Lovell, WY 82431
(406) 484–2583

Paintrock Outfitters, Inc.
Box 509
Greybull, WY 82426
(307) 765–2556

Shively Ranch
1062 Route 15
Lovell, WY 82431
(307) 548–6688

CARBON COUNTY

Moore Guest Ranch
Box 293C
Encampment, WY 82325
(307) 327–5574

Medicine Bow Lodge
Dave and Tani Cheney
Box 752
Saratoga, WY 82331
(307) 326–5439

Sand Lake Lodge
1634 Jim Bridger
Casper, WY 82604
(307) 234–6064

Boyer Ranch
Joyce B. Saer
Box 24
Savory, WY 82332
(307) 383–7840

CONVERSE COUNTY

Pellatz Ranch
Don and Betty Pellatz
1031 Steinle Road, Route 2
Douglas, WY 82633
(307) 358–2380

Deer Forks Ranch
Mr. and Mrs. Ben Middleton
Route 6, 1200 Poison Lake Road
Douglas, WY 82633
(307) 358–2033

FREMONT COUNTY

Bitterroot Ranch
Bayard or Meloena Fox
Dubois, WY 82513
(307) 455–2778

Cross Mill Iron Ranch
Mr. and Mrs. Larry Miller
Crowheart, WY 82512
(307) 486–2279

CM Ranch
Les E. Shoemaker
Dubois, WY 82513
(307) 455–2331

Absaroka Ranch
Dubois, WY 82513
(307) 455–2275

Double Bar J Ranch
Larry Stetter
Box 695
Dubois, WY 82513
(307) 455–2725

Triangle C. Ranch
Bill or Mary Ann Marr
Box 691
Dubois, WY 82513
(307) 455–2225
(307) 598–2213

Lazy L & B Ranch
Bernard and Leota Didier
Dubois, WY 82513
(307) 455–2839
off season: (312) 945–0107

Ram's Horn Guest Ranch
Ike and Margaret Prine
September–May:
2017 Hillside Drive
Laramie, WY 82070
June–August:
Box 564
Dubois, WY 82513

Timber Line Ranch
John and Barbara Wells
Box 308
Dubois, WY 82513
(307) 455–2513

Louis Lake Resort
650 Amoretti
Lander, WY 82520
summer: (307) 332–4324
winter: (307) 332–5020

JOHNSON COUNTY

Horton's Ranch (HF Bar Ranch)
Saddle String, WY 82840
(307) 684–2487

Pines Lodge
Box 100
Buffalo, WY 82834

South Fork Inn
Box 854
Buffalo, WY 82834

Paradise Guest Ranch
Box 790
Buffalo, WY 82834
(307) 684–7876
(307) 684–5254

Rafter Y Ranch, Inc.
Box 19
Banner, WY 82832

PARK COUNTY

Manager, **Pahaska Tepee Resort**
Box 2370
Cody, WY 82414
(307) 527–7701

Crossed Sabres Ranch
Fred and Alvie Norris
Box WTC
Wapiti, WY 82450
(307) 587–3760

Circle H. Ranch
M. E. Hall
Wapiti, WY 82450

Valley Ranch
Valley Ranch Road, West
Cody, WY 82414

Hidden Valley Ranch
Duane and Sheila Hagen, and
  Tony and Lin Scheiber
153 Hidden Valley Road
Cody, WY 82414
(307) 587–5090

Rimrock Dude Ranch
2728 North Fork
Cody, WY 82414
(307) 587–3747

Wapiti Valley Inn
Wapiti, WY 82450
(307) 587–3961

4-Bear Outfitters
1297 Lane 10, Route 1
Powell, WY 82435

Goff Creek Lodge
Gloria T. Schmitt
Box 155TC
Cody, WY 82414
(307) 587–3753

Bill Cody's Ranch Resort
Box 1390–T
Cody, WY 82414
(307) 587–2097

Mountain Shadows Guest and UXU Lodge
Box 110WT
Wapiti, WY 82540
(307) 587–2143

Castle Rock Ranch
Joe or Allison Tilden
412 Road 6 N.S.
Cody, WY 82414
(307) 587–2076

Hunter Peak Ranch
Louis and Shelley Cary
Box 1931
Cody, WY 82414
(307) 587–3711
winter: (307) 754–5878

Elephant Head Lodge
Wapiti, WY 82450
(307) 587–3980

Blackwater Lodge
Chris and Jane LaBuy
1516 North Fork Highway
Cody, WY 82414
(307) 587–3709

Line Creek Ranch
Bob and Penny Mehling
1058 Clark HCR
Powell, WY 82435
(307) 645–3114

Flying L Skytel
Cecil A. Legg
Box 1136
Cody, WY 82414
(307) 587–4029

Grizzly Ranch
Rick and Candy Felts
North Fork Route
Cody, WY 82414
(307) 587–3966

Siggins Triangle X Ranch
Stan and Lila Siggins
Southfork Route
Cody, WY 82414
(307) 587–2031

Broken H Ranch
Bert and Rosemary
Wapiti, WY 82450
(307) 587–5053
(307) 587–4606

Shoshone Lodge
Box 790WT
Cody, WY 82414
(307) 587–4044

7-D Ranch
Box 100
Cody, WY 82414
(307) 587–9885
(307) 587–3997

Absaroka Mountain Lodge
Box 168
Wapiti, WY 82450
(307) 587–3963

PLATTE COUNTY

Diamond Guest Ranch, Inc.
Box 235
Chugwater, WY 82210
(307) 422–3567
winter: (307) 422–3508

**Kamp Dakota Campground and
Guest Ranch**
Box 595
Wheatland, WY 82201
(307) 322–2772

SHERIDAN COUNTY

Bear Lodge Resort
Dayton, WY 82836
(307) 655–2444

Spear-O-Wigwam Ranch, Inc.
Box 1081
Sheridan, WY 82801
(307) 674–4496

Eaton's Ranch
Wolf, WY 82844
(307) 655–9285

Arrowhead Lodge
Box 267
Dayton, WY 82836
(307) 655–2388

Master Ranches
Dick and Jean Masters
Z Bar O Ranch
Ranchester, WY 82839
(307) 655–2386

SUBLETTE COUNTY

David Ranch
Daniel, WY 83115
(307) 859–8228

Flying U Ranch
Box 25
Cora, WY 82925
(307) 367–4479

Bridger Wilderness Outfitters
Tim Singewald
Box 561T
Pinedale, WY 82941
(307) 367–2268

Big Sandy Ranch
Bernie and Connie Kelly
Box 223-W
Pinedale, WY 82941
(307) 367–2905

Green River Outfitters
Bill Webb
Box 727
Pinedale, WY 82941
(307) 367–2416

Boulder Lake Lodge
Box 1100
Pinedale, WY 82941
(307) 367–2961

Spring Creek Ranch
Steve and Dallas Robertson
Box 1033
Bondurant, WY 82922
(307) 733–3974

Sweetwater Gap Ranch
Box 26
Rock Springs, WY 82901
(307) 362–2798

Ponderosa Lodge
Box 832
Pinedale, WY 82941
(307) 367–2516

Green River Guest Ranch
Box 32
Cora, WY 82925
(307) 367–2314

White Pine Lodge
Box 833
Pinedale, WY 82941
(307) 367–4121

Box R Ranch
Cora, Wy 82925
(307) 367–2291

Triangle F Lodge
Bondurant, WY 82922
(307) 733–2836

Game Hill Ranch
Pete and Holly Cameron
Bondurant, WY 82922
(307) 733–4120

TETON COUNTY

Moose Head Ranch
Box 214
Moose, WY 83012
(307) 733-3141

Triangle X Ranch
Moose, WY 83012
(307) 733–5500
(307) 733–2183

R Lazy S Ranch
Bob and Claire McConaughy,
   managers
Box 308
Teton Village, WY 83025
(307) 733–2655

Diamond D Ranch and Outfitters
Box 211
Moran, WY 83013
(307) 543–2479

Heart Six Guest Ranch
Carol Beeston
Moran, WY 83013
(307) 543–2477

Lost Creek Ranch
Wanda S. Smith
Box 95
Moose, WY 83012
(307) 733–3435

Trails End Ranch
Box 20311
Jackson, WY 83001
(307) 733–1616

Twin Creek Cabins
Walter and Susan Wyrick
Box 697
Jackson, WY 83001
(307) 733–3927

Beard Mountain Ranch
Lyle Beard
Alta, WY, via
Tetonia, ID 83452
(307) 576–2694

Flagg Ranch
Flagg Ranch Village
Box 187
Moran, WY 83013
(307) 733–8761
(307) 733–8761
1–800–433–2311

Togwotee Mountain Lodge
Box 91
Moran, WY 83013
(307) 543–2847

Mad Dog Ranch
Box 1645
Jackson, WY 83001
(307) 733–3729

Darwin Ranch
Box 511
Jackson, WY 83001
(208) 354–2767

Box K Ranch
Walter M. Korn
Moran, WY 83013
(307) 543–2407

Spotted Horse Ranch
Dick or Dian Bess
Jackson, WY 83001
(307) 733–2097

Flying V Ranch
Roy and Becky Chambers
Box 505
Kelly, WY 83011
(307) 733–2799

Grand Targhee Resort
Alta, WY, via
Driggs, ID 83422
(307) 353–2304

Elk Track Ranch
Kennis and Marsha Lutz
Box 53
Kelly, WY 83011
(307) 733–6171

Goosewing Ranch
Bill and Phyllis Clark
Box 70
Kelly, WY 83011
(307) 733–2768

Red Rock Ranch
Ken Neal
Box 38
Kelly, WY 83011
(307) 733–6288

Teton Valley Ranch Camp
Susie and Stuart Palmer, managers
Box 8
Kelly, WY 83011
(307) 733–2958

JACKSON HOLE SKI AREA

Teton Village Resort Assoc.
Box 220
Teton Village, WY 83025
(307) 733–4005
outside WY: 1–800–443–6931
in WY: 1–800–442–3900

Spring Creek Ranch
George Sporn
Box 3154
Jackson, WY 83001
(307) 733–8833
out of state: 1–800–443–6139

Turpin Meadow Ranch
Box 48
Moran, WY 83013
(307) 543–2496
(307) 733–6521

R Lazy S Ranch
Box 308
Teton Village, WY 83025
(307) 733–2655

WASHAKIE COUNTY

Deer Haven Lodge
Bill and June Littlefield, Bill and
Stella Hughes, owners
Box 76
Ten Sleep, WY 82442
(307) 366–2449

YELLOWSTONE

Roosevelt Lodge
TW Services, Inc.
Yellowstone National Park,
WY 82190
(307) 344–7311

Trail Creek Ranch
Elisabeth Woolsey, manager
Wilson, WY
(307) 733–2610

MONTANA
GLACIER COUNTY

Agape Bear Creek Ranch
Star Route Box 185
Bonner, MT 59823
(406) 244–5611

Bear Creek Guest Ranch
Box 151
East Glacier, MT 59434
(406) 226–4489

Bison Creek Ranch
Box 144
East Glacier, MT 59434
(406) 226–4482

Blue Spruce Lodge & Guest Ranch
451 Marten Creek Road, Box 1486
Trout Creek, MT 59874
(406) 827–4762

Broad Axe Lodge
1151 East Fork Road
Sula, MT 59871
(406) 821–3878

Broken Heart Guest Ranch
Box 107
Haugan, MT 59842

Bull Lake Guest Ranch
15303 Bull Lake Road
Troy, MT 59935
(406) 295–4228

Desert Mountain Ranch & Resort
Box 157
West Glacier, MT 59936
(406) 387–5610

Flathead Lake Lodge (DRA)
Box 248
Bigfork, MT 59911
(406) 837–4391

Hargrave Guest Ranch
Star Route
Marion, MT 59925
(406) 858–2284

Laughing Water Ranch
Box 157A
Fortine, MT 59918
(406) 882–4680
(800) 444–3833

Nez Perce Ranch
West Fork Route, Highway 89
Darby, MT 59829

Selway Lodge
Box 1100R
Hamilton, MT 59840
(406) 363–2555

Spotted Bear Ranch
Box 28M
Hungry Horse, MT 59919
or
801 P Street
Lincoln, NE 68508
(800) 228–4333

West Fork Lodge
West Fork Road
Darby, MT 59829
(406) 821–4423

Wildlife Outfitters Guest Ranch
992 Pleasant View Drive
Victor, MT 59875
(406) 642–3262
(406) 642–3869
(406) 642–3462

The Wilderness Lodge
Route 2 Box 41
Heron, MT 59844
(406) 847–2277

Willow Fire Inn & Guest Ranch
RR 1 Box 64
Eureka, MT 59917
(406) 889–3344
(406) 889–3343

CHARLIE RUSSELL COUNTY

Circle Bar Guest Ranch (DRA)
Utica, MT 59452
(406) 423–5454

Faber Ranch
Box 554
Big Sandy, MT 59520
(406) 386–2266

Foxwood Inn
Box 404
White Sulphur Springs, MT 59645
(406) 547–3918

Heaven on Earth Ranch
1605 14th SW
Great Falls, MT 59404
(406) 452–7365

Homestead Ranch
Utica, MT 59452
(406) 423–5301

JJJ Wilderness Ranch (DRA)
Box 310
Augusta, MT 59410
(406) 562–3653

Jackson-Snyder Ranch
Box 1099
Lewistown, MT 59468
(406) 538–3571

Pine Butte Guest Ranch
HC 58 Box 34C
Choteau, MT 59422
(406) 466–2158

7 Lazy P Ranch (DRA)
Box 178
Choteau, MT 59422
(406) 466–2044

South Fork Lodge
Box 56
Utica, MT 59452
(406) 374–2356

T Lazy T Ranch
South Utica Road
Hobson, MT 59452
(406) 423–5254
(406) 423–5304

Vanhaur Polled Hereford Ranch
Hilger, MT 59451
(406) 538–8693

MISSOURI RIVER COUNTY

Bar Y Seven Ranch
Brusett, WY 59318
(406) 557–6150

Hell Creek Ranch
Box 325
Jordan, MT 59337
(406) 557–2224
(406) 557–2864

YELLOWSTONE COUNTY

Almart Lodge
Box 220 Canyon Route
Gallatin Gateway, MT 59730
(406) 995–4253

Beartooth Ranch & JLX Outfitters (DRA)
Nye, MT 59061
(406) 328–6194
(406) 328–6205

Boulder River Ranch (DRA)
McLeod, MT 59052
(406) 932–6406

Burnt Leather Ranch (DRA)
West Boulder Road
McLeod, MT 59052
(406) 222–6795
(406) 932–6155

Covered Wagon Ranch
34035 Gallatin Road
Gallatin Gateway, MT 59730
(406) 995–4237

Firehole Ranch
11500 Hebgen Lake Road
West Yellowstone, MT 59758
(406) 646–7294
(406) 646–9093

G Bar M Ranch (DRA)
Clyde Park, MT 59018
(406) 686–4687

Hawley Mountain Guest Ranch (DRA)
Box 4
McLeod, MT 59052
(406) 932–5791

Lazy JH Guest Ranch
Box 1285
Red Lodge, MT 59068
(406) 446–3610

Lazy K Bar Ranch (DRA)
Melville Route
Big Timber, MT 59011
(406) 537–4404

Lone Mountain Ranch (DRA)
Box 69
Big Sky, MT 59716
(406) 995–4644

Montana's Wild West Adventures
Nye, MT 59061
(406) 328–6222

Mountain Sky Guest Ranch
Box 1128
Bozeman, MT 59715
(406) 587–1244
(800) 548–3392

9 Quarter Circle Ranch (DRA)
Gallatin Gateway, MT 59730
(406) 995–4276
(406) 995–4876

Rocking J Ranch
Park City, MT 59063
(406) 633–2222

Rocky Ledge Canyon Ranch
Nye, MT 59061
(406) 328–6200

63 Run Ranch
Box 979M
Livingston, MT 59047
(406) 222–0570

Skyline Guest Ranch
Box 1074
Cooke City, MT 59020
(406) 838–2380

Sweet Grass Ranch (DRA)
Melville Route, Box 161
Big Timber, MT 59011
summer: (406) 537–4477
winter: (406) 537–4497

GOLD WEST COUNTY

Benchmark Wilderness Ranch
Box 190
Augusta, MT 59410
(406) 562–3336

Black Tail Ranch
Wolf Creek, MT 59648
(406) 235–4330

CB Cattle & Guest Ranch (DRA)
Box 604
Cameron, MT 59720
(406) 682–4954

Diamond J Ranch (DRA)
Ennis, MT 59729
(406) 682–4867

Hildreth Livestock Ranch
324 East Court Street
Dillon, MT 59725
(406) 683–2007
(406) 681–3111

Klicks K Bar L Ranch (DRA)
Augusta, MT 59410
summer: (406) 467–2771
winter: (406) 264–5806

Lazy AC Ranch (DRA)
Box 460
Townsend, MT 59644
(406) 547–3402

Rush's Lakeview Guest Ranch
Red Rocks Lake
2905 Harrison
Butte, MT 59701
summer: (406) 276–3300
winter: (406) 494–2585

Sundance Ranch
Ovando, MT 59854
(406) 793–5633

YA Bar Livestock & Guest Ranch
Box 83
Dell, MT 59724
(406) 276–3382

CUSTER COUNTY

Happy Valley Working Ranch
Route 1 Box 2185
Miles City, MT 59301
(406) 232–4851

Walt Disney World College Programs
Walt Disney World Company
College Relations Department
Box 10090
Lake Buena Vista, FL 32830
Program length: semester
Cost: salary for work experience
Housing: available for rent
Age range of participants: college;
    must have matriculated

Number of participants: varies
Application process: application;
    interview; transcript;
    recommendations
Application due date: rolling
    admissions
Program location: Walt Disney
    World, Lake Buena Vista,
    Florida

Where better to learn about and work in the resort business than at Walt
Disney World? In fact, WDW hires students throughout the year to travel
to Florida and work and learn there. The program will give you thirty

hours of classroom instruction, while simultaneously putting you to work for at least thirty hours per week throughout the theme parks. You might find yourself giving a "spiel" (a narration) beside an attraction, working in one of the various restaurants, operating a people-mover, or learning the hotel business firsthand. You'll be paid for your work and in return will pay for your housing, although the cost of the apartments Disney provides is subsidized. This program is not meant to be a vacation. As the Disney literature points out, park employees work while others play. But Disney's employees also enjoy full use of the incredible facilities on their time off. So perhaps this is one place you can have your job and vacation too, not to mention learning about the entire operation.

Work Opportunities Abroad

◆ ◆ ◆

Working abroad can be broken down into some general categories: volunteering, working for room and board, and working for wages. In the latter two cases, the work might seem close to volunteering, since comparatively few jobs abroad will pay what you could earn in a comparable job in the United States. But once you've absorbed that realization, add to it the fact that you can live in many places around the world far more cheaply than in the United States. So you needn't despair. But don't count on getting rich, or, more important, don't count on earning enough to pay for your trip. What's more likely is that you can earn enough—if you're careful and lucky—to pay for your daily expenses. Below, you will find jobs that fall into the following categories: (1) work that will pay some or most of your expenses; (2) work that will keep you sheltered and fed; and (3) work that will pay you—if you pay first. These positions have an entrance fee attached.

WORK THAT WILL PAY YOUR EXPENSES

International Camp Counselor Program/Abroad

356 West 34th Street, 3d Floor
New York, NY 10001
(212) 563–3441
Program length: varies
Cost: $100 membership fee;
    transportation to/from camp
    location; stipend possible in
    some cases
Financial aid: none
Housing: provided
Age range of participants: 18 and
    up

Number of participants: varies by
    program
Application process: application
    with fee; photo; language-
    evaluation form (if applicable);
    personal letter from you to
    camp director; 2 letters of
    reference, 1 from YMCA
    director; interview with YMCA
    director if you aren't a YMCA
    member

Application due dates: September
  1 for Southern Hemisphere;
  January 1 for Northern
  Hemisphere

Program location: worldwide

So you've been a camp counselor? Had your cabin raided at midnight by those lovely children you were responsible for? If that experience brings back positive memories, the YMCA's International Camp Counselor Program is for you. Through the YMCA, you can work in camps in any of twenty-seven countries—and you don't have to wait until the summer, since opportunities exist not only in Australia and New Zealand but also in Peru. But it can be expensive: "I had to put everything on the line to come to Australia," said one counselor. Travel costs, passport and visa arrangements, medical examinations—even language study if you're ambitious enough to take on a situation where a new language is necessary: these are all your responsibility. "But I think it was absolutely meant to come, the way things fell into place."

The Y will do all it can to prepare you for this experience. ICCP provides written information, orientations, and possible training weekends; in addition, the French camps provide a special training course called Le Stage. Also available through ICCP are opportunities with work camps abroad, as well as with a few other programs staffed by ICCP. They should be contacted for information about these opportunities.

"I was part of the staff of a camp for Japanese people. I did a lot of hard work. I helped build roads, I help mend things, I helped clear trails. You have to have a real good sense of humor . . . you spend a lot of time with the kids. For a lot of the children I was the first American they'd ever seen. I did campfires, arts and crafts, nature hikes with them. . . . I basically became Japanese. I did what they did—which was hard sometimes. They do things very differently. . . . It was really interesting to experience their way of doing things.

Another counselor remarked: "The foreign travel has really changed my life. . . . It's different. If you are used to camping programs in the States, it's different overseas. Go in with an open mind, don't have too many expectations, and don't go over there trying to fix them, cause they're fine. But go and appreciate it. It's a wonderful experience, so relax and enjoy it. . . . I didn't speak much Japanese, and they didn't speak much English, but living and laughing transcends language. It was great."

PGL Adventure

Personnel Department
PGL Young Adventures Ltd.
Station Street
Ross-on-Wye,
Herefordshire HR9 7AH
England

001–44 + 0989 764211
Program length: November–
  February; summer, April, May
Cost: stipend, room and board
Financial aid: none
Housing: provided

Age range of participants: 18 and up

Number of participants: varies by program

Application process: application stressing experiences relevant to PGL; essays; 2 references

Application due date: rolling admissions

Program locations: United Kingdom, France, Austria, Holland

If you've had it with camp counseling in the United States but you hanker to apply those skills you've earned elsewhere, try PGL. PGL Young Adventures operates children's facilities, family camps, and adventure holidays across the United Kingdom and throughout France, Austria, and Holland. If you can sail—especially if you've taught sailing or windsurfing; if you can water-ski or canoe; if you can ski, scuba dive, play squash—all these and many more skills are in demand at PGL. In fact, the list also includes gym/aerobics, judo, tennis, fencing, softball, basketball, swimming, volleyball, abseiling, arts and crafts, performing, drama, grass skiing, archery, rifle shooting, American and European football, golf, hockey, and video film making. Cooks, nurses, drivers, and all kinds of managers also are in demand. Wages are reasonable—beginning at about $50 a week plus room and board for the bottom group of instructors. Group leaders, who must be over twenty-one, can make as much as $150 per week.

Obviously, pay is not the issue. You won't make enough to be rich, but you will get a very different slant on working in a job you know in a very different place.

World Teach

Phillips Brooks House Association, Inc.
Harvard University
Cambridge, MA 02138
(617) 495–5526
Contact person: Sidney Rosen
Program length: full 12 months; 2 years for Botswana
Cost: $2,850–$4,450, includes airfare and health insurance
Financial aid: will aid with fundraising
Stipend: available.
Housing: provided, homestays or own house

Age range of participants: graduate students or college graduates, primarily 21–25

Number of participants: 100 placed per year

Application process: application; essay; interview; recommendations

Application due dates: March 1 for August departure: May 1 for December departure

Program locations: Botswana, Kenya, and China

World Teach is essentially a job placement service. Created in 1986 by a Harvard undergrad interested in helping other young graduates and students gain volunteer placements as teachers in Africa, World Teach has since enlarged its opportunities to other developing nations. A year (or in the case of Botswana, two years) with World Teach will mean a year of teaching high school age kids in your chosen country. You will live in a remote village, probably with no running water and no electricity. Your day will be spent teaching from 8:00 A.M. until 3:00 P.M. and then most likely coaching a sport or being involved in some extracurricular activity. Evenings are quiet. You will either do work or read, most likely by the light of a kerosene lamp.

You probably will not be in a city (except in China), and unless you are married, chances are slim that you will be placed in the same school or town as another World Teach teacher. World Teach does place individuals in neighboring towns, however, so you do have the opportunity to visit with others in the program during the week. The actual teaching position placement is done by the governments of the host countries. World Teach acts only as the liaison. In this respect, its important to note that World Teach does not set governmental policy in the countries it serves but rather follows that policy. What this means is that the host countries decide what kind of teachers they want and how many, and Word Teach fills that bill.

You will be paid a small stipend by the host country to cover living expenses during your time abroad, but World Teach advises bringing along extra money in case of an emergency.

World Teach offers a wonderful opportunity for people interested in teaching and living in a developing country. The benefit of working in Africa through World Teach is in large part the thorough preparation you will receive before you leave: The literature is detailed and straightforward; the orientation period informative and energizing. As one World Teach veteran says: "We are primarily a service and education organization. We are not a study-abroad program. This is a full-time job, so expect to perform as a professional twenty-four hours a day. But the rewards of living in a third world village are intense, the appreciation for that environment is wonderful."

Although World Teach has an affiliation with Harvard, anyone may apply. The program welcomes college graduates with an interest in teaching and helping the cause of education around the world.

WORK THAT WILL KEEP YOU SHELTERED AND FED

Willing Workers on Organic Farms
See listings below
Program length: varies
Cost: none
Financial aid: none
Housing: provided
Age range of participants: 16 and up

Number of participants: varies
Application process: letter of introduction
Application due date: none
Program location: worldwide

While this organization has a perfect right to be listed among the options in this volume, it lacks many of the criteria most of its partners share. Anyone—and that certainly means you—can do it; it takes no money, just a willingness to exchange a little labor for room and board for a few nights. Most of all, WWOOF gives you a chance to learn a bit about organic growing methods, to travel around the country of your choice (see below for options), to help the organic movement—where labor is sometimes a problem because of the labor-intensive character of organic farming—and meet people around the world. Some WWOOF members offer more serious students of agriculture stays of up to six months. For example, in New Zealand, "with just over a hundred WWOOF farms in an area two-thirds the size of California, . . . we often had several farm choices within a day's journey. Whether you are a serious student of organic farming or just a traveler seeking to cut costs and enjoy a more intimate traveling experience, [New Zealand] WWOOF offers something for everyone."

So if the possibilities of some education mixed with low-cost travel appeal to you, check the list below and join WWOOF. Each of the following operates as an independent organization.

APOG; c/o Torbiern Dahl; Lekkeht 23, N-2600; Llllehammer, Norway

Integral: c/o Co-ordinadora de Agricultra Ecologica; Apdo 2580; 08080; Barcelona, Spain

MAWOOF; Jeanne Nye; 1601 Lakeside Avenue #607; Richmond, VA 23228; U.S.A.

Natur et Progrès Liste des Services: Alancourt; Nancy, 51200 Epernay; France

NEWOOF; New England Small Farms Institute; Box 937; Belchertown, MA 01007; U.S.A.

Sativa; Route 2, Box 242-w; Viola, WI 54664; U.S.A.

WEEBIO; Delisse Adolphe; Chaupreheid, 64, B-4081; Cherron, Belgium

WWOOF(UK); Don Pynches; 19 Bradford Road; Lewes, BN7 1RB, Sussex; England

Australia (AUS), Lionel Pollard, Mt. Murrindal Reserve, Buchan, Victoria 3885

(Germany), Stettiner Str 3, D-6301, Pohlheim, Germany

(NZ), Tony West, 188 Collingwood St., Nelson, New Zealand

(Erie), Annie Sampson, Ballymalone, Tuamgraney, Co. Clare

(California), 1525 Lakeside Drive, Oakland, CA 91342, U.S.A.

(Northwest United States), Neal Bittner, 3231 Hillside Road, Deming, WA 98244

(Canada) John Vanden Heuvel, RR1, Port Williams, Nova Scotia, Canada BOP 1TO

Farm Apprenticeship Schemes

Center for Local Food and Agriculture FAP; Candice Galik, Annabel Taylor Hall; Ithaca, NY 13617; U.S.A.

Horticultural Learning Opportunities; Box 1064; Tonasket, WA 98855; U.S.A.

Maine OFGA FAP; Box 2176; Augusta, ME 04330; U.S.A.
National Farmers Co-op FAP; Birdsfoot Farm; Start RT Box 138; Canton, NY 13617; U.S.A.
Natur et Progrès Service de Remplacement: Alancourt; Nancy, 51200 Epernay; France
Organic Farming Studentships, Australia—see WWOOF above
South Organic AP; Utopia Garden Centre; Box 45 OG; Utopia, TX 78884; U.S.A.
Tilth Placement Service, P.O. Box 95261, Seattle, WA 98145-2261; U.S.A.
WWOOF (UF) Training Scheme: 17 Bourn Bridge Road; Lt Abington, Cambridge, CB1 6BJ; England

Other addresses of organic farms willing to exchange labor for room and board, but not directly connected with WWOOF, appear below:
De Kleine Aarde: Munsel 17; Postbus 151. 5280 AD Boxtel; Holland. Contact Gijs van den Berg.
Andreas Wijgmans; Lindelaan 89. 3971 HB Dreibergen; Holland. Contact Biodynamics
Ferenc Fruhwahld; Magyar Biokertmuvelok Orszagos Klubja; Belvarosi lfjusagi Haz; 1056 Budapest, Molnar u. 9; Hungary
Jonathan Bar-Or; 12 Devora St; Beer Sheba, Israel
Kibbutz Shin Shizen Juku; Nakasetauri, Akan; Gun, Hokkaido 085-12; Japan
VHH (this organization does have WWOOF affiliations), c/o Bent and Inga Nielson; Asenvej 35; 9881 Bindslev, Denmark

Additional farm programs exist in the following countries (whatever details are available are included):

Finland: Finnish Family Program [see "Abroad," p. 158, for more detail about this program]: mainly agricultural opportunities are offered for one to three months in the summer, a minimum of six months in the winter.
Apply to: Ministry of Labor
    International Trainee Exchanges
    Fabianinkatu 32, SF00100
    Helsinki 10, Finland

France: work for a maximum of three months on farms throughout France.
Apply to: Centre de Documentation et Informations Rurales
    12, rue de Dessous des Berges
    75013 Paris, France

Switzerland:
Apply to: Swiss Farmer's Union
    Laurstrasse 10
    CH-5200 Brugg, Switzerland

United Kingdom: an international farm camp, operating in the summer only.
Apply to: Camp Organizer
  Tiptree
  Essex CO5 0QS, England
(See also American-Scandinavian Foundation, p. 60 for more details about opportunities in Denmark and Sweden.)

Atlantis–Norwegian Foundation for Youth Exchange

Rolf Hofmosgate 18
N–0655 Oslo 6, Norway
011–47 + 47 + 2 + 670043
Program length: from 4 weeks to 3 months
Cost: (1) 300 Norwegian kroner (NOK) to cover processing: this sum (approximately $40) must be sent in Norwegian currency to postal account 2 47 36 01 or bank account 8720.07.03349 at address above; (2) a fee of NOK 70 (about S12) for disinfection—also to be paid in kroner. Your local bank, American Express office, or AAA should be able to help you out here.

Financial aid: stipend of approximately $65 per week is standard once employment is secured
Housing: provided
Age range of participants: 18 and up
Number of participants: varies by program
Application process: application; fee as described above, with receipt accompanying application; medical certificate; personal recommendation
Application due date: rolling admissions
Program location: Norway

Despite the fact that you have to be disinfected in order to participate in this program, the Atlantic–Norwegian Youth Exchange is an inexpensive and fascinating way to join another culture and live with another family for a while. The program involves farmwork, from haymaking to milking to feeding cattle to home repairs, and maybe even housework and child care occasionally. But work is part of the reason the Norwegian government sponsors this program. It's a good way for cultural exchange to be combined with some needed help on the farm. What should be important to you is that you will be working for and with a family—your family for a few months. And you will be doing that somewhere in Norway, from above the Arctic Circle to the most picturesque of fiords. And the agricultural work is why the disinfection must happen. But beyond that? You will have from a month to three months in Norway, with a guaranteed salary of about $65 per week. This is an exceptional chance to become a part of another culture, enjoy a friendly and beautiful country, and even be paid a little bit for your trouble. Given the fact that you will work no more than thirty-five hours a week, you should still have time for some sightseeing.

However, please don't expect to make money from this program. You pay all travel expenses, including transport to the family with whom you'll be working, and the stipend is not huge. You also need a tuberculosis test; the Norwegians are extremely sensitive to the possible importation of disease. But you can have a minimum of four weeks in Norway, and you don't need to learn Norwegian first. English will do fine. If this sounds good, proceed. You won't be alone; the organization processes about five thousand applications a year. And you shouldn't expect to hear back from the Youth Exchange quickly. It receives five times as many requests as there are spaces available.

An alternative to Atlantis, modeled along the same lines, is:

The Finnish Family Program
Finnish Ministry of Labor
Fabiankatu 32, PL 30
SF–00101 Helsinki, Finland
358 + 0 90 18561

This experience will be less oriented toward farm help, since the primary focus of this program is language teaching. Moreover, the program operates mainly in the spring and early summer. But it is likely that you will be asked to join in family activities, including work, although your family might as well live in the city as in the country. Here, as in Norway, some spending money accompanies room and board.

If you're interested in child care, both as an end in itself and as a mechanism for getting abroad, you may contact the following address:

The Norwegian Ecological Agricultural Association
Langevn, 18
Bergen 5000, Norway

NOLL, as the foundation is called, will send you information and application forms. Upon completion of the forms you will be sent—eventually— an agreement obtained from the family with whom you'll be working and a letter of invitation. "These must be presented to the Norwegian embassy.... The procedure for getting a work permit seldom takes less than three months, so apply as early as possible."

Susan Griffith notes in *Transitions Abroad* (see Bibliography) that if you have sufficient Danish, Swedish, or other Scandinavian language to post an advertisement card or conduct a conversation while traveling in these countries, informal arrangements for exchanging English lessons for room and board are possibilities.

GOING DOWN UNDER

Probably one of the hottest locations in the world for travel in the past few years is the Antipodes, which for all you ungeographers means Australia and New Zealand. Between the subcontinent and the islands of New Zealand, you can find everything from surfing to skiing—or skiboarding to windsurfing. The scenery is fantastic; the people are friendly, and there's no language barrier for Americans. So what are you waiting for? Below are some details to consider.

Remember, their summer is our winter and vice versa. Since many of the opportunities described have to do with labor, particulary outside cities, climate becomes a most relevant issue.

Neither Australia nor New Zealand encourages immigration, hence it is difficult to gain a working visa. You need to investigate this issue if you don't sign on with one of the opportunities mentioned below. There are jobs to be had, but don't expect them to be professional or long-lived. However, you should be able to find short-term menial or clerical employment. If you approach the issue through CIEE (see p. 70), you may have more luck, but even under their aegis, working vivas are limited in both number and duration.

Also consider the problem of getting there. Airline rates to the Antipodes are based on seasonal considerations. One good place to look for reasonable rates is at travel agencies aimed at student fares. (Two possibilities would be Council Travel Services and Student Travel Agency, which originally was called Student Travel Australia.) If you see both New Zealand and Australia in your future, look to a multistop fare. Depending on your place of origination, the fare will be around $1,000 to $1,300 round trip.

If you're looking for a mix of travel and work, Australia might be just the thing. Skilled computer operators are less common in Australia than in the United States, so there's one place in which employment is possible; farm and vineyard laborers are always in demand, as, more recently, is staff for Australia's burgeoning tourist industry. Less popular but possibly available are positions on Australia's sheep stations, although here specific skills might be necessary. Above all, as one travel writer notes, many of these jobs mean living under very rustic conditions and are "not for fragile types of either sex."

Australian Trust for Conservation Volunteers
Box 423
Ballarat
Victoria, 3350 Australia
053–32–7490

Program length: minimum of six weeks: day, weekend, or weeklong work periods

Cost: $380, plus $42 for each additional week
Financial aid: none
Housing: provided
Age range of participants: 17 and up
Number of participants: varies by program

Application process: application with fee; personal medical insurance and travel insurance package advised
Program location: Victoria, Australia

This is a fair dinkum experience (a real doozer of one, that is) for anyone willing to put themselves in the hands of the trust. The projects the trust sponsors range from clearing land of dangerous weeds (yes, that's weeding for you gardeners) to making usable "trails or bird hides in national parks, etc. Accommodations might be in shearers' cottages, village halls, ski lodges, or under canvas." In fact, under canvas (your own tent or sleeping bag) is likely to be your lot until the weekends. Then you are given time in more urban settings, with rooms and showers, and other amenities.

For the initial cost of $500, Americans can be sponsored in Australia by the trust, for whom they agree to work for no more than thirteen weeks. In addition to finding tasks for applicants, the trust also includes transport directly from the airport and a one-week "recreation excursion canoeing, rafting, surf kayaking, climbing, ski touring or bushwalking . . . [hiking]." Actually, your $500 investment is your contribution to room and board. This program has few funds to speak of, so you really are paying your own way. As you might imagine, that small an investment doesn't mean a luxury cruise through the Australian Outback. "There were times I wanted to leave, but it was a good way to do the country really cheaply if you want to see the wildlife." Other advantages include the international flavor of each work group, peopled by individuals from around the world, as well as the opportunity to make contacts throughout the territory in which you are traveling.

Other possibilities for casual work in Australia include:
Opportunities on the "Sunshine Coast," north of Brisbane. Relatively inexpensive and quietly beautiful. Useful addresses are:

Queensland Government Travel Center
Alexandra Pde.
Alexandra Headland
Queensland, Australia
071–43241

For jobs:
The Commonwealth Employment Office
818 George Street
Railway Square, Broadway, Sydney
New South Wales, Australia

This employment office will have listings for temporary work and likely also those seeking help for harvesting, the latter lists on a state-by-state basis.

Also:

Northern Victoria Fruitgrowers'
  Association
21 Nixon Street
Box 394
Shepparton, Victoria 3630

Victorian Peach and Apricot
  Growers' Association
21 Station Street
Box 39
Cobram, Victoria 3644

WORK THAT WILL PAY YOU . . . IF YOU PAY FIRST

Interexchange
356 West 34th Street
New York, NY 10001
(212) 947–9533
Contact person: Mary Ruppel,
  program director
Program length: 1 month to a year
Cost: $75–$175 placement fee
Financial aid: None
Housing: May be available
Age range of participants: 17–25
Number of participants per
  program: varies

Application process: application
  and fee
Application due date: March 1 or
  April 15 depending on
  country
Program locations: Australia,
  Austria, Finland, France,
  Germany, Norway, Switzerland,
  and Yugoslavia

Interexchange is a nonprofit job placement service that places Americans in short-term working situations abroad. Work options through Interexchange consist primarily of menial jobs, many of which are located at resorts in Australia, Germany, Switzerland, and Yugoslavia. "You have to be completely self-reliant and realize that this is work."—"Before you go you should have an open mind, and you shouldn't have any expectations about what kind of job you want. As long as you go over willing to work, it will be a good experience." The service also includes positions teaching English in Finland, farming in Norway, and grape picking in France. Interexchange also has au pair openings in Austria and France for females only. Room and board and a small salary are provided in almost all instances. Even if salary is your only compensation, it should be enough to cover living expenses. And most of your prospective employers have dealt with exchangees before. "The people in charge at work were great and very helpful. They were used to having foreign students work for them and tried to make it easier for us. . . . It was wonderful." Interexchange will notify you of your job placement three to six weeks before your departure date. They cannot guarantee a job for every applicant, and if you are not placed they will refund your placement fee.

Interexchange offers interested individuals the opportunity to travel and work abroad. How better to experience another country than by living and working there? "You learn so much that way when you really live in the culture." Not only can you expect to become fluent in another language, you also never will lose your sense of life in a place different from your home. "[Now] . . . I know I have friends from all over the world . . . you learn all sorts of things that you never thought you would just by talking to other employees about their home country and their lifestyles." Interexchange offers you placements in a variety of countries—if you're adventuresome and open to hard work!

Internships

An internship means working for a person (or an institution) who knows something you don't and will teach you what it is, usually through on-the-job training. Also implicit in the concept of internships is the idea that you will find out about something you might want to do as a career.

Now that definitions are out of the way, what about it? Does an internship appeal to you? If so, you've got to follow a few steps. First, you need to figure out just what you might want to do. Identify an area of work, a profession or technical speciality. Then comes the hard part. You need to track down some possibilities, realistic ones. What follows are some comments and sources for specific types of internships, but it's possible to find an internship in almost any area of work if you look.

HOW TO FIND AND APPLY FOR AN INTERNSHIP:

To find an internship, for example, one college sophomore wrote dozens of letters. Before she began, however, she did some careful thinking. First she had isolated medicine as the area she wanted to try out. Among the questions she asked herself were: Where do I want to be (region of the country)? University or city or town or regional hospital—or other variety of medical service? What skills or training might they want me to have? (A question she answered by extensive questioning of medical staff at her university.) Do I need special skills or experience not directly related to profession in which I want to intern? Here's what she ended up with:

Rural Health Office
Department of Family and
  Community Medicine
University of Arizona
3131 East 2d Street
Tucson, AZ 85716

Job title: mobile clinic
  program coordinator
Program length: year
Cost: none; stipend possible
Financial aid: none

Housing: possible
Age range of participants:
  college junior and up
Number of participants: 1
Application process: letter of
  application; resume;
recommendations; phone or
personal interview
Application due date: rolling
admissions
Program location: Tucson,
Arizona

Next comes the introductory letter:

January xx, 1990
Rural Health Office
Department of Family and Community Medicine
University of Arizona
3131 East 2d Street
Tucson, AZ 85716

Dear Sir:
[Step 1: introducing yourself]

I am currently a sophomore at Any College. I am considering taking a leave of absence next year and am interested in an internship in medicine and medical services. I am taking those courses designed to prepare me for medical school. Because of my interest in medicine, I feel that a year of hands-on experience would be invaluable to me as training. I also believe this year will help me locate my academic knowledge in real life situations. Therefore, I am willing to consider any position that will allow me to gain experience. My only condition is that I be given the chance to learn from the situation.

[Step 2: vital statistics]

Enclosed you will find a copy of my resume. I will call you next week to discuss internship possibilities. Thank you for your consideration.

Sincerely,

[You will notice that you must force the issue. Don't assume that you can await a reply. Always call them.)

INTERNSHIPS IN THE UNITED STATES

What follows are a few examples of the variety of internships available domestically. The opportunities are out there for you, if you simply look carefully. Use the list below to refine your concept of what an internship might be, and, of course, apply to any of the opportunities that interest you.

Accuracy in Media
1275 K Street NW, Suite 1150
Washington, DC 20005
(202) 371–6710
Program length: varies
Cost: none
Financial aid: none
Housing: none
Age range of participants: 18 and up

Number of participants: varies
Application process: resume; writing sample and cover letter stating interest and dates of availability
Application due date: rolling admissions
Program location: Washington, D.C.

Here is an example of an internship with a small organization that publishes a monthly newsletter where you'll be involved in an variety of tasks including writing and public relations. AIM's interns are excepted to be able to use or learn to use a computer, to be involved in desktop publishing, in photography, and to be willing to write for the newsletter or other publications frequently.

AIM's opportunity is a hands-on internship, promising involvement in a small enough office that the intern is likely to do more than stuff envelopes and run the photocopying machine. All of this, however, goes hand in hand with something else often present in the politically charged atmosphere of Washington: an ideological or philosophical commitment. AIM has a definite and consistent political point of view; that view is one of ideological conservatism. If your approach to political questions mirrors AIM's, this is an internship to consider. If not, AIM is entirely inappropriate for you. Please understand that the notion of commitment to a point of view neither condemns nor extols any program or opportunity. But make sure you can support or at least tolerate the ideology of the program you're working for. Otherwise, your job might become unpleasant for you.

Amalgamated Clothing & Textile Workers Union
Organizing Department
15 Union Square
New York, NY 10003
(212) 242–0700
Contact person: Peter Goldberger
Program length: varies
Stipend: $100 a week
Housing: available

Age range of participants: college
Number of participants: several internships available
Application process: resume; cover letter
Application due date: rolling admissions
Program location: New York City

The AC&TWU is one of the largest labor unions in North America. The union is currently working to organize previously unorganized workers so that collective bargaining may be used to secure job security and rights on their behalf. An intern with AC&TWU will help with the organizational process and can expect to work closely with one or two staff members on regional organizational campaigns. An intern's responsibilities will include: analyzing corporate records of potential organizing targets, investigating local public records of organizational targets, interviewing workers about the conditions of their workplaces and jobs, and helping to carry out organizational drives. The AC&TWU is looking for motivated candidates with good attention to detail. If you want to learn the ins and outs of unions and negotiation, this is a good place to start.

Avenel Associates

1201 Connecticut Avenue NW,
 Suite 500
Washington, DC 20036
(202) 328–0199
Contact person: John Nystrom
Program length: 3–6 months
 commitment required; full-
 time preferable
Stipend: approximately $200 a
 month
Housing: none

Age range of participants: college;
 junior and senior preferred
Number of participants: 100–150
 applicants for 2–3 spaces
Application process: telephone call
 before sending resume
 requested
Application due date: rolling
 admissions
Program location: Washington,
 D.C.

This is an internship with a political consulting firm started by two former members of the Carter administration. Interns' responsibilities will include research and compilation of data, the writing and editing of reports and proposals, and the organization of documents. Interns also will attend Congressional hearings when necessary. In addition, other general office work is required. Interns must be persistent and resourceful. They must be able to work independently and demonstrate initiative. The ability to write clearly and concisely is a plus.

Center for Population Options

1012 14th Street, NW, Suite 1200
Washington, DC 20005
(202) 347–5700
Contact person: director of interns
Program length: full-time, 3-
 month commitment required
Stipend: $400 a month
Housing: none
Age range of participants: PG,
 college

Number of participants: varies;
 very few spots available
Application process: resume;
 cover letter; 2 letters of
 recommendation
Application due dates: rolling
 admissions
Program location: Washington,
 D.C.

The Center for Population Options is a national public-interest group that works on reducing the high incidence of unwanted pregnancies among teenage women. The center makes available information on family planning; its message is directed particularly toward young women so that they can make informed decisions about childbearing. An intern will assist in lobbying efforts in Congress as well as helping to track legislation. In addition, you will research and write public policy articles for the center's publications; you will prepare material for Congressional hearings; and you will help to analyze opposing arguments on family planning. Interns also will be expected to take part in general office work. The center is looking for an intern who is motivated and has excellent writing skills.

Center for Study of Responsive Law

Box 19367
Washington, DC 20036
Contact person: intern
  coordinator
Program length: summer, fall, and
  spring semesters
Cost: none
Stipend: available, for college-age
  students only
Housing: none

Age range of participants: 16 and
  up
Number of participants: 10–15
Application process: resume;
  writing samples; references
Application due date: rolling
  admissions
Program location: Washington,
  D.C.

The Center for Study of Responsive Law "is a nonprofit Ralph Nader organization that supports and conducts a wide variety of research and educational projects to encourage the political, economic, and social institutions of this country to be more aware of the needs of the citizen-consumer." What all that means is that the center is a lobbying group. An internship here will allow you to research various areas, for example, consumer law, and write reports on your finding. The center is looking for interns who are "self starters [and] people who are confident of their skill and competent." This is a meaty internship. You will have a lot of responsibility, and a lot of work. But if you are interested in law, government, and public advocacy this is something definitely worth looking into.

Circus Arts Foundation of Missouri: Circus Flora Internships

634 North Grand Boulevard, 10th
  Floor
St. Louis, MO 63103
(314) 531–6273
Contact person: intern director
Program length: 3-month
  minimum
Cost: none; small stipend provided
Housing: provided

Age range of participants: PG and
  up
Number of participants: 1–3
Admissions process: resume and
  interview
Admissions due date: rolling
  admissions
Program location: St. Louis,
  Missouri

One of the standard fantasies of childhood is running away to join the circus. What child hasn't wanted to become an expert tumbler, a lion tamer, a clown, or a trapeze artist? And the travel! Well, what would you say if you discovered that you, too, could be a part of the "big top"?

The Circus Arts Foundation can give you the chance. Originally Circus Flora, the Circus Arts Foundation has made the city of St. Louis its permanent home. The CAF has two distinct parts, the Circus Flora, which travels ten to twelve weeks a year, and the Arts Foundation, which runs a school for disadvantaged children. The school works with the children to teach them tumbling as a boost to their regular education. An internship with CAF is unlike almost any other—and understandably.

You might find yourself working in the main office, coordinating the running of both the foundation and the circus. Or you could work with the professional tumblers teaching children in the school. "Kids came after school and would practice with circus performers. The children were amazing at what they could do."—"The kids were great at it but hated the discipline required of it all. They didn't like standing in line or behaving."—"I would recommend this because it gets you totally involved and I was someone who was so uninvolved with people before this internship."—"You could learn about the animals and work with them. During the ten to twelve weeks that the circus travels, you can travel with them, putting on and then dismantling show after show across the country. You can learn the ins and outs of fundraising in the development office, or you can do some combination of all of the above." Expect to find some differences between genders. "Men will do much more labor-oriented stuff, while women will be in more managerial positions." In exchange for your work, Circus Flora will house and help feed you. You will be living with the performers in mobile homes. The Circus Flora is in the European tradition. The performers are talented people who take their work and their community very seriously. You will be with great people. But you will do a lot of hard work. However, if you're yearning to spend some time under the big top, this might just be for you.

Common Cause Internships

2030 M Street, NW
Washington, DC 20036
(202) 383–1300
Contact person: Kevin Ryan
Program length: summer;
  semester; year
Cost: none
Stipend: none
Housing: none
Age range of participants: 18 and
  up

Number of participants per
  program: 60
Application process: resume;
  phone interview; 2 references
Application due date: rolling
  admissions
Program location: Washington,
  D.C.

Common Cause is a grassroots lobbying organization that publishes a bimonthly magazine by the same name. Grassroots lobbying means that CC is dedicated to educating the public at large so that voters get involved in the system and push for changes. Make no mistake. CC has a definite point of view. You won't find it advocating greater military buildup, less government, and other conservative issues. CC is a lobbying group with a particular point of view on such issues as the environment, ethics in government, better government services for the poor. CC has over 280,000 members and forty-eight state offices. Its mission is to work at the local level, to get Americans involved in the system, to effect change via letters to members of congress, to get out the vote, and to encourage people to express their opinions about public issues. As an intern at Common Cause, you can be placed in one of several departments: Press Office, which puts together the magazine; the Issue Department, which selects and researches the target areas of concern; or the Legislative Department, which tracks the progress of Common Cause issues on Capitol Hill. Common Cause interns are given a great deal of responsibility. For instance, you will get the chance to see how government and lobbyist groups actually work, in addition to a fair share of clerical work. Your responsibilities will vary according to department, but as one intern summed it up: "It's a real job. You do valuable work and you definitely have a sense of accomplishment at the end of each day."

Common Cause offers you the chance to see how a lobbying organization works—and to enhance that observation by doing. This is one of the nation's biggest lobbying organizations. So you won't be likely to make much policy. But you might help to shape some. Here's an unusual chance to gain the perspective of an insider. You won't get paid; and you'll have to house and feed yourself. But you just might learn something.

Fourth World Movement Internships

172 First Avenue
New York, NY 10009
(212) 228–1339
Program length: semester, summer
Cost: $20 per week; stipend of $40 per week after the first month
Financial aid: none
Housing: provided
Age range of participants: 18 and up

Number of participants: 1–10
Application process: must have completed a year of college or equivalent work experience; expect interview or correspondence about intentions
Application due date: none
Program locations: New York City; Prince Georges County, Maryland

The Fourth World Movement in the United States is a branch of an international movement dedicated to "promoting the participation of society's most disadvantaged families." By joining the movement as an intern, you will become involved with the problem of poverty—through direct contact with the very poor—and you will learn about the Fourth World's course toward social justice, toward assisting those families living in extreme poverty. Fourth World has a clear agenda here. Its intent is to win the hearts of interns, to convince you of the worth of its cause: "No change is possible for the poorest families unless there is a serious, long-term effort to include those families in any programs designed to help."

Internships are available three times a year, roughly following a semester framework. As an intern, you might find yourself helping to prepare for a benefit concert or working with the library, which is a special part of Fourth World, indeed a key to its message. Fourth World seems to see itself as an instrument of educating the poor. Hence, one of its principal functions in New York is to operate street libraries, complete with traveling computers, to make education available to the very poor. Interns join the program's full-time volunteers in this and other tasks. In addition, interns also are exposed to the other mission of Fourth World, creating a storehouse of information on the disadvantaged, much of which is collected and published.

An internship with Fourth World is likely to be an intense experience, a confrontation with a part of the world you may have had little knowledge of or contact with.

Investor Responsibility Research Center

1775 Massachusetts Avenue, NW,
  Suite 600
Washington, DC 20036
(202) 939–6500
Contact person: director of interns
Program length: 3 months, full
  time
Stipend: $250 a week
Housing: none
Age range of participants: college;
  junior or senior preferred

Number of internships: 6
Application process: resume;
  cover letter; 2 letters of
  recommendation; brief writing
  sample
Application due date: rolling
  admissions
Program location: Washington,
  D.C.

The Investor Responsibility Research Center researches questions relating to the role of business in society. The center reports its findings to nearly 300 institutional investors, including 110 colleges and universities. Interns are expected to have strong writing skills and be able to analyze information clearly and logically. Interns will attend congressional hearings, interview officials at state and federal agencies, and meet with representatives of corporations and unions. Applicants are encouraged to call before applying to ensure that a position is open.

Population Institute

110 Maryland Avenue, NE
Washington, DC 20002
(202) 544–3300
Program length: 6 months

Stipend: $200 a week; dental and
  medical benefits
Housing: none

Age range of participants: 18 and up

Number of participants per program: 10

Application process: interview; resume; 3 letters of recommendation; transcript

Application due date: rolling admissions

Program location: Washington, D.C.

The Population Institute is a nonprofit lobbying organization founded on the belief that the root of many of the world's problems comes from overpopulation. Therefore, it is the mission of the Population Institute to introduce family planning via education and communication wherever possible. There's a small permanent staff, so the backbone of the agency is really its interns. An internship with PI will mean a great deal of responsibility and an introduction to life as a lobbyist in Washington.

Internships at PI exist in four areas: public policy, international, media coordinator, and community organization. The public policy liaison interns are responsible for the "Capitol Hill beat." That means that they spend their day covering important legislation, setting up meetings with members of congress or legislative assistants, setting up interviews with the press, and working on mailings that will help to educate the public. The international intern (there is only one) must be bilingual—no specific second language required—and will help translate documents and will work on lobbying at an international level. The intern keeps track of what is happening in family planning all over the world and how each and every development relates to the United States. The media coordinator assists in organizing media events and contributes to the Population Institute's newsletter, "Pop Line," by research, writing, and editing copy for it. The media coordinator also is responsible for news releases. Interns also serve as community organizers. According to Population Institute staff, these interns are the "backbone of the educational project." They are each assigned to seven or eight states and organize media and civic groups within those states. In each case, their goal is to set up population awareness days during which the president of the Population Institute speaks and shows slides to a local group. These speaking engagements are strung together to form a six- to seven-day trip to educate and involve the public in family planning at a grassroots level.

Interns at PI rave about the experience: "An unbelievable amount of responsibility. They are very organized and let me be very responsible. It's a lot of work. I could work as much as twenty hours a day. But it's super because I am really working." Another intern called the internship with PI "very fulfilling. . . . You make a difference and learn the real world stuff of Washington and politics."

Population Institute internships are as rewarding as you can hope to find in Washington. They will provide you with lots of responsibility, yet are structured enough to allow you to get help if you need it. They offer a stipend, which, while small, is more than you will find at most places. And they will give you an insider's view to the world of the Capitol Hill and the White House.

Project Vote

1424 16th Street, NW, Suite 101
Washington, DC 20036
(202) 328–1500
Contact person: director of interns
Program length: 3-month
    commitment, full time
Stipend: available
Housing: none
Age range of participants: college

Number of participants: "several"
    openings for interns
Application process: cover letter
    and resume
Application due date: rolling
    admissions
Program location: Washington,
    D.C.

Project Vote is an organization created in the early 1980s to register voters and form effective grassroots lobbying campaigns. An intern with Project Vote would have the following responsibilities: handling correspondence, research, fund-raising materials, press releases, and training manuals. An intern also would help to service and monitor field offices and activities for Project Vote. Interns participate in staff meetings, are involved in phone work, and perform general office duties. Project Vote needs interns with liberal arts backgrounds who can handle a great deal of responsibility and are self-motivating.

Public Affairs Television

356 West 58th Street
New York, NY 10019
(212) 560–6930
Contact person: Judy Doctoroff
Program length: full time;
    duration of internship is
    flexible
Stipend: $50–$200 a week
Housing: none

Age range of participants: college
Number of participants: varies by
    year
Application process: resume;
    cover letter; recommendations
Application due date: rolling
    admissions
Program location: New York City

Public Affairs Television is an independent production company formed by Bill Moyers. The company produces documentaries usually aired on public television. An intern's responsibilities will include general office work and research on program related activities. This is a chance to see how television production works and to get some hands-on experience. Interns must have good reading and writing skills, but no particular academic background is required.

Union of Concerned Scientists

1616 P Street, NW, Suite 310
Washington, DC 20036
(202) 332–0900
Contact person: director of interns
Length of internship: 3-month
commitment, full-time;
positions available starting June,
September, and January
Stipend: $500 a month
Housing: none

Number of participants: varies by
year
Age range of participants: college
Application process: resume;
cover letter; and 2 references
Application due dates: March 1
for June; June 1 for
September; November 1 for
January
Program location: Washington,
D.C.

The Union of Concerned Scientists is "a national organization of over 100,000 scientists and citizens concerned about the impact of advanced technology on society." The union has conducted studies on the strategic arms race, radioactive-waste disposal, nuclear-plant safety, and energy-policy alternatives. An intern with the union would monitor legislation and attend congressional hearings related to the union's work. An intern would also research and write on a number of important issues the union is working on, as well as perform general office work.

NONPROFIT AGENCIES

Volunteering for a nonprofit agency has all the criteria needed to make it an ideal way to spend all or part of a year away from academia: The experience is undeniably "real world"; it is practical and it is desperately needed. If all that's true, why shouldn't you just go and find one and sign up right away? The problem with volunteer internships is that you can't really tell what you're getting into until you're there. Since volunteer positions vary dramatically depending on the agency and the current need, there are no real hard and fast ways to tell if you're going to have a good experience. The best way is to simply try to get a sense of what your responsibilities will be before starting out: here are some questions to ask as you look for placement.

1. What will you be doing? Sure you will be a jack of all trades, but will you have focus, a specific area of responsibility or concern?
2. Do you have a staff adviser or boss? This is very important because the best internships need structure.
3. Do you like the tasks your volunteer agency provides? For example, if you are uncomfortable with children, it's probably not a good idea to work at the children's hospital.
4. How many hours a week do you intend to work? If your intention is to commit a minimum of time, then just running the photo-

copier wouldn't be so terrible; if you plan to spend a normal work week with the internship, you need to think twice about what your tasks will be.

5. How many people are on the staff? Will you have a core group you will constantly be working with, or will your coworkers, responsibilities, and position shift from time to time (and if so, how often? In some volunteer agencies, the turnover can be dizzying).

6. Is there a former volunteer intern you can talk with about his or her experience?

7. Remember that volunteer work is not glamorous. It's often likely to be unpleasant and frequently frustrating. For that reason it's important that you consider volunteering for a cause you really believe in.

Good luck. If you've made allowances for reality in your selection of an internship, you're likely to have a most rewarding experience.

INTERNSHIPS IN GOVERNMENT

So you want to work in Washington. You want to be where the action is, where deals are struck, bills debated, laws made, and vetoes handed down. You want to have an internship. You want to be part of the American government system. Or so you think. Well, internships are great ways to find out for sure, and learn a lot in the process.

First, what is an internship in government? they come in all shapes and sizes, and from some surprising places. An internship usually means that you will be part of a team in an office with a specific perspective working for some governmental goal. That goal might be the election of a candidate, the passage of a bill in Congress, the dissemination to the public of information about governmental issues, the investigation of a hot topic for a congressman.

What you do in an internship depends directly on the mission and the goals of your office. Every internship has its fair share of "grunt" work. It is not all glamour; in fact, it's a lot of envelope-licking, stamp-sticking hard work. But, when looking for your internship, the first thing to keep in mind is that you need to feel comfortable with the direction taken by your particular office. If you don't, that one's not the internship or office for you. Second, in order to have a successful internship experience it is important that you feel you will be alotted specific tasks, and that your responsibility will be allowed to grow as you complete them. It is OK to ask an office staffer how much responsibility you will gain. If the only thing you're going to do is lick envelopes, you might want to think twice about commiting to the position.

Where do you find these internships? The most obvious answer is your congressman. However, the internships in congressional offices are only a very tiny fraction of the internships available in Washington. Directories of internship positions exist (see Bibliography); indeed, there are several organizations devoted solely to placing interns in positions in and around the capital. So by all means contact your congressman's office, once you've exhausted the material in this book. Many of these organizations are lobby groups; they have a definite bias, so you need to keep that in mind. But if there is an issue that you feel strongly about, joining a lobbyist organization might be a good course to follow. It also is no small consideration that lobbyists often need volunteer help. If it is an election year, a campaign internship in your home state is a super way to see the democracy in action. Campaigns are always anxious to have interested, committed people, and are usually understaffed. Therefore, your chances of increased responsibility are great. You can find the names and addresses of the current members of Congress in either your school library or in your local library.

STATE AND LOCAL GOVERNMENT

There are at least fifty unusual opportunities for college juniors and seniors across the United States. Where? Right there in your own state government. If you go to school out of state, you have two opportunities, since most state legislatures will hire not only residents but those who attend college in their state. Moreover, many states have executive internships available also. If you have any interest in politics, an internship in state government is an ideal way to explore that interest. Interns find themselves deeply involved in legislative business, often doing research on upcoming bills, dealing with constituents' problems, and observing the legislative process firsthand. In addition, most state internships also involve periodic coursework and sometimes mock legislative sessions. Only natural that they would, since these internships usually award college credit, often as much as a full semester's work. Almost all pay a stipend, although it's seldom more than just enough to keep you housed.

You also can find internships at the local level. City mayors all take interns and provide them with a super view of what goes on in their part of the American democratic system. So, if city government interests you, in any and all of its aspects, write to your mayor or to your city councilperson and ask for information and an appointment.

Internships exist anywhere and everywhere, at every level and in every facet of government. Any public internship should prove a most satisfactory way to learn firsthand how government really works, but you need to find the best one for you.

NONGOVERNMENTAL INTERNSHIPS

The following are actually collections of internships—or programs organized around internships. Hence, their separate listing.

The College Venture Program

Contact through your college career services or career planning office

Program length: semester or year

Cost: none; stipend often provided

Financial aid: none

Housing: depends on opportunity

Age range of participants: PG, college

Number of participants: varies by program

Application process: You must be a student at one of the colleges and universities listed below. Apply through college career office; specifics might require a letter of introduction; a statement of purpose; and other supporting material.

Application due date: none

Program location: domestic United States

To leap to the bottom line, if you're not intending to be or are a student at Bates College, Brown University, the College of the Holy Cross, Connecticut College, Hobart and William Smith Colleges, Swarthmore College, Vassar College, or Wesleyan University, you needn't read further. At the moment, the College Venture Program serves only these institutions. However, if you are an applicant to any of these schools, have been admitted to any of them, or are currently enrolled at one of them, welcome to this opportunity. And be thankful, because it's an exceptional one.

Venture is a clearinghouse for internships. If you have been admitted to or are a student at one of the eight colleges above, you're eligible for a Venture internship. This means several things. It means you have a chance to have a break from school. "I wouldn't trade these past six months for three years of free college education. I have learned more and given more than I have at any other period in my life and now I feel ready to tackle the remaining years of my education."

It also means you have a chance to taste the "real world." As a result of his internship with a Washington-based public interest group, one Venture alumnus noted that he had "developed a thirst for knowledge of history and government, an interest in the law and a fascination with politics and public interest work. . . . I'm more aware of how the 'real world' operates and am not afraid of it anymore. I look forward to graduating from college. I know what courses I want to take. I know why I'm doing what I'm doing."

As almost every student reports, a Venture internship gives the intern a chance to gain a better sense of self. "Moving to New York City for six months, living on my own, earning my own living without help from my parents and coping with a full-time, nonsummer job has given me more self confidence."

If any of the above sound like good reasons for a break to you, then the College Venture Program is worth considering. Venture will not guarantee a placement, but the list is extensive and your chances extremely good.

Dynamy

57 Cedar Street
Worcester, MA 01609
(508) 755–2571
Contact person: director of
admissions
Program length: full academic
year, September–June;
semester option possible
Cost: $8,900
Financial aid: available
Housing: provided

Age range of participants: PG and
college, 17–20
Number of participants: 42 per
session
Application process: essays,
references, required; interview
strongly encouraged
Application due date: rolling
admissions
Program location: Worcester,
Massachusetts

Dynamy is an organized program that places students in internships throughout the city of Worcester. Interns choose from more than two hundred possibilities in the fields of media, business, education, government, human services, and the arts. Through the course of the year interns are placed in three to four different internships and thus gain the opportunity to experience several different fields, or in some cases, several sides of the same field. Dynamy requires that its interns switch internships at least three times in order to ensure variety and personal growth.

Dynamy is unique in its provision for students to have the opportunity to do independent internships in a supportive environment. Before even beginning the search for an internship, the Dynamy kids are taken on a three-week wilderness trip run from Dynamy with Outward Bound. This trip, called the North Country, is designed to foster self-confidence in and cooperation within the group. Upon returning from the North Country, interns choose their first internship in conjunction with filling out a Goal Sheet, which outlines the ways in which an individual wants to grow during the course of the year. These goals can be anything from increased public-speaking skills to assertiveness on the job. The Dynamy staff advisers work with the individual to achieve those goals. On the internship side, the Dynamy staff works with both the interns and the sponsoring organizations to find a good fit for both. Once the intern is placed in the internship, Dynamy advisers continue to help him/her adjust to and cope with the pressures of the working world. This is done through weekly meetings with the intern, and periodic sponsor/adviser/intern meetings.

The interns are housed together in furnished apartments owned by Dynamy. There are three apartment houses, and each has one apartment designated for an adult supervisor. The students are placed in groups of two to five depending on the size of the apartments. They are responsible for their own food, and are provided with an allowance of $45 per week to spend on food and entertainment.

The Dynamy experience is centered around the theme that its participants need to learn a bit about the real world and take some responsibility for their existence in that world. One Dynamy intern summed up the program's philosophy by saying: "This year is for you, and you have to take charge of it or it won't happen." Dynamy encourages its participants to adopt that philosophy. They strongly encourage interns to go out and find new internship opportunities, or to take existing opportunities to new depths of involvement. Staff members quickly point out that Dynamy returns exactly what each individual puts into it. That's not a new idea, but Dynamy's secret is in making that input/output function effectively. The program can have a profound impact because, as an alum said: "Dynamy makes you see things differently."

The Dynamy staff is quick to point out that the program is entirely what the individual puts into it. It can provide kids with a completely new perspective on the world of learning or be a way to fill the year. Yet, all the interns seemed to agree that if a participant is willing to give to the program, Dynamy will more than return the investment.

Interim

The Center for Interim Programs
Box 2347
Cambridge, MA 02238
(617) 547–0980
Program length; varies; almost always a semester or year
Cost: $800 fee
Financial aid: none
Housing: none

Age range of participants: high school, PG, college
Number of participants: varies
Application process: no formal process; interview if possible
Application due date: rolling admissions
Program location: Cambridge, Massachusetts

Interim, or the Center for Interim Programs, is an unclassifiable commodity. Although Interim advertises itself as a collection of programs, actually its head, Cornelius Bull, functions more as a facilitator. Bull uses his years of connections to make possible individual opportunities for students wishing to, as he puts it, "rekindle motivation . . . expand their awareness of self . . . [and redesign] their lives." As was reported in the *New York Times*, these efforts are usually successful. They can take the form of sailing on a research vessel in the Caribbean or working with wildlife in a variety of locations. Because these opportunities often rely on the client/mentor chemistry, their effectiveness is varied. The excitement of the placement sometimes doesn't live up to its reality. But the idea—taking time out from school—does, as the *Times* notes, "refuel the spirit and make[s] the return to traditional education more meaningful."

Playhouse on the Square

51 South Cooper in Overton Square
Memphis, TN 38104
(901) 725–0776
Contact person: Jackie Nichols

Program length: half or full season
Stipend: $60 per week
Financial aid: none
Housing: provided

Age range of participants: PG, college

Number of participants: varies

Application process: application; letters of recommendation; resume; 8 × 10 black-and-white glossy photo

Application due date: rolling admissions

Program location: Memphis, Tennessee

Do you think you belong in the theatre? Playhouse on the Square may be the way for you to find out. There you will be given a chance to work as an intern in the two theatres operated by Playhouse, as well as becoming involved in their youth theatre program. Internships are in both acting and in technical theatre; in either, you will be regarded as professional staff. That means being prompt, accepting all responsibilities visited upon you, and working with your peers. "The rewards are experience and extensive training within a successful professional theatre."

If this sounds like hard work, you're right. However, because of the demands put on you, Playhouse will house you and pay you a stipend sufficient to keep you healthy. Beyond those material benefits, you also can earn college credit—if your parent institution is so inclined. Playhouse's staff "will assist by providing reports to the school as necessary." The catch-22 of this program is experience. Not only will you get it, you also need some to make yourself eligible. So put together your resume and trot out everything you've done, from playing the tree in Macbeth on up (or down).

Here are a handful of other theater opportunities around the United States. All offer internships or like opportunities. Write for details.

Allenberry Playhouse
Box 7
Boiling Spring, PA 17007
Program length: summer
Cost: none; stipend provided
Financial aid: none
Housing: provided
Age range of participants: college
Number of participants: varies

Application process: cover letter; resume; photo
Application due date: rolling admissions
Program location: Pennsylvania

American Stage Festival
Box 225
Milford, NH 03055
(603) 673–4005
Program length: May–Sept.
Cost: none; stipend provided
Financial aid: none
Housing: provided
Age range of participants: college

Number of participants: varies
Application process: application; interview; letters of recommendation, possible audition
Application due date: March 15
Program location: New Hampshire

Florida Studio Theatre
1241 North Palm Avenue
Sarasota, FL 33577
Program length: November–June
Cost: none; stipend provided
Financial aid: none
Housing: provided
Age range of participants: college

Number of participants: varies
Application process: application
    form; cover letter; resume;
    photo; interview by phone
Application due date: rolling
    admissions
Program location: Florida

Glimmerglass Opera Theatre
Box 191
Cooperstown, NY 13326
Program length: May–September
Cost: none; stipend provided;
    possible academic credit
Financial aid: none
Housing: provided

Age range of participants: college
Number of participants: varies
Application process: cover letter;
    resume; 2 recommendations
Application due date: February 1
Program location: New York

John Drew Theatre of Guild Hall
158 Main Street
East Hampton, NY 11937
Program length: June–September
Cost: none; Equity and academic
    credit
Financial aid: none
Housing: provided

Age range of participants: college
Number of participants: varies
Application process: cover letter;
    resume; interview
Application due date: May 1
Program location: New York

Denver Center Theatre Company
1050 13th Street
Denver, CO 80204
Program length: all year
Cost: none; stipend provided
Financial aid: none
Housing; none
Age range of participants: college

Number of participants: varies
Application process: cover letter;
    resume; interview by person
    or by phone
Application due date: June 1 for
    early consideration
Program location: Colorado

**Rural Education Project and American/Mexican Indian Student
    Teaching Project**
Indiana University Cultural
    Immersion Unit
Project Options for Student
    Teachers

Room 321, Education Building
Indiana University
Bloomington, IN 47405
(812) 335–8579

Contact person: Dr. James Mahan, director
Program length: semester
Cost: varies according to semester hours
Financial aid: available
Housing: provided
Age range of participants: college juniors and up, graduate students
Number of participants: varies; you will be placed individually

Application process: application; essays; interview
Application due date: rolling admissions
Program locations: rural Kentucky, Kansas, Indiana, West Virginia, and on Indian reservations throughout the West and Southwest

If the idea of teaching appeals to you, if you also have a desire to go someplace really different—and to help people who need it—rural education might be an answer. The Cultural Immersions Unit at Indiana University offers students the chance to be placed in rural school systems and service agencies for a semester. Students divide up their semester, spending the first few weeks assigned as an intern to a community agency that provides some form of necessary relief work for that area. After learning a little bit about the history and problems of their community, students are then placed in the school system as student teachers. This advance time to meet the community and its issues before stepping into the classroom is an important component to the program. In the words of one past participant: "A community assignment lets you ease into the community, become familiar with the residents—their attitudes and lifestyles. After my agency work, I felt like I was just moving into the community instead of just being dropped into [student teaching]." A word to the wise, however: Teaching in these parts of the country can be lonely, and the normal stresses of teaching seem exaggerated here because of the isolation. But if you are committed to ideals that make up rural education, this is a terrific place for you to try your wings.

Shelburne Farms Environmental Internships
Shelburne, VT 05482
(802) 985–8686
Program length: semester
Cost: see stipend
Financial aid: none
Stipend: room and board
Housing: none until fall 1991
Age range of participants: 18 and up

Number of participants per program: up to 6
Application process: resume; cover letter; interview
Application due date: rolling admissions
Credit available
Program location: Shelburne, Vermont

Shelburne Farms is a thousand-acre working farm that functions as an environmental education facility. Students and teachers come for the day to experience "life on a farm." Shelburne Farms offers several daylong, hands-on adventures such as "Winter Tracking," which explores the age-old art of tracking animals in the snow, or "Super Soil," a hand-son scientific look at dirt and the creatures that live within it, as well as "The Harvest," an actual journey through fall harvesting on a large farm. The programs are designed for children from kindergarten through sixth grade and take place during the school day. Children learn by working with the soil, planting a garden, harvesting a crop, or touring the dairy. Shelburne Farms tries to get its visitors to understand agriculture and agricultural history by living it. As an intern, you will be one of the people responsible for giving these programs the breath of life.

Interns at Shelburne Farms are primarily responsible for teaching two field trips a week. You will attend special monthly training workshops, and you will have required reading and lesson plans. Interns may also help out with general farm upkeep, the feeding and grooming of animals, tending and harvesting of gardens and crops, and the upkeep of barn buildings. Each intern is expected to keep a journal of his/her teaching experiences.

Shelburne Farms is a great place to start if you are thinking about teaching young children. At the farm, you have the opportunity to work directly with kids—digging in the dirt or trekking through the snow. While there is no housing available yet, dorms are being built and will be ready for fall 1991. Shelburne intends to provide its interns with room and board at that point.

Smokey House Project Internship

Smokey House Project
RFD Box 292
Danby, VT 05739
(802) 293–5121
Program length: semester, year
Cost: see stipend
Financial aid: none
Stipend: room and board
Housing: provided
Age range of participants: 18 and up

Number of participants: varies, but no more than 4
Application process: resume; cover letter; interview
Application due date: rolling admissions
Program location: Danby, Vermont

Smokey House is a special-education project for adolescents who have had problems in the public school system—students with high rates of absences, low to failing grades, or chronic discipline problems—and works with them for half of every school day and full time in the summer on forestry, carpentry, and agriculture projects. Smokey House seems to give its students a sense of self-worth and concrete reasons to go on with school. All Smokey House projects are designed to incorporate the skills that the students learn in school. Students discover planting a garden or making a table requires basic math skills. They discover why their half day of regular classes is so important.

Making this program work requires unusual commitment and real effort. Smokey House clients are tough; they demand a lot of energy from the staff. So don't underestimate what doing this job will take. As an intern at Smokey House, you will be working with the crew leaders helping to train students in such skills as carpentry, agriculture, and forestry. You will live on the project with other staff members, and Smokey House will provide your board.

Starlight Foundation

5050 Eighth Avenue
New York, NY 10018
(212) 268–1545
Contact person: Lucy Mullen
Program length: 3 months and up
Cost: see stipend
Financial aid: none
Stipend: possible
Housing: none

Age range of participants: 18 and up
Number of participants per session: varies
Application process: cover letter; resume; interview
Application due date: rolling admission
Program location: New York City

The Starlight Foundation is in the business of making wishes come true for chronically and terminally ill children. The foundation's mission and name come from the children's rhyme "Starlight, star bright/first star/I see tonight/ wish I may/wish I might/have the wish/I wish tonight." Since its inception in 1983 the foundation has managed to grant nearly every child's wish. It's not an easy matter. Children's wishes have taken staffers to exotic places, to the offices and residences of the rich and famous . . . indeed to fantastic lengths on occasion. And that's where you come in. As an intern for the Starlight Foundation, you will be responsible for making wishes come true. Because the foundation is a nonprofit agency that relies on fund raising and volunteers for its funding and staff, your responsibilities will extend into a variety of other areas also. One of the pluses about an internship with the Starlight Foundation is that it operates with a small core staff. This means that the possibilities for an intern to really learn about the running of a nonprofit agency and to really get involved in the organization are tremendous. An intern with the Starlight Foundation will most likely work on the Wish Program, which means attending to the details that executing each child's wish requires. But the greatest part about an internship with the Starlight Foundation is that it is flexible. Interns will also be able to help out on fund raising and other aspects of the foundation's daily operations.

INTERNSHIPS ABROAD

Congress-Bundestag Youth Exchange Program for Young Professionals

CDS International, Inc.
425 Park Avenue
New York, NY 10022
(212) 593–2090
Contact person: William Brown
Program length: year, August–August
Cost: none for program, but at least $200 per month for pocket money
Financial aid: not needed

Housing: homestays, some dormitory
Age range of participants: must be at least 18 and no older than 24 at start of the program
Number of participants per program: 55
Application process: interview; form; recommendations; essay
Application due date: January 31
Program location: Germany

The Congress-Bundestag Program offers a terrific opportunity for those who want to study and work abroad. Set up in 1983 by the U.S. and the West German governments, the program was designed to strengthen the ties between the countries by allowing young adults from each nation to live in the other. Developed primarily for students who have specific and primarily—though not exclusively—technical career aspirations, for Americans the program combines two months of intensive German language, four months of classroom instruction at a German technical school or "other institution of higher education," and a six-month internship in a German company. While previous knowledge of German is suggested, it is not required. But alums strongly advise some previous exposure to the language. Not only is the ability to make early contact important but the brief scope of the language-training module, only two months, was called by one former student "a major drawback" to the program.

Whatever your language facility, you must bring to the program a strong career sense and the ability to work and communicate well with others. "[Your own] . . . initiative is so important. You have to do it. If you want to go to the bank, make friends, read a magazine. You have to do it. No one can do it for you." The program is, as one student termed it, a "real growth experience."

This program's principal advantage is its funding by the governments of the two countries, a virtue noted by several alumni. Funding makes the program's extreme flexibility possible. As an exchange participant, you will live with a German family, go to a German university or technical school, be "of Germany." 'What you learn about the Germans, yourself, and history is tremendous. It is a real character builder." Yet, you will be associated with other Americans involved in the program. This is a program that gives a student everything he or she could possibly wish to gain on an exchange—school, family, language, and work experience. But don't delude yourself.

As many graduates of this program have noted, the process of cultural immersion is a complex and difficult one. "[This was] ... the toughest year of my life and the best year of my life." But was it valuable? "I would do it again in a second."

International Association for the Exchange of Students for Technical Experience

Association for International
Practical Training
10480 Little Patuxent Parkway,
Suite 320
Columbia, MD 21044–3502
(301) 997–2200
Program length: 8 weeks to 12
months
Cost: $75, plus expenses
Financial aid: none
Housing: available

Age range of participants: college;
must have completed
sophomore year
Number of participants: varies by
program
Application process: application
with fee; usually transcript
and/or essay; teachers'
recommendations
Application due date: December 10
Program location: worldwide

Want to discover more about your field while living in another country? IAESTE is an organization devoted to placing students in technical fields (engineering, computer science, mathematics, agriculture, the natural and physical sciences, architecture) in appropriate positions around the world. Its parent organization, the Association for International Practical Training, was founded in London in 1948. AIPT's aim was to foster career experience and give its participants a working knowledge of other countries. IAESTE is the U.S. branch of this program.

This is a fantastic opportunity for anyone who wants to see his/her field from a different perspective. But there is another, equally valuable learning experience involved here. By living abroad, you will have a chance to understand another culture, an opportunity that goes beyond technical learning.

What are the drawbacks? First, you must be qualified—and that means majoring in one of the technical fields mentioned above. Second, you may need a particular facility in another language; and any linguistic ability will be of enormous help (although a foreign language is by no means a requirement; in fact, many applicants have no foreign language training). Finally, you must be a bit adventurous and have some experience with the field you're pursuing.

Hotel and Culinary Exchange Program

Association for International
Practical Training
Program length: up to 18 months;
generally 6–12 months
Cost: $75
Financial aid: none

Housing: provided
Age range of participants: 18 and
up
Number of participants: varies by
program

Application process: applicant
finds prospective employer;
AIPT application with fee;

Application due date: rolling
admissions

Program location: worldwide

This division of AIPT is "intended to benefit young people beginning a career in the hotel and food service industry." To enter this program, you must have completed a training program or university course, and should have had some practical experience. You also should have some fluency in the language of potential host countries. Beyond that, AIPT will assist you in placement and in obtaining the necessary visa and work permits.

Career Development Exchanges Program

Association for International
Practical Training

Program length: year round

Cost: $75

Financial aid: none

Housing: provided

Age range of participants: college
and up

Number of participants: varies by
program

Application process: application
with fee

Application due date: rolling
admissions

Program location: worldwide

The Career Development Exchanges Program is AIPT's answer to the problem of what to do with you if you aren't in a technical field or involved with food and hotel management. This program will find a spot for you to train in your field abroad: currently in Australia, Finland, France, Ireland, Switzerland, and the United Kingdom. The requirements remain as with AIPT's other options above: You need to have pursued your field previously; you need language capability where necessary; and you may need university or comparable background. If all that is under your belt, you might look to CDEP.

Internship in European Business

Washington University

Campus Box 1077

One Brookings Drive

St. Louis, MO 63130–4899

(314) 899–5175

Program length: year

Cost: varies

Financial aid: available

Housing: provided

Age range of participants: college
junior

Number of participants: varies

Application process: application
with fee; transcript; personal
essay; 2 faculty
recommendations (one from
French department); parental
statement; personal interview

Application due date: October 31
for fall

Program location: Paris

In the early 1980s, Washington University organized a new kind of year-abroad program. By combining a semester of coursework at the Ecole Européenne des Affaires de Paris with an internship position in a French-managed company, the university created a junior year for the nineties. Indeed, there is no better time for you to find out about European business than on the eve of European unity.

Given the quality of this concept, the Washington program has some daunting requirements. You need a solid background in French, including not only fluency but also a knowledge of what Washington calls "commercial French." You should have had introductory macro- and micro-economics, as well as a semester of financial accounting. In addition, other business and French literature and civilization courses are desirable, as is coursework in calculus and international economics.

Is all this worth it? Alumni of the program have responded with "Definitely! . . . I learned things I could never have learned in a classroom or from books. . . . I wouldn't trade the experience for anything!"—"The internship and the year in Paris were priceless."—"It was not only an investment in my future career but was an unforgettable experience that changed me for the better in a way no other experience could." Clearly, this program offers the qualified applicant an unusual opportunity.

London Internships

Beaver College Center for
  Education Abroad
Glenside, PA 19038
(215) 572–2901
Program length: semester, year
Cost: approximately $6,600 fall;
  $6,900 spring; $12,500 year;
  includes travel to Britain,
  tuition, housing in session
Financial aid: available, principally
  through home institution
Housing: provided; homestays
  possible
Age range of participants: college
  junior and above

Number of participants: varies by
  semester
Application process: application
  and fee; transcript;
  photographs; 1 faculty
  recommendation; signed
  approval by home college
  official; minimum GPA 3.0
Application due dates: depends on
  site to which you apply;
  usually October 5 for spring;
  April 20 for fall
Program location: London

Beaver's London Internship offers both semester and full-year opportunities for college juniors interested in a hands-on situation. These internships are available in an astonishingly broad range of areas, stretching from a variety of applied academic disciplines to areas of business, social and public service, the arts, communications, fashion, real estate, hotel management, and government. In addition, the program office is open to original proposals, of which there are a regular number annually. Interns also take a regular schedule of courses at the City of London Polytechnic. The distinct advantage of this program is its affiliation with the well-established machinery of the Beaver College Center for Education Abroad. Interns can rely on the security and predictability of tested experience.

London Internship Programmes

Boston University
725 Commonwealth Road, Room
   B2
Boston, MA 02215
(617) 353–9888
Contact person: Nancy Sullivan
Program length: semester or
   summer
Cost: $7,200
Financial aid: available
Housing: apartment living with
   other students
Age range of participants: 18 and
   up; undergraduate students
   preferred

Number of participants per
   session: 150–200
Application process: essays; 2
   recommendations; transcript;
   3.0 GPA
Application due dates: for fall:
   rolling admission until July 1;
   for spring: rolling admission
   until November 1; for
   summer: rolling admission until
   March 1
Program location: London

The Boston University internship program offers students the chance to have an internship at a London office (or theater) in one of five fields: political science, economics/business; journalism/communications; art/architecture; human services; and visual/performing arts. What is unique about the BU program is that before entering your internship, you spend four and a half weeks in "intensive classroom study." During this period, you will take two core courses relating to your field. For example, students with political internships must take British Political Culture and British Political Institutions, and journalism students must take courses entitled British Media, Culture and Society and Advertising Practices and PR in England. These courses are designed to give you a foundation for the work you will do during your nine-week internship. The courses meet from 10:00 A.M. to 4:00 P.M., with an hour break for lunch.

If you want an internship that will give you the real flavor of your area of interest, BU places its students in internships that give each student a high probability of involvement. For example, a student might be an intern in a member of Parliament's office. As an intern you can expect to spend four days a week in the office, from 9 to 5 and to spend the fifth day back in the classroom, devoted to a course you've selected to help you understand your internship. You also will be responsible for keeping a journal. Moreover, on this internship you won't just be stuck at the copy machine; B.U. sees to that. You really will get a good look at how things operate in Britain. You are there to learn, not be a flunkie, and your office staff knows that.

One of the nicest elements of the program is that you live with other BU interns in a flat. This automatically gives you friends and freedom. The independence of flat living is an important part of the BU experience. As one alum puts it: "This combination of [apartment] living and working was key for me because so many other programs seem to isolate the student as an American observer in a narrower academic arena with sightseeing excursions on the side." BU gets you involved in English life. Another alum says it this way: Bu provided "an opportunity to learn about the British firsthand by working directly with the people."

Minnesota Studies in International Development

MSID-Global Campus
202 Wesbrook Hall
77 Pleasant Street
Minneapolis, MN 55455
(612) 625–9383
Program length: year
Cost: $1,200–$4,000
Financial aid: available
Housing: provided
Age range of participants: 19 and up; college sophomore, junior, senior
Number of participants: 11
Application process: application with fee; transcript; language fluency in Spanish or French; previous introduction to other indigenous languages (Hindi, Arabic, Swahili); resume; statement of purpose; autobiographical statement (in French or Spanish if that is language of destination); 1 academic reference; 1 personal reference; interview; predeparture quarter spent at the University of Minnesota
Application due date: early applications, February 15; deadline, May 15
Program locations: Colombia, India, Jamaica, Kenya, Morocco, Senegal

Here is an opportunity for you to learn about development in the third world and get academic credit for it. If you are willing and qualified, you could spend most of a year working on development projects in Jamaica, Colombia, India, Kenya, Morocco, or Senegal. For most of these projects, you will need at least a nodding acquaintance with the national language; in the case of Colombia, Morocco, or Senegal, you must come to this program fluent in Spanish or French. Also, this probably is not a program for someone majoring in art or literature. As the program director notes: "A typical intern is a junior or senior with a major in internal relations, political science, or other social science. [M]ost have previous travel or study abroad, experience, demonstrate good people skills, independence, flexibility, and maturity; most have previous involvement in community service, environmental projects, or other voluntary service." If you don't fit all of these criteria, don't be discouraged. That's why the word *most* is used. But don't miss the implication. Backgrounds like those described here make the most sense. If yours is radically different, examine carefully why you want to take this opportunity.

You also should note that the University of Minnesota requires you to be in residence for the fall quarter of the year of your internship. This also suggests the necessity for admission to the university. Clear that with your college early on. In addition, you should expect to be living in a homestay situation, probably in a village with a family, for part or all of the internship.

Overseas Development Network Opportunities Program

Box 1430
Cambridge, MA 02238
(617) 868–3002
or:
Box 2306
Stanford, CA 94309
(415) 725–2869
Contact person: Rebecca Zeigler
Program length: semester, summer
Cost: $600–$3,000, depending on location
Financial aid: available

Housing: homestays or dorm
Age range of participants: 18–25
Number of participants per program: 6–20
Application process: 2 essays; 2 recommendations; interview
Application due dates: March 1 for Appalachia, Latin America, and the Philippines; March 10 for Bangladesh, India; October 1 for Zimbabwe
Program locations: worldwide

In their own words, "ODN is a national student-run consortium of college and university groups which seeks to raise awareness of global issues on campuses." Translated into layman's terms, this means that ODN attempts to educate young Americans about the conditions that exist in other nations around the world, particularly in third world countries, and in other regions of the United States. In order to achieve this, ODN sponsors learning internships in Appalachia, Latin America, the Philippines, Bangladesh, India, and Zimbabwe. The point of the internships is not to change those regions but to allow students interested in grassroots development to observe the culture and lifestyles of the regions most in need. As one former intern said: "ODN is dedicated to allowing you to see realistically what you can do. Some people have the idea that they can singlehandedly change a third world country. What ODN says is that change needs to come from within the country itself." As a result of this philosophy, the internships sponsored by ODN consist of "observing, not doing." An intern can expect to spend his/her days abroad assigned to one specific human service agency. But it is important to note that this placement will not be anything like an internship in the United States. An intern for ODN will not be answering phones, dealing with bureaucracy, or aiding in any specific way. In fact, you may do nothing for the entire time but observe what the agency you are assigned to does, and how it does what it does. One former intern, who went to India and was assigned to an agency for the promotion of women's rights, spent her six months "following a staff member, watching him and watching how the people interacted with him." As she said: "You aren't going to be helping. You will feel powerless. You must realize that you can't possibly hope to understand the intricacies of what's going on [in a developing nation's society] in six months. It can be frustrating to realize how hopeless you are, so it is important that you be very interested in development."

But if you are interested in development, this program may offer you a lot. Interns are sent to locations in which problems are displayed graphically. Interns cannot avoid noticing the vivid contrasts of development amid traditional cultures. In fact, you might experience these contrasts more directly than could be imagined. For example, housing opportunities for interns vary enormously from site to site. According to ODN's director, Rebecca Zeigler, housing "depends on the country, location and agency. You may be living in a home, sleeping on a floor in a room with ten other people or you may have a bungalow all to yourself that the agency provides." Whatever the conditions, you can be guaranteed that living will be rustic; yet, in the words of an ex-intern: "I didn't think [the living conditions] required being especially tough . . . it is a shock culturally . . . but the living was in general better than I'd led myself to expect."

An important piece of the ODN experience is the education of other Americans about the country you visited. Interns are expected to keep diaries of their time abroad and write several short pieces, each with a separate focus on some aspect of the society they were observing. Upon their return to the United States, interns are expected to help educate other Americans, through either their writing or speech giving at universities and local schools. This fulfills ODN's desire to educate American about how development is best promoted. As one former intern says: "Grassroots is the only way to go. . . . We [developed nations] can't impose technology, it must come from the community itself." It is ODN's mission to help Americans understand that.

Another sums up the ODN experience best in the following: "This is not a vacation and it is not for personal growth. The idea behind this program is to give people a global perspective on grassroots organizations so that they can transfer it back home. ODN is designed for people who are really interested in development as a career. It is a wonderful launching ground for a development career."

The Ohio International Agricultural Intern Program

113 Agricultural Administration
  Building
2120 Fyffe Road
Columbus, OH 43210-1099
Program length: 1–3 months or 4–
  12 months
Cost: $90
Financial aid: available

Housing: provided
Age range of participants: 19–30
Number of participants: varies
Application process: application
  with fee; resume; references
Application due date: rolling
  admissions
Program location: worldwide

OIAIP offers blossoming agriculturalists and horticulturists the opportunity to intern abroad for either a short (one to three months) or a long (four to twelve months) stay. In the former program option, interns "are placed in a wide range of agribusinesses: from family-run farms to larger businesses operating crop and livestock units. Placements are also made on nurseries, vineyards, and hops farms." Why should you consider this program? "The answers range from obtaining new techniques to just establishing a network of global colleagues. . . . International programs often provide a fresh look at "the way we've always done it.' . . . The internship program is like a conduit that brings people together."

If any aspect of agriculture of horticulture interests you, this program offers an unusual opportunity. But you must have some previous schooling and preferably some experience. In addition, you should be prepared to pay your own air transportation, health insurance, and incidental costs. You will be paid a wage by the host family or families; in many instances, you will be housed and fed. But don't overlook the language issue. You should be prepared for language training if you go to a country whose native language is not English.

If none of this sounds too formidable, then OIAIP may be for you. As one American who went from California to Wales remarked: "The working atmosphere was great. The people tried hard to make me feel at home. I still miss the life I had in Wales. . . . I learned something technical and earned enough money to pay for room and board and the occasional pint."

FUTURE FARMERS OF AMERICA

Other opportunities exist for those interested in farming, particularly if you belong to the Future Farmers of America, an organization that sends interested members abroad on a semester or full-year basis to a variety of locations. If you want details, write to:
International Department
National FFA Center
Box 15160
Alexandria, VA 22309

YMCA Intern Abroad

Director, International Programs
National Capital YMCA Service
  Center
1711 Rhode Island Avenue, NW
Washington, DC 20036
(202) 862–9622
Program length: varies; minimum
  2–3 months
Cost: varies by program, but
  ranges from $500–$2,500
Financial aid: possible
Housing: provided
Age range of participants: 18 and
  up

Number of participants: varies
Application process: application
  with fee; 2 professional
  recommendations, 1 personal
  recommendation; 1-page
  statement of purpose; 2 photos
Application due dates: January 1
  for spring; March 1 for
  summer; 3 months before
  program beginning for all
  programs
Program locations: worldwide

The Washington Metropolitan YMCA offers internships around the world for volunteers interested in teaching in recreational work and in community development work. But be aware that you will work hard; that you may need to be fluent in Spanish, French, or Portuguese; and that the entire process may end up costing you some money for travel, food, and incidental expenses. Finally, you may arrive at your destination only to discover that "their image of what the program description implied, and the reality of the situation are quite different."

If you're flexible enough to deal with that kind of change, consider the YMCA. You can go to Brazil, Chile, Jamaica, Uruguay, Egypt, Kenya, or India at any point in the year. Once there, you probably would be teaching, but it might be sports or secretarial skills or English. You also might be able to find your way to Australia or New Zealand during their summer (January and February), with camp counseling or sports programs as your agenda. There also are a variety of summer opportunities around the world.

The YMCA could be your ticket to exotic climes and meaningful work. Of particular interest to them are any special skills, especially the nontraditional variety: computer training or fitness training are two examples.

Apprenticeships

The dictionary calls an apprentice a learner of a craft. Below you will find ways to learn a wide variety of crafts and skills. The opportunities described are likely to be hands-on and probably hands dirty.

APPRENTICESHIPS IN THE UNITED STATES

Apprentice Alliance
150 Potrero Avenue
San Francisco, CA 94103
(415) 863-8661
Contact person: Anne Marie
  Theilen
Program length: varies according
  to apprenticeship
Cost: $25
Financial aid: none
Housing: none

Age range of participants: 18 and
  up
Number of participants: varies
Application process: resume; $25
  fee; an additional $50 upon
  placement
Application due date: none
Program location: San Francisco
  Bay Area

The Apprentice Alliance is a clearinghouse for internship and apprentice positions in businesses throughout the San Francisco Bay Area. It is dedicated to the notion that labor can be exchanged for education in a specific field. Apprentices are not paid and are responsible for their own housing. But they gain the kind of knowledge that can come only from working with a professional in their chosen field.

Apprentice Alliance annually publishes a directory of introductory and part-time positions available in a variety of fields located in and around San Francisco. Apprentice Alliance members have access to this publication and the resources of the staff at AA. Apprentice Alliance has placement opportunities in the following areas: architecture, art, law, business, computers, construction, furniture and related trades, fabric, food, galleries, gardening, graphic arts and illustration, health and fitness, interior design, music, performance, photography, public relations, publishing, printing, repair services, service and nonprofit organizations, travel, visual and sound production, as well as writing and editing. Each opportunity included in the directory is detailed with a brief job description and a biographical sketch of the professional an apprentice would be working with. The write-ups also include the number of hours per week and minimum time commitment required of the apprentice. People looking to secure a specific apprenticeship can contact the professional and arrange an interview.

Apprentice Alliance offers people interested in learning more about a potential career the opportunity of working closely with a professional in the field. Apprentice Alliance is not a placement agency but a resource network. Yet the opportunities within the directory are fascinatingly diverse and funky. They run the gamut from architectural and commercial photography to harpsichordist. If living and working in the Bay area appeals to you, or if you want to pursue a special interest, particularly a crafts-oriented one, and haven't been able to find a place to do it, try Apprentice Alliance.

The Seafarers Harry Lundeberg School of Seamanship

Piney Point, MD 20674
(301) 994-0010
Program length: 12–14 weeks
Cost: initiation fee to union; quarterly dues
Financial aid: none
Housing: provided
Age range of participants: 18–24
Number of participants: 20 per class

Application process: physical examination; drug screen; dental exam; state-issued birth certificate; 10 photos; U.S. citizenship; must have completed 8th grade.
Applications can be obtained at any office of the Seafarers International Union
Application due date: rolling admissions
Program location: Maryland

This is an institution that grew up to support the American maritime industry. But the training provided by the three months one spends at the Seafarers School will give the graduate seaman's papers (actually, seaperson's, since the Seafarers School is coeducational), and thus the ability to sign on and ship out on any merchant vessel. Further, the training will make its recipient a skilled boatperson. The twelve-week program provides training in CPR, first aid, and firefighting procedures, the entire range of shipboard deckwork, engineering, and stewardship.

Also be aware, however, that the program is quasi military. Seafarers school is run like a military academy. Everyone wears issued clothing (which is free, as is the rest of the program); everyone learns together; everyone eats together. The trade-off is professional training and the acquisition of a most salable skill. For some people, the imposition of such discipline would be unbearable; for others, the price is a small one to pay for such training and for a very different kind of experience.

The Shipbuilding Apprentice Program

The Maine Maritime Museum
Washington Street
Bath, ME 04530
(207) 442-7401
Contact person: staff
Program length: 19 months
Cost: $35 application fee; $200 deposit for holding volunteer space, refunded at the end of the monthlong volunteer placement; $1,000 deposit for apprenticeship, refunded with interest at the successful completion of the 18-month program

Housing: none
Age range of participants: 18 and up
Number of participants per program: 12
Application process: volunteer form; essay; woodworking experiences; successful completion of the volunteer program
Application due date: rolling admissions
Program location: Bath, Maine

The Maine Maritime Museum offers interested woodworkers the chance to learn and refine an age-old skill and profession that is almost extinct: the art of shipbuilding. In the ancient tradition of apprenticeships, at Maine Maritime you learn by doing. As an apprentice you will exchange labor for knowledge. For eighteen months you will work under the supervision of master craftsmen and will learn and refine the skill of boat building. Apprentices will be exposed to every conceivable aspect of boat building, from the designing of new boats to the restoration of ships that date back to the early 1800s. These disparate tasks are accomplished through a unique curriculum of doing and studying. While most of your day will be spent in the shop working on boats, the program also includes library and classroom facilities and museum artifacts for the apprentices' use. Work in the apprenticeship goes on from eight to five, five days a week. Apprentices receive four vacation weeks a year, two at Christmas and two during the summer, as well as nine holidays during the year. The apprenticeship requires that all of its apprentices volunteer for a one-month period prior to being admitted into the apprentice program so that both the future apprentice and the apprenticeship staff can make sure that a full apprenticeship is an appropriate step. Housing and board are not provided. An apprentice must have the financial stability to support him/herself during the eighteen-month period. The Maine Maritime Museum's apprenticeship offers you the unique opportunity to learn a challenging and complex skill by doing it. "I first came one and a half years ago with no woodworking experience. Now, I feel very confident. I feel like I have been working with tools and wood all my life."—"Here I had the chance to build two boats; I learned a great deal about designing boats; and I had the chance to sail quite a lot in a traditional eighteenth-century fishing vessel. It's quite an experience, an internship here. The best thing about the shipbuilding program: Everything is the way it used to be a long time ago. That is very difficult to find."

APPRENTICESHIPS ABROAD

The International Agricultural Exchange Association

817 2d Street South
Great Falls, MT 59405
(406) 727-1999
Program length: varies; at least a semester
Cost: varies; there is a stipend paid once on the program
Financial aid: none
Housing: provided
Number of participants: varies by program

Age range: 19–28
Application process: applicant must apply to program of choice; application with fee; interview; 2 letters of reference; autobiographical essay
Application due date: rolling admissions
Program locations: worldwide

Probably it's best to begin with what you need to have even to consider this program: some farming experience. If you've got it, if you've spent any time on a farm, then IAEA might be for you. However, spending time on a farm doesn't mean living in a farmhouse. It means working: working with animals, growing things—horticultural experience is also applicable here. Opportunities also might include home management—domestic chores and child care or some minimal agricultural or horticultural experience with a willingness to learn more. Through this organization, you will live on a farm in Denmark, Germany, Scotland, Ireland, England, Norway, Finland, Austria, Sweden, Holland, Switzerland, or in New Zealand or Australia. In the words of one participant: "[It's a] really good experience for people who have never been overseas, and a great way to get involved in the agricultural community."

The program is not without cost. A prospective traveler might have to give IAEA as much as $5,000. In return, however, all travel arrangements and some training and excursions are arranged by IAEA. In addition, applicants must have that year of experience, have a driver's license, and be healthy. Beyond that, "It's not a very competitive program. As long as there is a family to stay with, you can go."—"You go over and work with a family on their family farm. It's a great experience because you can learn their farming techniques and share ours with them. It really is an exchange in that way."—"I would never have gone overseas by myself without the IAEA, and to have the combination of agricultural techniques and culture was terrific."—"It made me a lot more aware of the world."—"The best part was being able to interact with people from all over the world and study agriculture." But graduates of the program have this reminder: "You need to be committed to the purpose of the program: agriculture. Then, it's great. If you're just going over to travel, party, and play, this isn't for you. This really is a *working* exchange."

Travel/Study Programs

The following programs represent unusual travel opportunities, either because they combine some other feature with the specifics of the travel experience or because they take you to unusual places.

Foundation for Field Research
787 South Grade Road
Alpine CA 92001
(619) 445-9264
Program length: varies, but usually short term: from a few days to a few weeks throughout the year
Cost: varies by program
Financial aid: available for students and teachers
Housing: provided
Age range of participants: 14 and up

Number of participants: varies by program
Application process: completion of "I Want to Volunteer" form and deposit
Application due date: "first come, first served" basis
Academic credit obtained through parent institution
Program locations; worldwide

This organization is a clearinghouse and funding organization for research studies around the world. Its opportunities are diverse. There are programs studying primatology, paleontology, marine biology, marine archeology, and so forth. The downside here is that most of these programs don't last for more than several weeks, although their costs are commensurately low (about $900 for a fourteen-day expedition to find an underwater settlement off Grenada). So the opportunities may be fascinating, but the time frame is limited. Those searching for longer term opportunities should look elsewhere. But if intensity is the desired commodity—along with the possibility of association with professionals—the foundation might be your cup of tea.

This from a pyschologist volunteering to study Indian artists of the Colorado River: "Walking the California desert with two experienced anthropologists is very different from walking it alone. . . . [W]hen I stumbled past another meaningless pile of rocks . . . [one anthropologist] called me back . . . and described . . . a . . . perfect example of an [Indian] workshop. . . . Nearby were 'sleeping circles.' . . . Suddenly, this dry, desolate place came alive as we envisioned ourselves among families or tribes of an ancient people."

Remember also—as the above suggests—these field studies will take any able-bodies; so there's no issue of experience for this opportunity. As the program director notes, all you need is the desire to "physically work on a scientific project."

Galapagos Island Adventure

Office of International Studies
Eastern Michigan University
Ypsilanti, MI 48197
(313) 487-2424
Contact person: Dr. George J. Klein, director
Program length: summer, 3 weeks
Cost of program: $2,595, including airfare from Miami and all meals
Financial aid: none

Housing: provided on cruise boats
Age range of participants: 17 and older
Number of participants per program: 20
Application process: $250 deposit; form
Application due date: May 1
Program locations: Galapagos Islands and Quito, Ecuador

The Galapagos Island Adventure is a wonderful opportunity to re-create Charles Darwin's famous voyage on the *Beagle*. Called a "living laboratory of evolution" by Darwin, the Galapagos, a wildlife sanctuary untouched by the hand of man, are a rich area in which to study biology and learn about the islands and the wildlife that inhabit them. During your three-week trip, you will be led by an experienced naturalist and an Eastern Michigan University biology professor. You will explore the islands on foot as well as by boat. You will be housed aboard the cruise ships that bring you to the islands, and while the accommodations are not luxurious, they are comfortable. As a bonus, three semester hours of biology credit are offered by Eastern Michigan University at the end of your journey. No course prerequisites are needed, just a sincere interest in the environment of the islands. This is a great opportunity to experience the site of the foremost scientific discoveries—just as it was.

Mountain Travel

6420 Fairmount Avenue
El Cerrito, CA 94530
1-800-227-2384
Contact person: staff
Program length: 2–6 weeks
Cost: $1,000–$5,000 depending on trip; air travel not included
Housing: provided

Age range of participants: 16 and up
Number of participants per program: 4–16
Application process: application plus deposit
Application due date: rolling admissions

If you're looking for a wondrous travel tour that will make you an active participant—there's no riding around on crowded tour buses with these folks—this is your place. Mountain Travel is one of a new breed of travel tours that gets you actively involved. For example, they offer trips that take you trekking in Nepal or mountaineering in South America. These trips are active, but don't let that scare you off; there is something for even the most sluggish of you in this catalogue. Many of the more exciting trips require that you be in good physical condition, and require camping. But while you won't have the luxury of a hotel, the scenery and the experience will be well worth the sacrifice. And don't worry about eating hot dogs for two weeks straight, because Mountain Travel also knows how to put on a campfire dinner. It's what you might expect to find at the Ritz, that is, if the Ritz had campfire dinners. So, if you are looking for an adventure trip, with other adventuresome people, this is a good place to check out.

Other adventure travel tour companies:

Equitour
Bitterroot Ranch
Route 66, Box 1042
Dubois, WY 82513
1-800-545-0019

This program organizes worldwide tours on horseback. If you love to ride, Equitour allows you to combine that interest with expeditions all around the world.

Putney Student Travel
Putney, VT 05346
(802) 387-5887
Contact persons: Jeffery and Peter Shumlin
Program length: summer: 5–6 weeks
Cost: $2,440–$5,990, depending on the trip
Financial aid: available
Age range of participants: completed 8th grade–completed senior year in high school

Number of participants: 16 per trip
Application process: essay required; 2 teacher recommendations
Application due date: rolling admissions
Program locations: worldwide

Founded in 1952, Putney Student Travel has been offering summer travel/study tours for kids ever since. Run by the Schumlin family, Putney does its best to provide kids with exciting experiences in foreign enviroments. Trip options include China and the USSR as well as Europe and Australia. Putney also offers language programs that provide its participants with travel and the support of a peer group, yet total emersion in the language and culture of the host country via a homestay. As one Putney alum said of the Spanish-language program: "I learned as much as I could have in a year at school. Meeting Spanish people, visiting museums, hiking, talking to fishermen, farmers and stone cutters, tasting Spanish food and life. The beaches, having freedom to explore in a city—it was all great."

Special attention is paid by the Schumlins to the choice of staff. Each group is led by two staff members who are rigorously screened and must be fluent in the language(s) of the host country(ies). The group leaders add a great deal to the student's experience and make the program complete. As one student said: "Our leaders were great! We could not have asked for two more energetic, fun, cheerful, nice, helpful leaders; their persistent urgings that we speak French were just what we needed—their interest and enthusiasm for the language was inspiring. I hope to major in French in college as well as return to France as soon as I can; the trip would not have been the same without them."

Each travel/study tour incorporates some form of athletic activity during the four to six weeks; for example: biking in China, skiing in Australia. Perhaps what is most striking about Putney is the dedication of the program to the growth of the child, through both group experiences and independent achievements. Putney does a super job of showing kids the world and getting them to profit from the experience.

University Research Expeditions Program

University of California
Berkeley, CA 94720
(415) 642-6586
Contact person: Jean Colvin, director
Program length: approximately 2 weeks per session
Cost: $700–$1,600 tax-deductible contribution
 Financial aid: limited
Housing: provided; some camping depending on trip

Age range of participants: 16 and up
Number of participants per program: 5–10
Application process: application form and $200 deposit
Application due date: rolling admissions
Program locations: worldwide

Ever wondered what it would be like to go on a scientific expedition? Through University Research Expeditions you can find out. UREP sponsors more than twenty trips a year and places interested individuals on actual research expeditions led by university professors from the California state system. The projects take place all over the world and encompass a variety of topics. For example, you can go to Costa Rica and work with a research team on the development of a wildlife reserve or to an archeological dig in Ireland. Once on the trip you are no mere tourist but a member of a scientific expedition led by a professor doing research in his field. You are responsible for collecting data and for learning how to interpret what you observe. UREP takes you into the greatest science lab of all—the world—and provides you with teachers interested in conveying their passion for their work to you. As a team member in Costa Rica you will "observe and record behavior and habitat locations of bird and bee populations." In Ireland you will "map church sites and examine settlement patterns associated with the sites." Every expedition has a definite goal; you will play an active role in helping to achieve it. Housing accommodations vary dramatically from trip to trip, depending on the location of each. In some cases you will stay in hotels; in other cases you will camp. UREP has seen to it that each trip description includes housing arrangement information. The trips are divided into two-week blocks, and you are welcome to stay on until an expedition is over, provided you pay accordingly. Your fee is considered a tax-deductible contribution because you are acting as a volunteer on a scientific expedition. This is a super way to get a firsthand glimpse into the scientific community and have a vacation with a difference all at once.

Language Study Programs

Listed below are programs designed to teach foreign languages. Some of these programs offer substantive investigations of the relevant cultures; others are more like language factories, dedicated to cramming you with basic linguistic skills and then sending you on your way. Some language teaching facility, perhaps dozens of them, will exist in almost every major city you visit. More-over, there are language facilities around the world that will teach you a variety of languages. So don't worry; you can learn the language of your choice. But as you read through the sections below keep in mind that there are different programs for different purposes. The factory approach has its advantages; so do the more complex programs. It depends on what you need.

GENERIC LANGUAGE PROGRAMS

EUROPE

Eurocentres
Seestrasse 247
CH-8038 Zurich, Switzerland
Country code + 01-4825040
Program length: varies
Cost: varies by program
Financial aid: none
Housing: available
Age range: 16 and up
Number of participants: varies
  by program
Application process:
  application with fee

Application due date: rolling
  admissions
Program locations: French in
  Paris, LaRochelle,
  Amboise, Lausanne, and
  Neuchâtel; Italian in
  Florence; Spanish in
  Madrid and Barcelona;
  German in Cologne and
  Lucerne

Here is the first variation on the theme of language learning: Euro-centres, a language conglomerate that teaches you your language of choice in the city of your choice (with limitations), with the traditional homestay available. The program has the advantage of being tried and true, the disadvantage of being part of a much larger and therefore more bureaucratic whole. You should be careful—as always—to check on class size and make sure you're placed where you should be. Otherwise, with Eurocentres you have the privilege of choosing from a variety of locales, while knowing that your choice is likely to result in quality instruction. Rates are competitive.

STUDYING A FOREIGN LANGUAGE ABROAD

If learning a language is your goal, the most effective method is to go where that language is spoken and learn it there. If you choose this option, it is effectiveness you're after, not inexpensiveness. Nor are you interested in saving time, because it will take you at least two to three weeks and more likely a month (the standard duration of most programs) to become relatively proficient. Note the term *relatively*. These programs cannot make you a fluent speaker. But they will set you on the road to fluency, and much farther along than any equivalent American preparation. These programs are able to do so because they are intensive, meeting usually four hours a day, but with some programs offering up to eight hours of instruction; and they take place in an environment saturated with the language you're learning. You may hear English in your own mind, but you're going to hear the language you're learning everywhere else from the moment of your arrival.

What do these programs have in common? The Italians, the French, and the Mexicans have the edge in terms of environment. You can learn Italian almost anywhere you want to be in Italy, and always by the conversational method in relatively small groups, about six to twelve students. Most programs are located in Rome and Florence, but many have summer offshoots on either coast, and virtually every other major Italian city has at least one *scuola* offering instruction by the month. Most also offer homestay situations. Similarly, many French programs are in Paris, but several also exist in towns and cities along the Riviera or along the Channel or Atlantic Coast. Others exist at a variety of sites inland. In France, however, many of the language programs are associated with universities, and so housing might be in dormitory situations or in pensions, as well as in homestays. Most language programs, wherever they are located, offer several options for accommodation. It is always possible to find at least one in any given language that will suggest several ways to satisfy accommodation. Moreover, within each country costs remain relatively constant, and it's fair to say that, with the exception of Mexico, most language programs cost about $100 per week for twenty hours of instruction.

In Mexico, language programs exist in several locations, one of the many attractive settings being Cuernavaca. There the rules discussed above apply: about twenty hours per week, normal program duration about one month, conversational method, small classes. But the housing is almost exclusively homestay, and the cost is packaged with instruction for a total of about $100 per week.

The situation in Asia is rather different from that in Europe. Programs of language instruction in China and Japan often, although not always, begin by expecting some previous training. Also, their guarantee is even less precise than that of the programs mentioned above. Given the complexities of the respective languages, these programs simply cannot promise much fluency. Moreover, most housing provided in China and in Japan is dormitory based. Otherwise, the programs remain similar. They offer a conversational approach, with attention to the written language. In terms of cost, partially because of the travel, these programs far exceed the European and Mexican options.

There are also some problems of which to be aware. Remember, the glossy attractiveness of the brochure is not a guarantee of the quality of the course. Try to get some sense from the program's directors about what they promise in terms of your success before you send the check.

Also, see if you can get names and numbers of some alumni—and make sure they're American. Some language programs look like the UN in terms of their constituency. That may make for a wonderful experience in some respects, but it increases the teacher's burden and may affect your progress negatively.

CHINA

CET—Wellesley College Chinese Language Study Program
1110 Washington Street
Boston, MA 02124
(617) 296-0270 or 1-800-225-4262
Contact person: Mary Jacob
Program length: semester, full year, and summer options
Cost: varies between $4,477 and $5,562 and includes airfare
Financial aid: none
Housing: dormitory
Age range of participants: 18 and up

Number of participants: 50–70 per session
Application due date: February for September; November for February; March for summer
Application process: essay; transcript; recommendations; phone interview
Program location: Beijing, China

The CET-Wellesley Program is an intensive Chinese language study program. The CET participant, whether a beginner or an advanced language student, will return from China with an extraordinary amount of proficiency in the language as well as experience in the culture. The program is intensely academic. Its participants spend between fifteen to twenty hours a week in Chinese-language classes and another fifteen to twenty studying outside the classroom. The participants are housed in special "Western" dorms. This means that the standard of living for CET students will far surpass that of their Asian counterparts. but don't expect conditions to be like home. Relative comfort in this case needs to be balanced against the fact that the standard of living in China is below that of America. Thus, Americans should be prepared to go without some of the creature comforts of American life, such as daily showers and stereos. However, if one can get over such minor inconveniences, CET has a great deal to offer. The program is held on the campus of the Beijing Foreign Languages Normal College, and participants get a chance to interact daily with the Chinese students enrolled at the college. Furthermore, participants are housed and attend classes with Americans enrolled in the other CET run programs. Thus, CET allows for a wide range of interaction with both other Westerners and Chinese students.

Classes are taught by CET's own faculty. Faculty members sign on for at least two-year stretches so that the program has continuity, unlike some other programs abroad. The classes are small, and language tapes as well as tutors are a regular part of the learning experience. Further, participants can stay for one semester or a twelve-month period as a result of CET's trimester system. Because of the flexibility within the CET program, it is not uncommon for students to extend their stay to include the following term. Indeed, some begin during a summer session and leave in December. CET also offers a new program and campus for more advanced language students in Harbin, Manchuria. Participants may now choose to divide their stay in China between the two campuses.

CET also prepares its students for what they should expect during their stay. The program publishes a detailed packet of information that answers questions ranging from what living conditions will be like to where to buy personal hygiene products. The detail of the packet makes it clear that CET's staff wants to eliminate surprises upon arrival. Furthermore, CET takes care of all travel and visa plans for its participants. Participants need only have a valid passport and show up at the airport, CET does the rest.

CET has a stringent application process that is highly selective. Participants must be in good academic standing with a strong desire to be in China and to learn about the language and the culture. Besides the application essay, recommendations, and transcript, CET strongly encourages each participant to speak with its academic program manager by phone.

The most striking thing about CET is the breadth and depth of its planning. Details are treated with the utmost attention, and one can be assured that CET will provide an extraordinary experience for its students.

FRANCE

Studying in France requires one of two things: participation in a recognized program or acceptance at a French university. The former is possible for almost any high school graduate or college undergraduate (depending on the program's requirements); the latter is at the least extremely difficult, requiring that the applicant meet a variety of conditions. For instance, you must be at least a junior; you must pass an extensive examination verifying your fluency in French but incidentally testing your level of proficiency in the subjects you intend to pursue at your French university. For example, you must pass an examination in biochemistry in French. If this isn't enough, there is a hedgerow of other requirements, mostly attestations to your health, both physical and financial, your lodging, and so forth. Then you must be admitted to the particular university you want to attend. French universities are organized according to discipline—science, art technology, humanities. Acceptance is by no means automatic.

The alternative—participation in a recognized program for Americans—is preferable for those less fluent. Most of the programs that follow fall into this category; some are organized by American colleges and universities that liaise with French universities. None have requirements as stringent as those set by France and French universities. To be fair, nor are any quite as inexpensive. So if your French is sufficient to carry you through tests in your subject area, and if you can gain admission to the French university of your choice, by all means seek your degree in that way. If not, read on, and perhaps some of the possibilities listed below can be of help.

Institute for American Universities

27, place de l'Université
13625 Aix-en-Provence
France
Program length: summer, semester, year; January interim
Cost: varies by program
Financial aid: none
Housing: available; homestays
Age range of participants: college
Number of participants: varies by program

Application process: application with fee; transcript; teachers' recommendations; personal statement; health certificate; photos
Application due date: rolling admissions
Program locations: Aix-en-Provence, Toulon, Avignon, Leo Marchutz School of Painting and Drawing (in Aix)

The Institute for American Universities serves not only as an educational institution but as a conduit for students to study in other locations in France. As such, IAU is a perfect vehicle for the American student who wishes to learn French in France, to take courses in English in France, or—if qualified by virtue of fluency—to take courses in French at the Université d'Aix–

Marseille, the Institute d'Etudes Politiques, or the Conservatoire de Musique. Because of IAU's connection with the Leo Marchutz School of Painting and Drawing, you can take advantage of programs there in drawing, painting, and aesthetics (see the description of the Leo Marchutz School, p. 100).

To make this program more accessible, IAU helps you select your courses by offering French-language courses at various levels, with companion courses in either English or French, depending on your fluency. All coursework is transferable, with credit recommendations being made by IAU. The institute offers a variety of summer programs, including courses in accelerated French and a January term intensive French course (at its Avignon location).

All this may sound wonderful, but how do you gain acceptance? You need to be willing to take a lot of French—you needn't have taken any before applying; you must be in good standing with your college—or you must have graduated from high school and be an acceptable matriculant, willing to spend your first semester or year at IAU. In either case, school representatives must attest to your emotional and intellectual preparation for study abroad. You also must apply for a student visa from your local consulate or from the French embassy.

Institut de Touraine

1, rue de la Grandière
Boîte Postale 2047
37020 Tours Cedex
Country code + 47 05 76 83
Program length: 3 months or
  longer
Cost: varies by program
Financial aid: none
Housing: available

Age range: 18 and up
Number of participants: varies by
  program
Application process: application
  with fee; transcript; student
  visa
Application due date: rolling
  admissions
Program location: Tours

The Institut provides another option in the spectrum of ways to learn French in France. This program is conducted entirely in French (including the application) and therefore requires you to have some understanding before entertaining it seriously. Costs are reasonable, corresponding to other language programs outside Paris. The advantages of living and learning in a provincial town should be considered when this program is evaluated as a possible choice.

Institut Européan des Hautes Etudes Internationales

9, avenue de Fabron
06200 Nice, France
Country code + 93 86 39 12

This program offers both language courses and a full range of studies revolving around the concept and practice of European community. As reorganization of Europe in 1992 nears, this area of study takes on special importance. In addition to independent application, Americans can gain access to the Institut's programs through overseas offerings from the universities of Georgetown and Vermont.

GERMANY AND AUSTRIA

If you want to study abroad—and not in an English-speaking country—you need to learn the language. Quite possibly, that's a major reason for going to the country. But if Germany is your choice, the problem is a bit more complicated than just going and learning the language. If you want to study in a German university you may find it more complicated than just going and taking a few German-language courses. All universities in Germany are state run; therefore, all requirements are standardized. On the one hand, that's great: you know what you're getting into; it's just a question of picking the disciplines and the place you want to go. Incidentally, tuition is free.

But don't overlook the serious downside. Or, to rephrase that, what might be a downside for you. You must be ready to enter your junior year. You must have completed at least five courses in English, one other language (not English, although it may be German), and a math or natural science course. In addition, you must take a German proficiency test given at the beginning of each semester. It's a good idea to plan on at least some refresher training in the language, if not a full-blown program, before taking the test. If you write to the German Academic Exchange Service (see below), you'll receive information about every university, including courses available. Some language options appear below.

Academic Studies in the Federal Republic of Germany

German Academic Exchange Service
950 Third Avenue, 19th Floor
New York, NY 10022
Program length: year
Cost: varies by program
Financial aid: home institution; various government programs
Housing: available
Age range: college junior and up
Number of participants: varies by program
Application process: application; transcript reflecting 2 years of university study with at least 5 liberal arts courses, among them English, a foreign language, mathematics and/or courses in the natural sciences; essay; teacher's recommendation; test proving proficiency in German
Application due date: applications must be received by January 15 for the summer term (April–September) and by June 15 for the winter term (October–March)
Program locations: any federal university in Germany

The great advantage of attending any German university—beyond the obvious attractions of going to school in another country, the high repute of German higher education, the rich cultural life of German universities—is that they are tuition free. So send for the booklet describing all of them (individual catalogues don't seem to exist). But don't forget the serious requirements.

Sprachinstitut Tübingen

Eugenstrasse 71
D-7400, Tübingen, Germany
Country code + 07071/34018
Program length: minimum of 2 weeks
Cost: varies by program
Financial aid: none
Housing: available

Age range: 16 and up
Number of participants: varies by program
Application process: application with fee
Application due date: rolling
Program location: Tübingen

The Sprachinstitut is a straightforward language course, no frills included. Housing is available either in the form of homestays or at the institute itself. The principal advantage of this program is its location in one of the most beautiful German cities, Tübingen, located near the Swabian Alps, amid national parks.

Deutschkurse für Ausländer

Ludwig Maximilians Universität
Adelheidstrasse 13 b
8000 Munich 40, Germany
Country code + Munich + 2712642
Program length: 2 months minimum
Cost: varies by program
Financial aid: none
Housing: none
Age range: college junior
Number of participants: varies by program

Application process: high school diploma; application with fee; transcript showing successful completion of 2 years of mathematics, 2 language courses (English may be one of them) and at least 2 courses in science or social studies
Application due date: rolling admissions
Program location: Munich

Operated in conjunction with the greater university program, this language program is aimed at preparing foreign students for study in the federal university system. See above for more information.

German Study Abroad Program

International Center
Macalester College
1600 Grand Avenue
St. Paul, MN 55105

Program length: spring semester
Cost: $6,200 plus transatlantic travel
Financial aid: none

Housing: available
Age range of participants: college
  junior and above
Number of participants: varies
Application process: application
  plus fee; 2 recommendations;
  essays; transcript

Application deadline: October 15
Program locations: various Goethe
  Institutes in West Germany;
  then Vienna, Austria

This program provides a vehicle for your attendance at a Goethe Institute
in Germany, coupled with courses provided through Associated Colleges of
the Twin Cities and taught by Viennese and ACTC resident professors. Its
advantage to you: the possibility of transferable academic credit and packaged housing and transportation costs. You must have taken four semesters
of college-level German language. As an added attraction, the program will
give you a chance not only to live in Germany but also to spend two months
in Vienna, where some cultural instruction will take place, focusing principally on the visual arts, music history, and German/Austrian language and
literature.

International Courses in German Language and Literature

International German Courses
Franz-Josef-Strasse 19
A-5020 Salzburg, Austria
Country code + 0662-76595
Program length: 3–10 weeks
Cost: varies by program
Financial aid: none
Housing: available
Age range of participants: 16 and
  up

Number of participants: varies by
  program
Application process: application
  with fee
Application due date: rolling
  admissions
Program locations: Salzburg and
  Zell am See, Austria

In addition to offering a variety of language courses for all levels of ability,
IFK has art and music history courses, teacher-training courses, and seminars in German philology and Austrian literature and culture. Add to this
panoply the advantages of Salzburg and learning by the lake in Zell am
See; the result is a wonderful environment for language training. Skiing
and watersports are also available, depending on season, in Zell am See.

ITALY

British Institute of Florence

Program length: month, semester
Cost: approximately $500 per
  month
Financial aid: none

Housing: assistance finding
  accommodations; homestays
  possible

Age range of participants: 16 and up

Number of participants; 10 or less

Application process: varies according to program

Application due date: at least 1 month before program begins

Program location: Florence

The British Institute of Florence has been in the business of teaching language to English speakers for almost fifty years. It is distinguished from other language programs available for those who wish to learn Italian in Italy by its bilingual quality.

The mainstay at the British Institute remains its monthlong programs in Italian. But in the last decade the institute has broadened its programs to include opportunities in the history of art, the Italian Renaissance and mannerism, in studio art, particularly drawing, and in the history of Florence. Not only have these programs been shaped to provide A-level instruction for young Britons, the same opportunities now exist for individual instruction and through the vehicle of university exchange. Tony Buckby, the school director for the institute, is anxious to encourage American students to take advantage of the semester programs the institute offers. Doing so means beginning in the Palazzo Feroni, in which the institute occupies the third floor, with a seemingly endless and circuitous corridor of rooms. Many of these rooms share a view of the Arno, on whose bank the Palazzo rests.

From this thirteenth-century building, students may tour and study in the Uffizi and the Duomo of Florence, among other centers of Italian art and history. Instruction is provided by resident faculty of the institute and by a variety of visiting lecturers. Currently, James Madison University grants credit for the institute's semester courses in the United States; the institute is recognized as an A-level preparer by the requisite British authorities.

Although the institute cannot guarantee accommodations, there is an accommodations office to assist students in finding appropriate housing. Homestay opportunities are possible, as well as bookings in Florentine hotels and pensions. The office will find accommodations in almost all cases and then leave negotiations to the student.

One of the most attractive aspects of studying with the British Institute is the automatic membership in the British library that is a feature of enrollment. The library is located on premises owned by Sir Harold Acton, grandson of the British historian. That former residence, the Palazzo Lanfredini, contains an extensive collection of English-language works, newspapers, and periodicals, as well as a variety of services open to its members, such as study aids and work and accommodations information. In addition, because of the extensive English-language training for Italians offered by the institute, the library serves as a locus for the meeting of two cultures. There, as well as on the school premises, English and Italian speakers are encouraged to meet and help one another share languages and cultures.

It is this sharing of language and culture that gives the British Institute its unique character among the multitude of language programs in Florence. As one American teacher noted: "The language instruction at the institute is a lot better than others I sat in on. There are top people also in their nonlanguage courses. The institute hasn't relied solely on the University of Florence for its instructors. Instead, it has tried to find the best people in each field, people really committed to teaching what they know."

Italian University for Foreigners

Università Italiana per Stranieri
Palazzo Gallenga
Piazza Fortebraccio 4
06100 Perugia
Perugia 64344
Perugia, Italy
Program length: minimum 2
  months, semester, year
Cost: varies by program
Financial aid: none
Housing: available

Age range of participants: PG,
  college
Number of participants: varies by
  program
Application process: application
  with fee
Application due date: rolling
  admissions
Program location: Perugia (similar
  programs exist in Siena,
  Florence, and Pisa)

This program begins as instruction in Italian but provides access to the broader offerings of the university. It is open to anyone who has graduated from high school or is in college in the United States. Courses run two or three months and cost from $200 per month for tuition. Intensive courses, July–September (by month or more), cost $300 per month. Cultural courses begin in January and also cost $300 per month. The university also runs a social program, shows free films, and offers sports facilities, including gymnasiums, tennis courts, and swimming pools. Accommodations are homestay or pension.

GENERIC LANGUAGE PROGRAMS IN ITALY

The proliferation of language courses in Italy began with the work of K. Katerinov, whose book (translated as *Italian Language for Foreigners*: Perugia, 1974) revolutionized the teaching of the language. Virtually every school—from a room or two in Como to an entire facility in Florence or Rome—uses the same method. It's for that reason that one student remarked: "I wrote to all the language schools in Florence and chose the one that seemed least expensive.... I've since learned that I could have paid more for a course of similar quality." So how do you choose? If possible, you should visit a few, talk to students or former students. Differences among schools have to do with the ways in which the staff and students interact, with the extracurriculars provided (which will cost, sometimes significantly more), with class size, with the attention taken to restricting speaking within the school to Italian. And so on. Below are a few schools in major locales. There are many others, of no less repute.

FLORENCE
ABC—Centro di Lingua e Cultura Italiana
Borgo Pinti. 38
50122 Florence, Italy
Country code + 055-2479220

Open to applicants 16 and up; standard course about $300 (four weeks), depending on exchange rate; application with fee anytime thirty days before admission. As with most language schools, the method is didactic, but ABC also offers ceramic and studio art courses, about nine hours per week.

Centro Linguistico Sperimentale
Instituo di Lingua Italiana
Via del Corso, 1
1-50122 Florence, Italy
Country code + 55/210592

This school, located in a house next to Dante Alighieri's alleged residence in the historic center of Florence, offers a variety of trips and nonlanguage activities in addition to its ten-person class size.

Scuola Botticelli
Lingua Arte e Cultura Italiana
Via Artina, 120
50136 Florence, Italy

Koine
Via de Pandolfini
50122 Florence, Italy
Country code + 055213881

Koine is a cooperative, which means a looser, more relaxed approach to classroom work. In addition, the program moves to Ortobello and Cortona in the summer, two attractive locations in which to learn Italian (while enjoying the Italian Riviera or the Tuscan countryside).

Centro Linguistico Italiano Dante Alighieri
Via de Bardi 12
Box 194
50100 Florence, Italy

This is one of several programs around Italy operating under the aegis of the Dante Alighieri association for linguistic studies. Other programs exist in Siena and in Rome.

Niccolò Machiavelli: Cooperativa di insegnanti
Centro di Lingua e Cultura Italiana per Stranieri
Piazza Santo Spirito 4
50125 Florence, Italy

ROME
Torre di Babele Centro di Lingua e Cultura Italiana
Via Bixio, 74
00185 Rome, Italy
Country code + 06-7008434

Open to all applicants: standard course about $250 (two weeks), depending on exchange rate; application with fee anytime thirty days before course beginning. Particular advantage of Torre di Babele is its summer program in Cilento, in Sicily. Torre di Babele also offers an intensive course in modern Roman architecture.

Italiaidea
Associazione Culturale
Piazza della Cancelleria 85
00186 Rome, Italy

Another alternative in Rome.

Isitituto Italiano
Centro di Lingua e Cultura
Via Carol Alberto, 43
00185 Roma, Italy
Country code + 06-732328

Yet another Roman alternative.

MILAN
Società Dante Alighieri
Via Napo Torriani, 10
Milan, Italy

COMO
Corsi "Cazzulani" di Lingua Italiana per Stranieri
Via Rovelli 41
22100 Como, Italy

This program poses an attractive alternative, located as it is on the shore of one of the most beautiful lakes in Italy.

GENOA
Centro Internazionale di Studi Italiani
Università degli Studi di Genova
Via Balbi 5
16126 Genova, Italy

BERGAMO
Lingua e Cultura Italiana per Stranieri
Istituto Universitario di Bergamo
Via Salvecchio n. 19
24100 Bergamo, Italy

BAGNO DI ROMAGNA
Scuola Palazzo Malvisi
Via Fiorentina, 36
I-47021, Bagno di Romagna
Ravenna, Italy

Should these schools prove unacceptable for some reason, contact the Italian Cultural Foundation, 686 Park Avenue, New York, NY 10021, (212) 879-4242. This organization will supply you with a much fuller list of programs around Italy. Depending on the exchange rate, the minimum cost for four weeks of instruction should be between $350 and $450.

JAPAN

Keio University
International Education Division
International Center
2-15-45, Mita, Minatu-ku
Tokyo 108, Japan
Country code + 453-4511. ext. 2310
Program length: semester
Cost: varies by program
Financial aid: none
Housing: none
Age range of participants: college
Number of participants; varies

Application process: $55 application fee; application form; academic record; proof of graduation from last school attended; health certificate; letter of recommendation from faculty member; letter of guarantee from a resident of Japan or foreigner living in Tokyo
Application due date: end of October for spring; end of April for fall
Program location: Tokyo

The International Center at Keio University will provide you with the opportunity to learn Japanese and to absorb something of Japanese culture simultaneously. The International Center is for students interested in becoming fluent in Japanese. While some Japanese studies courses are available, the majority of the courses open to foreign students are language related. You will take thirty hours of language training per week and are required to miss no more than 30 percent of your classes or you will not be allowed to take the final exam. Students do not live on campus, and the university is not particularly helpful about housing. Keio doesn't make study easy for foreign students, but it does provide you with superb instruction in Japanese.

Kansai Gaidai

Kansai University of Foreign Studies
16-1 Kitakatahoko-cho
Hirakita City
Osaka, Japan
011-81-0720-51-6751
Program length: semester, with extension to full year possible
Cost: $3,800 per semester; housing is another $2,077
Financial aid: available
Housing: dormitory or homestays
Age range of participants: PG and college

Number of participants: varies
Application process: application; transcript; 3 letters of recommendation; medical form; financial form; 10 identification photos; $20 application fee
Application due dates: rolling until May 31 for fall; November 20 for spring
Program location: Osaka

The greatest part about Kaisai Gaidai is that you needn't be fluent or near fluent in Japanese to go. All you need to take part in this foreign study experience is the desire to learn about the Japanese culture and language. A beginner can enter the program without the usual misgivings about fluency. Classes are taught in English (except for the required Japanese-language course) and are offered in a wide range of fields. Class offerings include: Japanese economic development, marketing foreign products in Japan, women in Japanese society, and survey of Japanese art. This is a great program for people who want to learn about Japan. You will take four courses, one of them a required language course designed to fit your level of fluency. You will take all your classes with other foreign students. That is the biggest flaw in this program. There is not much opportunity for you to mingle regularly with the Japanese students at Kansai. But Kansai does offer its foreign students the opportunity to take part in a homestay with a local family. If you combine this option with coursework, you should be able to complete your sojourn at Keio with some sense of life in Japan.

MEXICO

As you prepare to choose a language program in Mexico—or, for that matter, to go to Mexico for any study or volunteer work—you need to keep in mind a few essentials peculiar to life in that coutnry. To begin with, the standard admonition—"Don't drink the water"—continues to hold true. There are lots of bottled alternatives, and they're all preferable to the perils of the local water. As for food, well, as one traveler has put it: "Visit the . . . market and sample the goods from a food stall if you feel reckless." The good news has to do with transportation. Mexico has a most widespread and efficient (within limits) bus service, adequate if slow train transportation, and reasonably inexpensive plane travel. In fact, some travel writers advise flying to Mexico and then relying on internal Mexican airlines to save money. Similar advice has been given regarding bus and train travel in Mexico. It may not be the most rapid method, but buses particularly are safe and virtually ubiquitous. Some other tidbits of advice: Don't travel with pretentious luggage; it's not in your best interest to accentuate the economic differences between you and your hosts. Bring a small flashlight, toilet paper, wash'n wipes, disinfectant spray, and, just in case, Lomotil. Finally, given the vast difference between U.S. and Mexican currencies almost constantly during the last decade, any American traveling in Mexico can expect to do so fairly cheaply. Lodging can be obtained for under $20 a night—and that's a luxury rate—and sampling a *comida corrida* at a local restaurant can be both filling and remarkably inexpensive. This "running meal" is a tag-team challenge for your appetites, a three-or four-course "succession of soup, rice, refried beans, and meat. . . . [And] it is served in the afternoon, thus eliminating the need for an expensive . . . dinner." Cost? Probably under $3.

Keep in mind that most of the programs mentioned below expect to immerse you in Spanish—language and culture—during your time with that program. You should expect to live with a Mexican family. You should expect to spend at least four hours per day actually "doing" Spanish: grammar, vocabulary, informal conversation, listening to lectures, etc. The presumption of almost all language courses in Mexico—and certainly of the good ones—is that you are there to learn Spanish, as swiftly and efficiently as possible. Your peers will probably be a wild assortment of people: all nationalities, all ages, all walks of life. The result is likely to be an excellent grounding in oral conversation. "It is no exaggeration to say that, depending on the student's abilities, the . . . language schools can achieve in four to six weeks the equivalent of two semesters of instruction in the average U.S. college or university."

Cemanahuac Educational Community

Apartado 5-21
Cuernavaca, Mexico
52-73 12-1367
Program length: at least 1 month
Cost: varies; at least $500 for 4
  weeks including room and
  board

Financial aid: none
Housing: provided
Number of participants: varies by
  program
Age range of participants: 16 and
  up; median age: college or
  older

Application process: application
with fee

Application due date: rolling
admissions

Program location: Cuernavaca

The Educational Community is a language program that describes itself as Spanish-language study "in a cultural context." Consequently, Cemanahuac offers an ongoing Latin-American studies program at no extra cost. The great advantage of this program is its bilingual faculty, aware of the needs and concerns of English speakers but determined to immerse their students in the study and speaking of Spanish. The second advantage enjoyed by Cemanahuac is its location. Cuernavaca is a resort city, full of gaiety and life. As an alternative, there is a companion program in a far more bucolic town about an hour from Cuernavaca, where Cemanahuac operates another facility. Both offer homestay situations to insure a Spanish-speaking environment; each has its virtues. The Educational Community provides what an Ohio State professor called "a model program" for those who wish to initiate or improve their ability to speak Spanish.

Nor are the accommodations less than fitting for such a "model." There are "open-air 'classrooms' . . . with three out five students go[ing] through the language drills under the careful and patient guidance of an instructor." However, what makes this school most valuable is its selection of coursework in intercultural and interdisciplinary studies, particularly in Latin-American studies. Because of its connections with American universities, its transcripts are usually readily accepted by U.S. schools.

Universal

Apartado Postal 1826
CP 62000, Cuernavaca, Mexico

Program length: minimum 1
month

Cost: varies by program

Financial aid: none

Housing: homestays available

Number of participants: varies by
program

Age range of participants: 16 and
up

Application process: application
with fee

Application due date: rolling
admissions

Program location: Cuernavaca

Beyond the virtues of being in Cuernavaca, Universal offers the advantages of a small school with bilingual instructors dedicated to immersing students in Spanish for the duration of their stay in the program. Students work with instructors for about twenty-four hours a week, then go off to live with their homestays, who often are working-class families with no English whatsoever. Thus, the program fulfills the promise of total immersion in Ibero-American culture. In addition, Universal rotates instructors through the classes in each session. With a teacher-student ratio of about 1:4, this means that instructors and students become acquainted anew each week. Since that acquaintanceship is being done in Spanish, learning possibilities are enhanced significantly. Despite the fact that this program lacks the frills of other Cuernavaca language programs, its instructors are all veterans; its methods are laudable; and the chances of successful immersion with Universal are likely to be good. Perhaps the best news is that this program costs about $170 per week inclusive.

The Center for Bilingual Multicultural Studies

San Jeronimo 304, Apartado 1520
Cuernavaca, Moreles
62000 Mexico
Overseas code + 17-05-33 or 17-10-87 or 13-04-02
Program length: minimum 2 weeks; average stay 4 or 6 weeks for minimal proficiency
Cost: varies by program
Financial aid: none

Housing: provided
Number of participants: varies by program
Age range of participants: 16 and up
Application process: application with fee
Application due date: rolling admissions
Program location: Cuernavaca

Why go to the Center for Bilingual Multicultural studies? Because you will "leave with a confident . . . command of Spanish and greater understanding of Mexico." Or because of the quality of the teaching staff and their use of the immersion method (plus an agreement that you speak no English: "Students do nothing but live, eat, and sleep Spanish . . . and that's the best way to learn"). Or perhaps because "four weeks at the center in Cuernavaca costs less than four days at a first-class hotel. Professional instruction while sharing the warmth of a Mexican family."

Clearly, there are many good reasons to go the center for your training in Spanish. It's also worth noting that the center offers a range of courses in the history and politics of Mexico, Central and Latin America. But what's best about this range of training is its cost. Tuition is $125 per week; room and board with a Mexican family ranges from $70 to $105 per week. Considering that Cuernavaca, often called the City of Eternal Spring because of its gentle climate and beautiful setting, is a popular resort, what better locale in which to learn a new language or perfect a familiar one?

Instituto Allende

San Miguel de Allende
Guanajuato, Mexico 37700
465-2-01-90
Program length: minimum 1 month
Cost: varies by program and level of Spanish teaching
Financial aid: none
Housing: available
Age range of participants: 16 and up

Number of participants: varies by program
Application process: application with fee
Application due date: rolling admissions
Program location: San Miguel de Allende

Instituto Allende has several characteristics that distinguish it from many of the other language schools in Mexico. It is located in San Miguel de Allende, a university town in the mountains several hours north of Mexico City. The institute is affiliated with the University of Guanajuato, making credit transfers a possibility. The institute offers a variety of fine arts and crafts programs, from graphic art to ceramics, silverwork, weaving, and textile design. Because this is a university town, housing is a bit harder to come by and may require more advance planning than might be necessary elsewhere in Mexico. But homestays are available, costing about $16 per day. In addition, hotels and apartments are relatively cheap by American standards. It should be noted that the cost of language instruction varies by intensity. All programs run for one month, but different levels cost different rates. As a standard, an intensive four-hour per day program costs $250 for a month

Spring Term in Mérida

International Programs Office
Box 2759
Rollins College
Winter Park, FL 32789
Program length: semester, spring
   term
Cost: $5,750
Financial aid: if available from
   home institution
Housing: hotel

Age range of participants: college
   sophomore and up
Number of participants: 20
Applicaiton process: application
   with fee; transcript;
   professor's recommendation;
   dean's statement of
   permission; parent consent form
Application due date: November 1
Program location: Mérida

If your interest in things Mexican extends beyond language training, this program offers a variety of courses in English, as well as an affiliation with the University of Yucatán. Anthropologists can begin this program in January with the special winter term program in Yucatán offered by the Rollins College anthropology department.

SPAIN

If you're considering studying or traveling in Spain, remember the following: It's bigger than you think; Spanish has more dialect varieties than you might imagine (so don't think your four years of Spanish will be the passport to linguistic comfort). Also, Spain as a country stands somewhere between the eighteenth and mid-twentieth centuries, with a foot in each. Finally, and this is an admonition applicable beyond Spain, the ideological charge of many issues is far more significant than in the United States. Remember, politics has been a life-and-death matter in Spain as recently as the Spanish civil war, still within the memory of many Spaniards.

   Where is good to go and why? If you're in Spain to learn the language, proprietary programs abound. There is at least one in virtually every major city. Choosing the right location is important. For example, the most dedicated of students would find it almost impossible to study on a summer program in Seville, where temperatures regularly exceed 105 degrees. Those who abhor gigantic cities would do well to avoid Madrid and Barcelona—polluted, traffic-snarled megalopolises of 5 million people. A program located in a small city (Granada or Seville, for example) offers more to the student who likes quick access to the countryside.

Course in Hispanic Studies

Sr. Director del Curso de Estudios para Estranjeros
Facultad de Filosofia y Letras
Universidad de Valladolid
47002 Valladolid, Spain
Program length: semester: January 10 to May 30
Cost: approximately $900; room and board approximately $10 per day

Financial aid; none
Housing: available
Age range of participants: 18 and up
Number of participants: varies
Application process: application with fee
Application due date: rolling admissions
Program location: Valladolid

This program, operated under the aegis of the University of Valladolid, provides an excellent introduction to both Spanish language and Spanish culture. Through a daily regimen of intensive language instruction (two hours daily), as well as instruction in Spanish literature, culture, geography, and history, you should emerge with not only a working knowledge of Spanish but also of Spain.

This acculturative process is enhanced further by your residence with a Spanish family during your time in Valladolid. If your intention is to learn Spanish in a short period of time, this program is worth your investigation.

Other programs in Spain and the Canary Islands include:

Eurocentro, Institutos Mangold S.A.; Rambia de cataluna 16; Barcelona 7
Eurolingua, Calle Prats de Mollo 6; jto. a Pza. Adriano; 08021 Barcelona

CANARY ISLANDS:

Academic Year in Spain/Dialogue International.
This is a year or semester language and university program that has a resident director, excursions, field trips, and other features. Contact Timothy Langenberg; Academic Year in Spain/Dialogue International; Grand Plaza Place, Suite 210; 220 Lyons Square; Grand Rapids, MI 49503.
Contact Mr. Langenberg also for similar programs in Madrid, Pamplona, or Seville.

Gran Canaria School of Languages (an intensive language program that offers some potential for credit) c/o Tomas Morales; No. 54, E-35003 Las Palmas; Gran Canaria, Spain
or (in Malaga)
Centro de Estudios de Espanol: language and Hispanic culture. Contact F. Mario Fernandez, Centro de Estudios de Espanol, Avenida Juan Sebastian Elcano 110
29017 Málaga, Spain

There are also several university- or school-oriented programs:

In Málaga contact the Sr. Director, **Cursos para extranjeros;** Apto. 310; 29080 Málaga, Spain.

In Valencia contact **Luis Vives Escuela de Profesores de Lengua Espanola;** Calle Periodista Llorente 8; 46009 Valencia, Spain.

In Santander contact Trevor Fitt, **Inlingua School of Language,** Rualasal 23; 39001 Santander, Spain.

Cultural Exchange Programs

The following programs offer travel and education, but do so in a way that focuses more on the concept of contact between cultures. So if learning about another culture is your principal goal, these programs will have special value for you.

Citizen Exchange Council
12 West 31st Street
New York, 10001-4415
(212) 889-7960
Contact person: staff
Prices and deadlines vary from group to group

The Citizen Exchange Council is an exchange program that arranges tours of the Soviet Union for special-interest groups. However, CEC deals only with groups and will not act as the organizing body. Interested parties need to approach CEC with a readymade group and a special interest. Then, CEC will arrange a two- to three-week tour built around that interest. If, for example, photography happens to be your passion—and you belong to a group of enthusiastic photographers—CEC will arrange for your group to meet Soviet photographers, visit photography exhibits, and participate in related activities. You supply the group, and CEC will take care of the rest of the details.

Institute for International Cooperation and Development
Box 1063
Amherst, MA 01004
(413) 268-9229
Contact person: Ted Lewis, executive director
Program length: 9 months

Cost: $4,000–$8,000, covers tuition, room, board, and travel expenses
Financial aid: possible
Age range of participants: 18 and up

Number of participants per
  program: 12–18
Application process: application;
  essay; interview
Application due date: rolling
  admissions

Program locations: Latin America,
  Africa, USSR, China, and the
  Philippines

IICD specializes in travel/study "tours" that provide two months of language and culture preparation in the United States followed by five months of overseas traveling. The final two months of the nine-month program are spent back in the States preparing and giving lectures on your experiences to community groups up and down the East Coast (location of talks is limited to the East Coast by lack of funds).

IICD is not your average travel/study tour. It will take you to settings not frequented by tour buses, like Nicaragua, for example. The purpose of the program is to allow its participants to observe and explore the cultures of the countries they are visiting. Participants are not ushered around in a bus. Rather during the preparation process, the participants, along with their group leader, decide what shall be visited and studied while abroad. Once overseas, participants break into small groups of three or four. They will spend ten days to two weeks at a time in these groups investigating their particular area of inquiry. Perhaps one of the more unsettling parts of the program occurs here. Once separated from their team leader, the "satellite" groups have no planned contact with the program, nor does the program know precisely where they are or, perhaps more importantly, where they aren't until the whole group is reunited at a prearranged location. Furthermore, once a satellite group goes out, its members are responsible for finding their own housing. So keep in mind that when you reach your destination country, it's just going to be you and that country—or you and its inhabitants. IICD does not interpose any structure, protective or otherwise, between you and them. You have to cope—and it's worth considering that coping in the third and fourth worlds requires skills not always found in a jaunt around Italy or the French Alps.

IICD requires program participants to document their experiences through video or audio tape, photography or journalism, or in most cases a combination of the four. It is this material that allows students to get involved in the culture of their destination country and have some tangible evidence of that involvement. Students use their documentation projects as the basis for their lectures back in the States. One of the most important things program participants need to understand is that IICD is completely group oriented, and participants must be committed to that ideal. Decisions at IICD are made consensually, and there is a strict no alcohol, no drugs policy.

IICD offers a terrific opportunity for those interested in experiencing parts of the worlds not traversed by mainstream travel/study programs. Moreover, IICD enriches that experience by preparing you for the trip.

While this program should not be seen as the ultimate learning device, it is a valuable complement to textbook learning. There's little doubt that a veteran of IICD will find that experience breathes new life into the classrooms to which they return.

LEX America

68 Leonard Street
Belmont, MA 02178
(617) 489-5800
Contact person: staff
Program length: 1 month or 6 weeks, summer only
Cost: $2,500–3,000, includes airfare
Financial aid: none
Housing: homestays

Age range of participants: 12 and up
Number of participants per program:
Application process: essay; interview; application form; parental consent
Application due date: rolling admissions
Program location: Japan; Korea

LEX America offers you the opportunity to enter the exciting and unique culture of Japan. But you won't be staying in the best resorts or riding around in a tour bus. Rather, you will join a typical Japanese family. You will play the games they play, be part of their conversations, eat the same food; in short, you will live as if you were a member of the family for six weeks. LEX America carefully screens its host families so you can be sure that you will be welcome. But because you're entering the daily life of another culture, much of what you experience is likely to be unexpected. Just think about how interesting it would be for someone to become part of your family. As one parent says of the LEX America experience: "They're not really sight-seeing. They are really living as a family member. They're given chores." LEX America offers a terrific way to learn about Japan and yourself.

The Oomoto Foundation School of Traditional Japanese Arts

American address: Patricia Ryan, coordinator
168 Grand View Avenue
San Francisco, CA 94114
(415) 641-4841
Program length: 1 month, summer only
Cost: $1,900, airfare not included
Financial aid: none
Age range of participants: 18 and up

Number of participants: 24
Application process: letter of intent; photograph
Application due date: rolling admissions, but spaces in this program go quickly, so write early!
Program locations: Kameoka-shi, Kyoto-fu, Japan

The Oomoto Foundation School of Traditional Japanese Arts specializes in instruction for the foreigner in Japan's four most important art forms: the tea ceremony; budo, a martial art form performed with a wooden stick; No dance; and calligraphy. You will not just learn about these arts, you will learn to do them.

Oomoto is a strictly hands-on place. During your monthlong stay, you will experience Japanese culture from the perspective of Japan's sons and daughters. You will wear a kimono, eat Japanese food, learn the art of meditation, bathe in communal baths, and sleep on tatami mats while studying the four arts daily. This is not Club Med. Oomoto is intense. While English translators are present, classes are taught in Japanese, which is the language of choice outside the classroom as well.

Oomoto was founded in 1976 by David Kidd, an American-born professor who has spent his adult life in the Orient. It is his desire to provide foreigners with a more insightful view of the Japanese culture through the practice of traditional arts. Kidd says of his school: "There is no place in or out of Japan where so many arts can be practiced together at one time, nor is there, we believe, any country in the world that has preserved the tremendous range of traditional arts still found in Japan today." As a result of that tradition, students can gain cultural insight into the country as a whole through their training in Japanese art and meditation. As one former student put it: "The traditional arts of Japan represent a synthesis of Oriental cultures and philosophies. They combine the Shinto emphasis on purification and the spirituality of nature; Zen concepts of simplicity, discipline, and introspection; Taoism's quest to become one with the harmony of nature."

The school is located at the Oomoto Center in Kameoka City, in a near perfect setting. Originally an ancient castle, and currently the home of a Shinto organization, the Oomoto Center has been refurbished beautifully to preserve its charm and create a functional living space for its students. Within the castle walls, students will find stages for drama and dance, tea rooms, traditional gardens, shrines, and studios.

Students at Oomoto can expect a great deal of structure. Because each day will consist of experiential classes, there will not be much free time. In many of these classes, a professor will demonstrate, and a student will mimic his or her actions. You will be corrected—the rituals of every artistic aspect are meticulous and delicate—and then will try again. Such mimicry is likely to take place in every class from budo to acupuncture. Students are expected to take part in all lessons, and study all art forms.

In addition to classes, Oomoto organizes several day trips to points of interest. Oomoto offers foreigners a path toward understanding not available through books or guided tours of Japan. This is a trip into the rituals that are themselves the heart of Japanese society.

People to People International
501 East Armour Boulevard
Kansas City, MO 64109
(816) 531-4701

Contact person: Dr. Alan M.
Warne, vice president for
programs

Program length: summer only; trips last between 2½ weeks and 1 month
Cost: $1,600–$3,950
Financial aid: available
Housing: combination of hotels, homestays, and dormitories
Age range of participants: 16 and up
Number of participants per program: 16–30 per trip
Credit available through the University of Missouri–Kansas City

Application process: application; brief essays for London internship program; certification by another institution form; interview and/or recommendation
Application due date: rolling until April 10
Program locations: traveling seminars in Washington, New York, London, Paris, Stockholm, Edinburgh, Brussels, and other major cities in Europe

So you've got a long summer ahead of you. Nothing to do, nothing that sets you on fire—really interests you. How about Europe, with a twist? Traveling to Europe with People to People is the ultimate field trip.

People to People International was founded in 1956 by President Dwight Eisenhower as a way to help American citizens gain a greater understanding of the rest of the world through education and travel. Today, People to People offers summer travel courses that take its participants to several world cities and several different countries. Each course is structured around a main theme, and course subjects vary from a theatre course in England to a business course entitled Direct Marketing: International Perspectives, mastered by traveling to New York, London, and Paris. Other offerings touch on disciplines ranging from political science to education, from sociology and economics to history.

One of the perks of traveling with People to People is that you will be admitted to places and have access to people not usually available to the average tourist. "One of the highlights of this trip was meeting the people. They may not have had all the material things, but when it comes down to it, they were just like us. While we would walk down the streets, people would come up to us and want to talk and ask questions about America. I realized how America has such a large impact on the rest of the world. What we do affects them."

On the Global Security Issues trip you will get briefings on world security issues at NATO and talk with British security experts while in London. As one former PTP partaker remarked, it was just what he had hoped it would be. "I participated in the program because of its incredible opportunity: the coursework, the ability to study the Western Alliance and, with the PTP name, to talk with key leaders in each country. We got to hear their views in their own setting."

While the People to People courses offer tremendous travel experience, one must also remember that they are very definitely academic courses, and as such have homework—reading and writing assignments. Most have either a paper or an exam due at the end of the trip so that academic credit may be given for your effort. People to People staff stress that these trips are in fact courses, and they are interested in serious participants. If you are looking for a travel tour, this is not the place for you. If, however, you are excited by the subject matter of a course and want to delve into it with gusto, these are the trips for you!

It is worth mentioning that People to People also sponsors a summer Internship in London program. This program is open only to college students and graduate students. There are internships in four fields: education, political science, public administration (graduate students only), and business administration. In conjunction with the London office of the English-Speaking Union, People to People places students in unpaid internships and helps them find housing. Airfare and insurance are included in the $2,150 fee; housing, which can be located with the help of ESU for about $110–$125 a week, is not.

Up with People

Admissions Department
3103 North Campbell Avenue
Tucson, AZ 85719
 (602) 327-7351
Contact person: admissions staff
Program length: 11 months
Cost: $10,000
Financial aid: available
Housing: homestays/dormitory
Age range of participants: 18 and up

Number of participants per program: 550
Application process: application; references; interview; essays
Application due date: rolling admissions
Program locations: travels worldwide

What follows is gleaned from the Up with People literature. (Their busy schedule seems to preclude time for interviews.) But the authors' difficulties in communicating with them should not detract from the value of the program. Many prospective applicants have better luck getting their attention. Up with People is an organization founded in the mid-1960s to "build peace through understanding." The idea was to create a musical show with an international cast to entertain audiences around the world. Can entertainers break through culture barriers? Apparently, yes. The program has worked.

As a participant, you are a performer. You and your coperformers/coparticipants will travel the world performing for local schools, civic groups, and towns, and staying with local families in most cases. You'll become more than a singer; you'll be an ambassador of goodwill. This all may sound a bit corny, but it's true. As one young woman noted: "I can still remember the great feeling I got when Up with People came and performed in my town when I was only ten. Somehow the multinational cast and the songs from other parts of the world seemed to make the globe a smaller and more pleasant place. And what I most wanted to do that day was join Up with People as soon as I was old enough."

You probably have some questions: Do I have to be a terrific singer? Just how will I spend those eleven months? The answer to the first question is no. You have to have a great personality, and you must be enthusiastic for the adventure. But singing talent, while nice, is not a necessity. Now about the eleven months. Most of that time will be spent touring in the United States and abroad. This is no luxury trip. You will be quartered in private homes or stay in youth hostels. But it is a wonderful way to travel, make some great friends, and have a blast.

United States Servas Committee, Inc.

11 John Street
New York, NY 10038
(212) 267-0252
Contact person: Randi Metch-
  Ampel
Cost: $45 membership fee; $15
  returnable deposit for host
  book

Age range of participants: 18 and
up
Number of participants: unlimited
Program locations: Worldwide

Servas is a peace organization based on the philosophy that bringing people from all over the world together in one another's homes will establish greater understanding and an appreciation of different cultures. Servas arranges homestays but it is not a placement agency. If you join Servas, you will receive a "host" book that lists members by location, interests, knowledge of languages, birthdates, and so forth. You are expected then to contact your potential host and arrange the dates when you will visit. And the stress is on "dates," since Servas's intention would be belied by any arrangement that seemed to be a simple bed-and-breakfast situation. All Servas members are expected to spend enough time with their hosts to get to know their families, to enjoy the sensation of being guests of members of a different culture, and to learn about each other.

Host families and travelers alike take part in an interview and orientation program that helps both parties to understand fully the nature of the program. Servas stresses "person-to-person contact" between traveler and host. The parties need to understand that and be interested in that kind of arrangement. Servas officials admit that their program is not for everyone, and because travelers are guests in the hosts' homes they should come prepared to stay in a hotel in case of some emergency within the host family.

Servas operates in ninety different countries, helping to make the world a smaller place through fulfilling homestays.

Environmental Programs

◇ ◇ ◇

The programs in this section share one characteristic: They will put you in touch with the environment and give you the chance to learn and work outside, not in an office or classroom. And here's a warning: When you finish reading this section, you may be a bit bemused. "But I thought internships were a different place," you might say, or, "Weren't academic programs listed a couple of hundred pages ago?" This section focuses on what many people in alternative education consider the core of a nonmainstream experience: experiential education at its best. Below you will find programs that give you a chance to experience the environment—and to learn from it, whether as a student, intern, apprentice, or instructor of others. So remember: What makes this section different is that it centers on the environment. If that feature interests you, read on.

American Farm School in Greece
1133 Broadway
New York, NY 10010
(212) 463–8434
Contact person: Henry Crawford
Program length: summer: six weeks, mid-June until the end of July
Cost: $2,350 plus airfare
Financial aid: none
Housing: homestays and dormitory
Age range of participants: high school, 14–18: summer after freshman year in high school through summer after senior year

Number of participants: 44
Application process: 3 essays; 2 recommendations; $500 deposit (will be returned if you are not accepted, will be applied to tuition if you are accepted); 2 pictures; interview
Application due date: December 31
Program location: Thessaloníki, Greece

How are your summer plans shaping up? Do you know what you want to do? How does travel, friends, adventure, and hard work sound? Not bad, but where are you going to get all that before you get out of high school? Don't those opportunities go to college-age kids? The answer is no, not at the American Farm School's Greek Summer for American high school students. The Greek Summer offers forty-four American high school kids the opportunity to live with a Greek family in a small village (all farm school participants are located in the same village). In return for the village's hospitality you will work on a much needed project within the village, such as the building of a road or structure. While the work is hard, past participants rave about their summer in Greece, especially their Greek families. One alum talks about the way his adopted family made him welcome: "I had two brothers and a mother and a father, and they really did feel like my other family. . . . At the end we had a farewell dinner and it was a really emotional thing." Your time with your Greek family serves to do more than provide you with a place to live. Participants learn to communicate, to grow, and to accept a life entirely different from life in mainstream America. In the words of one alum: "Greek Summer opened my eyes to a completely different society, one I appreciated in many ways more than my own. The Greeks seem to base their attitudes on simple morals, whereas we base ours on science and economics. I think Greek civilization makes people give more of themselves."

While the time in the village is the most talked about and remembered part of each alum's summer, participants also spend several weeks at the farm school learning the basics of farming and animal raising. They then embark on a weeklong tour of Greece and some of its major points of interest.

The American Farm School's Greek Summer seems to have come up with a super answer to the summer doldrums. You will get the chance to stretch and grow as never before; you will make both American and Greek friends; and you will experience a completely foreign culture. One alum says of her time on Greek Summer: "Even after ten years, I still have to say that Greek Summer was the greatest experience I've ever had. I wish I were seventeen and could do it again." And that, folks, is the best recommendation you can get.

Appalachian Mountain Club—Trails Crew Jobs

Box 298
Gorham, NH 03581
(603) 466–2721
Contact person: Trails Program director
Program length: 3–8 plus weeks
Stipend: room, board, and small wage in some cases
Age range of participants: 18 and up

Number of participants: varies
Application process: letter of application
Application due date: rolling admissions
Program locations: Appalachian Trail in New Hampshire, Massachusetts, Connecticut, and New York

If you like to work outside in physical situations (trail clearing and construction) and you love the mountains, think about joining the Trails Program of the Appalachian Mountain Club. The work is often "frustrating, particularly when it rains and the mosquitoes come out" . . . and it's "rigorous."— "You have to think carefully about the physics and gravity of the task you are doing. You are working with huge rocks and very heavy objects. If you don't think it through, you are destined to fail."

AMC has both voluntary and paid positions available for the maintenance of its trails and the running of its shelters. You could manage a backcountry shelter, clear trails, or work in some other capacity. Sometimes, the days are really long, "twelve hours or more." And there's more than just you to worry about: "It's really important that you have the ability to keep your own morale up and your determination and patience with you—as well as the morale, determination, and patience of the rest of your crew."

AMC has openings in the spring, summer, and fall. The living accommodations are rustic, but if you're a mountain person there is some real satisfaction to be gained from the work. "Great people and a great bonding experience" was one alum's report. Nor do you have to know trail work: "Success is based on the character you bring to trail crew, not the experience you bring." Indeed, what AMC wants most is the attitude expressed by another veteran: You just "need to really want to be there and contribute."

Breckenridge Outdoor Education Center Internships

Box 697
Breckenridge, CO 80424
(303) 453–6422
Program length: December–April;
  June–September
Cost: board provided
Financial aid: none
Housing: provided
Age range of participants: 18 and
  up

Number of participants: varies
Application process: application; 3
  references; interview
Application due date: mid-
  September for winter; mid-
  March for summer
Program location: Breckenridge,
  Colorado

The Breckenridge Outdoor Education Center offers interns the opportunity to ski, snowshoe, dog-sled, even to camp in winter; to swim, raft, and canoe; and to climb and to camp in summer. You're right. All this sounds extremely exciting—if you know something of outdoor leadership and of the technical skills needed to master some of the above. The reason for such concern is that you will be working, and working hard, with special-needs populations. That means with the physically and emotionally disabled, as well as with recovering substance abusers and youth-at-risk.

BOEC has set itself the task of using the wilderness environment as a tool for making the lives of its students better. You will be helping instructors deal with these students, as they come to learn in courses of 1 to 4 days in length, and it's a grueling routine. As BOEC notes: "Internships

are demanding of your energy, good humor and communication throughout the season."

What's the return for all this outlay of energy? What you learn. You have
to bring to this program at least a certification in first aid/CPR, with some
experience in either the skills mentioned above or in experiential education.
Your principal reward has to be the satisfaction gained from helping people
gain confidence in themselves. But you'll also take away a lot more knowledge—in some or all of the skills above—than you came with. And you get
to live in one of the most beautiful locations in the United States—and ski
in winter, swim and camp in summer, for free.

This program requires commitment—and some background. But if you
can meet its qualifications, the experience promises to be more than worthwhile. As one intern noted: "Breckenridge is magical because of the people
who work and live there and because of those who participate in the
program. . . . We lived in a small community in an isolated cabin. We had
no TV, no phone, but we had each other. . . . And we [were encouraged to
push ourselves beyond our limits and to encourage others] to do the same.
In most cases, they did and great things happened. . . . I saw people learn
to trust themselves and each other. Participants surprised themselves and
those around them. They demonstrated who they could be and what they
could do when they shed their traditional roles." And ex-staffer summed
all this up by saying that Breckenridge simply encourages you to "think in
different terms."

Environmental Action Foundation

1525 New Hampshire Avenue,
  NW
Washington, DC 20036
(202) 745–4870
Program length: semester
Cost: none
Financial aid: none
Housing: none
Age range of participants: college
  and up

Number of participants: varies by
  program
Application process: letter of
  application; interview
Application due date: rolling
  admissions
Program location: Washington,
  D.C.

Environmental Action was founded by the organizers of the original Earth
Day (circa 1970). Ever since, this organization has worked to lobby for a
variety of environmental issues. The causes Environmental Action addresses
need constant research, most often are forwarded by grassroots activism and
education, and usually are directed toward corrective legislation. Interns are
involved in decision making because of the collectively styled management
structure by which Environmental Action operates. Your duties as an intern
would include all phrases of promoting progressive environmental policies,
possibly through journalism and marketing efforts. Unfortunately, Environmental Action has no funds for supporting its volunteer staff. Valuable

experience with the byways of Washington and a chance to work for the betterment of the environment are its principal benefits.

Interns have found the positions at Environmental Action instructive and rewarding: "I was lucky with the internship. I spent 60 to 70 percent of my time writing. I did reporting and helped solicit donations. I also go to a great deal of press conferences."—"The internship is flexible and geared to what you can do and want to do with it. . . . The best part is learning to write and learning about the environment." Other interns remarked: "They've been great about helping me in my writing and in my learning about the environment." "It's been good to see myself in perspective as an apprentice to a trade." Interns have found the conviviality of the group rewarding. "I like the people a lot, and that's crucial. They are great and very supportive."—"Opportunities definitely open up. It's really positive to talk and network with other people. You see what else is out there that you otherwise never would have found."

Five Rivers Environmental Education Center

Game Farm Road
Delmar, NY 12054
(518) 453–1806
Program length: 12-week sessions
Cost: none; $50 per week stipend
Financial aid: none
Housing: provided; not handicapped accessible
Age range of participants: 18 and up
Number of participants: varies by program
Application process: application; resume; list of environmental education-related college courses, if available; 3 references
Application due date: rolling admissions
Program locations: Delmar, New York; also programs in Sherburne, New York (Rogers Environmental Education Center, Box 716, Route 80 West); and in Wappingers Falls, New York (Stony Kill Farm Environmental Education Center, Route 9D)

The state of New York offers opportunities for naturalist training at any of three environmental-education centers in the state. What makes these internships distinctive is the range of opportunity at each center. You will be expected to complete your internship by producing a "nature walk" or workshop, by creating a major exhibit in one of the interpretative buildings on site, by preparing an audio-visual presentation or by writing an article. Sound formidable? It is, but such a range of options also gives you a chance to focus some collateral skills that take you beyond the necessary interest in environmental education. Moreover, in order to make you ready for such production, you will spend your internship learning these collateral skills at the hands of your supervisors at the center. The New York State program is a very professional program, with long-established goals and daily routine. You could spend your day teaching "a visiting school group, answering telephone queries, recording weather data, preparing exhibit materials, observing a staff member conduct a special program, work[ing] with the live animal exhibits."

One of the best features of this opportunity is the arrangement New York State has provided for your residence at each center. All three centers maintain an apartment for the intern on site, as well as paying that intern a stipend sufficient to cover board. So if you have a strong interest in "and enthusiasm for communicating to the public environmental messages and natural history information," this program could be for you. If your background reflects some experience in natural history or previous training in environmental education, so much the better.

Hidden Villa Environmental Education Program

Hidden Villa Ranch
26870 Moody Road
Lost Altos, CA 94022
(415) 941–6119
Contact person: Dave Brodky
Program length: semester, summer, year option available
Cost: none
Financial aid: none
Stipend: $50 per month
Housing: room and board included
Age range of participants: 18–28

Number of participants per session: 4 paid interns; up to 70 part-time volunteers
Application process: resume; references; interview—either on site or by phone
Application due dates: August 1 for fall; November 15 for spring; January 15; March 15 for summer.
Program location: Los Altos, California

Hidden Villa is an environmental education center for children that lies five minutes out of Los Altos, and only fifty minutes south of San Francisco—but could be worlds away. Bought by the Duveneck family in the early twenties, Hidden Villa sits on 1,600 acres of wilderness. The center is a working farm with cows, goats, pigs, poultry, ducks, and horses. Also it has more than five acres of gardens and many wilderness trails for children and adults to enjoy.

The Intern program has been in effect for nineteen years. Started by the Duveneck family as a way to allow college students and young graduates the chance to develop skills and training in environmental education, the intern program has been thriving ever since. Interns can expect to spend a great deal of their time working with children. They will lead farm tours, nature walks, gardening expeditions, and help the children understand how nature works by working with nature. The overriding teaching method is learning by doing, feeling, and seeing. The overriding ethic is, according to former farm manager Penny Sirota, "people taking care of the land and each other." One intern I spoke with labeled this the caretaker ethic. As she put it: "My teaching strategy is to make kids aware that they are responsible for themselves and nature, if they drop a piece of tissue, it's their responsibility to pick it up. If every child did that, then we would have less of a pollution mess on our hands." So the keyword to understanding life at Hidden Villa is caring, caring about the environment, but also about each other. Interns have a supportive network of full-time faculty and staff. The latter provide a welcome resource for discussion of teaching techniques and experiences. Similarly, the four full-time interns develop a close living and working relationship. The interns share a house on the ranch, where each is provided with his/her own room. Interns regularly help each other in chores and teaching issues; all mentioned "the wonderful people" as the best part of life on the ranch.

Hidden Valley provides a neat way to experience life on the farm. If your interests include teaching or learning about and working with the environment, Hidden Villa meets the bill. Interns work a forty-hour week, and when not teaching take an active role in the running of the farm, for which they earn very little pay. Yet the rewards appear to be great.

Inner Quest Apprenticeship Program

Inner Quest, Inc.
220 Queen Street, NE
Leesburg, VA 22075
(703) 478–1078 or 771–4800
Contact person: Sara Smith
Program length: 3 months: spring semester, fall semester, and summer
Cost: none
Stipend: $600–$700
Housing: none

Age range of participants: 18–27
Number of participants per program: 10–20
Application process: application; interview; 3 references
Application due date: rolling admissions according to nearest start date; contact Inner Quest for specifics
Program location: Leesburg, Virginia

Inner Quest is an "experiential education organization encouraging holistic growth through safe, challenging adventure." Its main goal is to run outdoor adventure programs that challenge a person's body and mind. Clients include schools, community groups, and businesses. Inner Quest strives to leave its participants feeling physically tired and mentally exhilarated at the end of each day.

To help participants achieve these goals, Inner Quest provides several trips, ranging in length from one to twenty-eight days, whose focus can be anything from rope courses to caving, mountain climbing, kayaking, canoeing, skiing, or any combination thereof.

Not only can you and a group do a trip, you also can choose to become an Inner Quest leader through their three-month Apprentice Program, which provides the trainee with twenty days of formal training and then another thirty-five of supervised work experience. Like the kind of activity you will be trained in providing, the Inner Quest Apprenticeship Program is oriented toward hands-on activities. As an apprentice you will be trained in outdoor skills and outdoor safety, including first aid. Before moving on to the student-teaching phase of the course, Inner Quest requires that you pass technical tests, thereby demonstrating your competence in the skills you will have learned. "Three months of intense training program . . . training program includes lots of different areas, first aid, rock climbing, caving, CPR, kayaking, and more. It was great." Another IQ veteran felt "getting introductory training in the hard skills areas" was the best part. Another intern remarked: "I would want to know: Was it safe? And the answer is yes. They don't take chances; it's very safe." It's "a wonderful program I really recommend!"—"People intern here and go off and teach for Outward Bound and other programs like that." Once you have finished the technical side of the program, you begin assisting certified instructors in their courses, the length and difficulty of which escalates as you gain experience and confidence.

The Inner Quest Apprenticeship Program provides terrific experience for those interested in pursuing outdoor education. It offers its apprentices the chance to gain both hard technical skills and some experience and confidence in the field. In addition, Inner Quest provides stipends for its apprentices, a rare thing indeed. Also an added bonus is that once you have completed the program, you are eligible to join the Inner Quest staff.

International Crane Foundation

E–11376 Shady Lane Road
Baraboo WI 53913
(608) 356–9462
Program length: at least 2 months in spring, summer, fall
Cost: none; stipend of $150 per month
Financial aid: none
Housing: provided
Number of participants: 5 per season

Age range of participants: 20 and up
Application process: letter of application detailing interests and background: resume; 3 recommendations; interview (often conducted by phone)
Application due dates: January 1, April 1, and July 1
Program location: rural Wisconsin

The International Crane Foundation is dedicated to the conservation and preservation of the world's cranes and of their wetland habitats. At this Wisconsin site, interns have opportunities to learn and work in aviculture (the raising of birds—in this case cranes), in the restoration of the crane's habitat, in art/photography, and in dealing with visiting scientists and educators. The facility is approximately 160 acres, about a quarter of it open to the public, another area in which interns provide service and learn more about working with groups.

Through this program, interns are exposed to a variety of tasks involving this endangered species. In addition, interns have the chance to be involved in the full range of educational functions present at the Wisconsin facility—and will work in the "Ecosystem Restoration Program, the reestablishment of prairie, oak savanna, forest and wetland communities on ICF's property."

Prospective interns should note that they are paid a small stipend and housed while working at the facility. Interns will be encouraged to embark on their own projects; therefore, they should have completed their sophomore year in college and have a background in an area of interest relevant to the activities of the facility, such as biology or botany.

What is the advantage of an internship like this one? It offers a chance for hands-on work in conservation, and embellishes that work by involving participants in saving an endangered species.

Land Between the Lakes

Golden Pond, KY 42231
(502) 924–5602
Program length: all seasons
Cost: none; $65 per week stipend
Financial aid: none
Housing: provided
Age range of participants: 19 and up
Number of participants: 40–50 per year

Application process: application; resume; faculty letter; phone interview
Application due date: rolling admissions
Program locations: western Kentucky, Tennessee

Land Between the Lakes is located on a peninsula established by the Tennessee Valley Authority in the early 1960s. The peninsula is almost evenly divided by the Kentucky-Tennessee border. On this peninsula visitors can find an observatory, a re-creation of a mid-nineteenth-century farm, several campgrounds and environmental education sites, a working farm dedicated to self-sufficiency and conservation, and a buffalo herd. Why detail all this? Because if you become an intern at LBL maintenance of these locations might be part of your responsibility.

Interns at LBL might find themselves working with outdoor education, promoting LBL at schools in the area, planning and supervising outdoor education programs at LBL, helping with (and learning more about) resource management, or assisting permanent staff in the daily tasks of orientation and management of the more than 2 million visitors LBL receives every year.

This is a learning experience of unusual quality. Because of the size and scope of LBL, students in a wide variety of fields—from environmental education to law enforcement, from journalism to astronomy—might find it an attractive choice. And the population is eclectic geographically as well. In 1988, twenty-one students from fifteen states served as interns at LBL. From TVA's point of view, that's just fine, since one of the goals of this program is to give students a taste of the workings of a federal agency.

Equally important here is the variety of training open to you as a prospective intern. The trade-off, as might be expected, is qualification. As a valid applicant, you must be enrolled in a college or university; you must be at least a sophomore, with a declared major; and you might have taken certain courses in order to be prepared for some of the programs LBL offers. In return, you will be housed in individual rooms in house trailers on site and paid an average of $65 per week. And you may be able to get academic credit for your experience through your home institution.

If some of the above sounds formidable, remember that dealing with government agencies does suggest some bureaucratic complications. Don't let that discourage you. If the outdoors interests you enough to consider spending a semester or year in a setting full of different opportunities, LBL should be on your list.

Longwood Gardens: Internships for College Students

Box 501
Kennett Square, PA 19348
(215) 388–6741
Program length: 3–9 months
Cost: none
Financial aid: none
Stipend: $700 per month
Housing: provided
Age range of participants: college
Number of participants: 25–35
Application process: application; transcript and essay;

recommendations from major adviser and current or former employer
Application due dates: November 15 for March or April; February 15 for June; May 15 for September
Handicapped access: yes; but housing access may be limiting physically
Program location: Longwood Gardens, Pennsylvania

Their own literature says it best: "Longwood Gardens offers college students an unmatched opportunity to gain practical experience, learn gardening skills, and study plants amid one of the world's finest horticultural displays." There it is, folks. Your opportunity to live, work, and study in a garden that makes gardeners the world over salivate. If horticulture and related fields are not of interest, you can stop here. But if you're currently involved in a college program relevant to horticulture—or want to be—this opportunity is a unusually valuable one. Longwood will house you, provide a substantial stipend ($700 per month), and give you the chance to work with experts who deal with 1,060 acres of cultivated gardens, the former estate of P. S. duPont.

But don't think any of this will come easy. To qualify for this internship, you must be a registered college student and maintain that status throughout the duration of the program. In addition, Longwood's staff will scrutinize your transcript; your essay; your recommendations, one of which must comment on work experience—"preferably horticultural"; and rely on your familiarity with the "stuff" of your proposed internship: plant identification.

If you make it on Longwood, be prepared for some hard work. You will be asked to put in about thirty-five hours a week dealing with various aspects of the gardens, including arboriculture, maintaining the conservatory areas (of which there are more than two acres), working with some of the 800,000 visitors who come to Longwood annually, and even doing some field research. But what better way to begin your career—to find out whether this is the right choice for you?

National Audubon Society Ecology Camps and Workshops

613 Riversdale Road
Greenwich, CT 06831
(203) 869–2017
Contact person: staff
Program length: 1- to 2-week
  sessions
Cost: U.S.: $500–$1,000; Kenya:
  $4,000
Financial aid: none
Age range of participants: 18 and
  up

Number of participants per
  session: 10–20
Application process: form and
  deposit
Application due date: rolling as
  space allows
Program locations: U.S. and
  Africa

The Audubon Society offers some fascinating trips and workshops for those interested in nature and wildlife. You might go to Wyoming's Wind River Mountains and Grand Teton National Park with guides who can lecture on the wonders of geology and wildlife—as you observe them. Or you might go on a photo safari in the Tetons and the Wind Swept Mountains. Your guides will be accomplished photographers who can help you with the techniques of nature photography. The western part of the country is also the setting for the Audubon's Wilderness Research Backpack Program. There, you will join staff biologists engaged in ongoing extensive research of the Yellowstone ecosystem. The groups are limited to ten people and will cover five to seven miles of hiking per day at high elevations. In addition, there are camera safaris in Kenya. Similarly, the Audubon Society offers several workshops in ecology, located in Connecticut and Arizona. The Audubon trips are a fascinating way to have an educational and adventuresome vacation.

National Audubon Society Expedition Institute

Northeast Audubon Center
Box 170
Readfield, ME 04355
(207) 685–3111
Program length: semester, year
Cost: $6,100 per semester;
  $10,400 per year
Financial aid: available
Housing: provided
Number of participants: 19–20
  per bus
Age range of participants: 16 and
  up; 18 and up (see below for
  differences)

Application process: preliminary
  application; selected readings
  supplied by Institute (see
  Bibliography); secondary
  application; interview
Application due date: rolling
  admissions
Program location: throughout the
  U.S.

Yes, they really do live in a bus. And so will you, if you make it to the Expedition Institute. What this program is all about is what Mike Cohen captured in the title of his book *Our Classroom Is Wild America.* Expedition Institute's classroom is America. Don't be misled by the *Wild.* What it seems to stand for is nature and, by implication, the interconnectedness of man and nature. But to find that essential connection, participants in the institute's traveling classroom aren't restricted to life in the wild. They also explore and learn about Americans, both native and immigrant. They learn how all sorts of American lifestyles coexist with nature unbeknown to most of us in this country.

How do these twenty or so students do all this? They travel together with three or four staff members, but they function as a group. "Most mornings we meet, often to decide how the day will go or where we'll head next. For instance, several of us had suggestions that eventually led us up to Massachusetts and to Cape Cod. But the decision was the group's. We all listened and then voted." Their mission is to traverse a certain number of miles. Where they go within that constraint is up to the group, which makes decisions by consensus based on the convictions and interests of individuals. Staff members serve as referents, as helpers, and, as they are in fact called, as guides when needed.

Where does this busload of intrepid nature students go? (Actually there are four buses, three of which travel for a year, one by semesters.) It traverses the East Coast or heads across country. Students view their life as based outdoors; the bus is only a facility to carry them from one outside classroom to another. When the bus stops, the students learn. "We met an old horse-and-buggy Mennonite family in Pennsylvania who needed help on their farm. We swapped ten days' worth of working for them in order to share ten days' worth of their eighteenth-century farm life. We gathered eggs, built a wagon, and cleaned sunflower seeds, which gave the farmer time to meet with us and answer our questions."

As for the bus itself, each person has a seat with a personal box underneath. Overhead racks hold packs and suitcases. In the rear are bins for heavy coats, a library of books, food storage, and other paraphernalia. More gear goes on the roof. But remember, this experience doesn't take place on the bus. The program takes place out of doors. That's where you live: eating, recreating, and sleeping are done for the most part outside, under the stars. That's where you work, whether it's exploring a new place, hiking, or working for someone who needs help. You also read and learn outside, equipped for night with miner's lamps if necessary.

The Expedition Institute is a truly educational experience. All those aboard are involved in learning, and the students gain credit for their experience. All students take a variety of courses, which are truly experiential. Courses range from overviews of natural history to geology, stopping along the way at American history and English as a means of self-expression. Yes, you do write papers and read books. But what better way to learn about history than to visit the places where it happened, to infer geological processes from observation, to see ecosystems in action (or in disruption). This is a school on wheels, a school for high school students (some finish their high school education through a year with the institute); for thirteenth-year students; and for students in or finished with college (Leslie College grants credit for work done in the institute's programs, both undergraduate and graduate).

All this is Expedition Institute. This is not a program for those who think travel requires access to air conditioning and indoor plumbing. It is a program, as virtually every graduate of the experience seems to maintain, that introduces the individual to his/her place in nature in ways previously unimagined. It is for this reason and because of the necessity for workable consensus that entrance into the program requires a significant effort: reading and understanding the founder's guide to the essence of the program (*Our Classroom Is Wild America*) and then undergoing an extensive interview (to which you may have to travel some distance, since the interviews are usually held wherever one of the buses is). If you succeed, the program is likely to be right for you. Its alumni also maintain the process is self-selecting. It's a big responsibility, they say, because the person you become responsible for is yourself.

National Outdoor Leadership School (NOLS)

Box AA
Lander, WY 82520
(307) 332–6973
Fax: (307) 332–3631; MC or Visa
 accepted
Contact person: admissions staff
Program length: courses from 2
 weeks to semester length
Cost: prices range from
 approximately $1,500 for a 2-
 week to 3-week trip to $6,500
 for a semester-length
 program.
Financial aid: available but limited
Housing: none (in the wild or in
 bunkhouses during periodic
 respites)

Age range of participants: 14 and
 up
Number of participants per
 session: 10–14
Application process: registration
 form: $300 deposit
Application due date: rolling
 admissions; registration fee,
 name and address and program
 choices will place applicant on
 lists in advance of application
College credit available for
 semester programs
Program locations: U.S. Rockies,
 Kenya, the Baja, Alaska

Picture yourself learning to rock-climb in the Rockies . . . or learning to white-water kayak! How about learning to build a quin-zhee and heat yourself to a toasty 75 to 80 degrees after a day of nordic skiing, without ever going inside? Picture yourself in Kenya, the Baja or Alaska, learning to trek through the cloud forest, climb a snow-covered volcano, or travel safely in a sea kayak. Does any of this sound appealing to you? If your answer is yes, perhaps some time with NOLS is just what the doctor ordered.

NOLS is an environmental outdoor education school whose purpose is "to teach people in a commonsense way how to live safely and comfortably in the wilderness, without harming the land." NOLS is experiential education at its best. While on NOLS, you will spend no time sitting in a classroom, but your instruction will be unceasing. You will have no printed textbooks; instead, your textbook will be the stuff of your experiences. Your courses will be in rock-climbing, kayaking, sailing, skiing, or camping. The curriculum at NOLS is best summed up by a staff member: "Students get to learn natural science, outdoor-living skills, and leadership in the best classroom available." Whether you are on NOLS for two weeks or a semester, you will learn the same way—by plunging in and doing, with the help of a very talented staff.

But don't let all this talk about the wilderness and rock-climbing scare you off. So you aren't a fabulous camper, you haven't ever rock-climbed, you don't know how to ski. That's the whole point! NOLS is not just for the outdoor pro; it is for anyone who would like to learn and would like to be outdoors for a while. The only requirement is that you be in good physical condition. Nor is panic in order once you've heard that requirement. NOLS doesn't expect you to be a marathon runner; the programs simply require you to be fit enough to be able to test yourself physically.

NOLS offers courses that will explore only one area, such as sea kayaking or mountaineering, or longer courses that will take you through different locations and teach you different skills and techniques for handling the environment. During your time with NOLS you will be taught to work with the environment, safely and responsibly. The emphasis will be on you as a member of the NOLS community to take responsibility for helping with group issues, whether it be how to scale the face of a mountain or how to cook dinner. A NOLS course is not always easy, but as one alum of the semester program said: "The memory of living, playing, and working with a group of individuals for ninety-five days in the wilderness is not an easy one to describe, even to someone who went through the same experience . . . but it is a memory I will cherish always."

NOLS is an intense experience. It is outdoor education at its finest. You will spend almost your entire trip outdoors. You will be confronted with situations you may never have dreamed of. You will achieve goals you never thought yourself capable of. And you will be in constant contact with the ten to twelve members of your team. NOLS will test your mettle repeatedly, but the program will give you much in return. In the words of a NOLS instructor: "Students get a very good idea of their strengths and weaknesses. Usually they find they can accomplish much more than they ever thought possible."

Crucial to the application process is the reservation. If you have any interest in a NOLS course, call them, have a catalogue forwarded, and then respond by mail or phone (with credit card in hand) to reserve a place in the course or courses of your choice. Your deposit will be at least partially refunded, and you will be assured of a place in the often overcrowded NOLS semester courses.

Nature's Classroom
RD 1
61 Harrington Road
Southbridge, MA 01550
(508) 764–8321
Program length: varies
Cost: none; board provided;
  possible stipend
Financial aid: none
Housing: provided
Age range of participants: 18 and
  up; college sophomore and up
Number of participants:
  maximum of 10
Application process: application;
  at least 3 references; interview

Application due date: rolling
admissions
Program location: 7 sites around
  New England: Andover,
Connecticut; Becket,
Massachusetts; Colebrook,
Connecticut; Ivoryton,
Connecticut; Prindle Pond,
Charlton, Massachusetts;
Sandwich, Massachusetts,
Wakefield, Rhode Island;
Brewster, Massachusetts

"Children are the reason for our program's existence," says its director, Dr. John Santos. And as an intern in Nature's Classroom, you will be faced with about twelve of these kids, ages eight to fourteen. And you'll be faced with them for five days at a time, because NC is a residential program. Its aim is to expose children to the world around them and, by doing that, "help them learn—learn about themselves, other people, the reason why they're in school, and [about] the environment."

Those are lofty goals, and they translate into a lot of planning and work for you, the intern. But the experience is invaluable. Not only will you gain a more precise sense of your ability to teach (and even to deal with) children on a long-term basis, you also will broaden and deepen your knowledge of the field of environmental education.

In return for being on duty twenty-four hours a day, five days a week, NC will house and feed you, perhaps even pay you a small stipend for your time with the program. And although your interest in and love for children is a basic prerequisite, you also need to know something about the environment and about teaching skills and have some experience camping and dealing with recreational groups. Any time you've spent around the seminar table and around the campfire will enhance your qualifications for this position. Anyone who has a degree will be hired as an instructor, although as an intern you will do the same job as an instructor.

Nature's Classroom—and its comparison summer program, Life Tech Ventures (summer counselor positions may be sought from the address above, with similar qualifications)—wants to raise ecological consciousness. If you share that goal, and if you like children, this program might make sense for you.

New Alchemy Institute
237 Hatchville Road
East Falmouth, MA 02536
(508) 564–6301
Contact person: Virginia
 Rasmussen, educator director
Program length: 8 months
Cost: none
Financial aid: none
Housing: aid in finding housing
 provided
Age range of participants: 18 and
 up; program geared toward
 upper division college level

Number of participants: varies
Application process: application
 and fee; essay; 2
 recommendations; resume;
 transcript; background in
 basic biology and ecology
Application due date: rolling
 admissions
Program location: East Falmouth,
 Massachusetts

No, this isn't a place for making gold from dross. Rather, it's a place in which everything is put to use, where natural resources are managed in an ecologically responsible way. But don't be put off by that high-falutin' phrase. At New Alchemy, nature is revered and served, while human beings are provided for. All this is done through organic gardens, solar greenhouses, fish ponds, and energy-efficient buildings. What you will learn here is how to live with your environment and make the most if it. You also will have the opportunity to give of this newly acquired knowledge to others, to the more than fifteen hundred school children who visit New Alchemy each year.

The process by which you will acquire that knowledge is through New Alchemy's student internship in Sustainable Design. New Alchemy's program is simple: an experiential program in sustainable agriculture, community systems, and ecologically sound technologies. And, through connections with the Audubon Society's Expedition Institute and Leslie College, the program has years of experiential education as well as a place through which you can receive academic credit. Your classroom will be New Alchemy's site. There, you can make use of the program's ongoing research and demonstration projects in agriculture, energy-efficient design, and resource conservation. Your goal is simple: to improve the ways we must, as the program staff put it, "bond ourselves anew to what Thoreau called 'the essential elements of life.'" In order to accomplish this goal, it's likely that New Alchemy will give you new insight. "The Student Internship has changed the way I think. I developed a healthy questioning of much that I took for granted," was the comment by one recent student. Said another: "Central to the uniqueness of the New Alchemy Institute and the Student Internship is the shared vision of a better world."

Your day will be filled with New Alchemy's ongoing projects: organic market gardening—they even operate a roadside stand; solar and composting greenhouse management; integrated pest control in garden and greenhouse; home-scale resource systems. A model house is under way on the site, eventually to house the products of technology and the minds of New Alchemy. Meanwhile, visitors arrive daily to tour, to visit the book shop, to get advice about their own projects.

New Alchemy will expect you to be committed to the program, including hands-on work of about twenty hours a week. But New Alchemy cannot house you. Until spring blossoms, that's not a real problem in a seasonal community. But you should expect to undergo some expense for housing as summer approaches. Is it worth it? This is a program unlike any other in the area. Here you will be exposed to a world of alternatives to a lifestyle and an environment imperiled by pollution, contamination, and waste. If you think that's worth learning about, prepare to conjure with New Alchemy.

New England Aquarium Internships

Central Wharf
Boston, MA 02110
(617) 742–8830
Contact person: supervisor of
  volunteer programs
Program length: varies
Cost: none
Stipend: in some cases
Housing: none
Age range of participants: 18 and
  up

Number of participants per
  program: varies
Application process: cover letter;
  resume; interview
Application due date: rolling
  admissions
Program location: Boston,
  Massachusetts

If you always have found the song of the whale unusually alluring, if you've ever traveled to see whales at play off Cape Cod, if you've been fascinated by porpoises playing off the coast, if the idea of swimming with seals fascinates you, the opportunity to work at New England Aquarium might be very appealing. This is a volunteer position, with no housing available, but the New England Aquarium does offer you a chance at positions of all kinds, from researcher to fish feeder. Some even pay a small stipend. There is something for everyone to do here, and they will happily take you on a full-time basis, or as seldom as once a week. What is important to the New England Aquarium staff is that you have the desire to learn and a commitment to the place and the animals. As one young woman notes: "A friend of mine currently is volunteering once a week and working with the penguins. She calls it 'the coolest thing I've ever done.' " Also, if you have a specific time frame that you wish to fill, such as a January break or a summer vacation, the aquarium will be glad to help you find a way to spend it there.

Outward Bound

384 Field Point Road
Greenwich, CT 06830

1–800–243–8540 or (203) 661–
  0797

Contact person: staff

Program length: semester or 3- to 6-week courses

Cost: $3,300–$5,500 for semester; $1,100 and up for shorter courses

Financial aid: available

Housing: tent

Age range of participants: 14 and up

Number of participants per session: 8–12

Application process: application; $50 nonrefundable application fee; financial aid form, if needed

Application due date: rolling admissions

Program locations: primarily in the U.S., but there are program locals in Nepal, Mexico, USSR, Canada

No doubt you've heard of Outward Bound; it's been synonymous with outdoor education since the early 1970s. Outward Bound was founded on and lives by the following philosophy: If you push yourself physically, you will grow mentally and emotionally. It must work. Many schools and other institutions have created programs modeled after it. Outward Bound is famous for its work with drug abusers and emotionally troubled youth. But its programs are equally successful for the average person.

Challenge is something Outward Bound guarantees. During your expedition you will learn techniques in rock-climbing, hiking, sailing, river rafting, and general outdoor living. Of course the skills you learn vary from course to course. But in all programs you will learn by doing. Your instructors are highly trained professionals who teach you to push yourselves while showing you the techniques and finer points of the sport you are pursuing. For example, you will learn sailing by spending time in a boat. You will learn to rock-climb by attacking a mountain face. But don't panic. Outward Bound takes every safety precaution. You only do what you feel comfortable doing. Yet you would be amazed at just how much you will do, and will learn. As one alum puts it: "Outward Bound isn't easy nor is it impossible. It is a great stretching experience. I learned so much about myself and others. I discovered the potential each person has to overcome and endure. I had a wonderful time. I want to go again and again."

While the instruction and the group adventures are the heart of your time with Outward Bound, the solo is the soul of the trip. Each participant spends some time (varies depending on total length of Outward Bound program) on a solo. You are dropped off in the wilderness and expected to spend your days reflecting on your experiences and writing in your journal. You are provided basic food at a pickup spot, and you must periodically display a signal that shows Outward Bound you're all right.

If your signal is not at the pickup spot every morning and evening, a search is started immediately. Outward Bound past participants speak of their solo as the high point of their journey. They comment on the ways the solo provided them with an invaluable sense of self-reliance and self-worth. They could live alone in the wilderness for three days!

Outward Bound offers those interested in a wilderness experience a challenging adventure to help them grow and develop. The effects of an Outward Bound course are best summed up by one former student: "Never again will I be satisfied with just getting by."

Pocono Environmental Education Center

RD 2, Box 1010
Dingman's Ferry, PA 18328
(717) 828–2319
Program length: 6–12 months
Cost: none, stipend depending on position, but minimum of $300 per month
Financial aid: none
Housing: provided, as is board
Age range of participants: college and graduate students

Number of participants: varies by program
Application process: cover letter and resume
Application due date: rolling admissions
Program location: Delaware Water Gap, Pennsylvania

PEEC gives its interns a chance to live and work in one of the most beautiful settings on the Atlantic seaboard: the 140,000 plus acres of the Delaware Water Gap's National Recreation Area. This is about as rural as you can get in the Middle Atlantic, since PEEC exists only twenty miles southeast of the meeting of New York, New Jersey, and Pennsylvania. But the center's comparative isolation provides a magnificent setting for the environmental education of those less advantaged and more citybound. It is this purpose that PEEC serves, and whether you come to this program as intern or as potential instructor, you will be teaching about the environment. As intern, you will also share responsibilities with permanent staff as guides and teachers for the students who come to learn about that environment.

In return, you are fed, housed, and paid at least $75 per week. But what's most important about the opportunity at PEEC is that it gives you the chance to explore your interest in working with the environment and teaching about it. PEEC also offers internships in public relations, providing you with a chance to tell others about the wonders of this center.

Being an intern, particularly in a place as busy as PEEC, means having a chance to step right into a job that elsewhere an "adult" might occupy. That means responsibility and a lot of experience fast. And those qualities translate into an excellent opportunity.

Slide Ranch Internships

2025 Shoreline Highway
Muir Beach, CA 94965
(415) 381–6155
Contact person: program director
Program length: 5 1/2 months

Cost: none
Financial aid: not necessary
Stipend: none
Housing: available; board included
Age range of participants: 19–25

Number of participants: 3–5
interns per session
Application process: letter of
intent; 3 references; personal
interview where possible.

Application due date: rolling
admissions
Program location: Muir Beach,
California

To be an intern at Slide Ranch is to experience an unusual combination of
breathtaking settings and challenging tasks. Located forty-five minutes outside of San Francisco on a cliff at the ocean's edge, Side Ranch is a nonprofit
environmental-education center. Its primary goal is to provide inner-city
communities in the Bay area with the opportunity to experience farm life
and the coastal wildlands. Slide Ranch is also a working farm, complete with
chickens, turkeys, goats, sheep, rabbits, gardens, and compost piles. Interns
take responsibility for helping care for the farm as well as running programs
for the visiting students. An intern can expect to spend a great deal of time
teaching about the farm, helping students understand what life on a farm
means. Teaching at Slide Ranch is done in a very hands-on way—teaching
about the chickens means leading a group of children into the coop and
allowing the chickens to eat out of their hands; teaching gardening means
having the visitors plant lettuce, weed the garden, and see how things grow
by being among them. While instructing is the main thrust of the Slide
Ranch internship, community living is its soul. Slide Ranch has a small
permanent staff, and only the program director and the farm manager live
on the ranch with the interns. Interns live together in one house, although
everyone is guaranteed his or her own room. Food is bought by the ranch,
but each staff member and intern is responsible for cooking one dinner a
week. There is a strong emphasis on honesty, communication, and understanding within the community of the ranch. Interns have daily meetings
in which they talk about their day. Each intern is encouraged to speak about
feelings and responses to situations that have arisen in the course of the
day's work. Slide Ranch is about support: support of each other, support
of the environment, and support of the community at large.

The ranch proves to be a wonderful place to spend time whether you
want to try out your teaching wings, live on a farm, experience a close-knit
community, or just live by the ocean.

Smithsonian Environmental Research Center

Work/Learn Program
Smithsonian Environmental
Research Center
Box 28
Edgewater, MD 21037
(202) 261–4190
Program length: varies; usually
academic semester or summer

Cost: none; stipend of $70 for
undergraduates; $90 for
graduate students
Financial aid: none
Housing: provided
Age range of participants: college
and graduate students

Number of participants: varies by program

Application process: application; transcript and 4- to 6-page essay; 2 recommendations

Application due dates: July 1 for September; December 1 for February; April 1 for August

Program location: Chesapeake Bay area, Maryland

This is a serious program that involves students in hands-on environmental research. To a nonscientist, a project title like Community Structure and Population Biology of Benthic Invertebrates in an Estuary sounds daunting. But to a student studying zoology, this project translates into working with sea creatures that reside in the mouth of a river. Since this study also involves microbiology and chemistry, as well as ecology, the opportunity is open to a variety of fledgling scientists. And what better place to pursue your interest than at the mouth of a river opening into Chesapeake Bay in late spring or early summer?

The Smithsonian has made available in its Environmental Research Center a limited number of openings for students with an interest, some background, and a desire to further their study in a nontraditional setting. There are opportunities among the center's projects for students interested in chemistry, microbiology, zoology, biology, environmental science, environmental education, mathematics (there are studies involving computer modeling, for example), and botany. Normally, students will be working with researchers on a designated project, assisting them wherever needed and often producing a piece of independent work or a presentation within the project's limits. Moreover, the center will accept proposals for independent projects within the center's scope.

As an internship or study opportunity, this program is first rate. Its value is enhanced by the fact that most colleges and universities recognize the Smithsonian's program as worthy of academic credit. Yes, this break may well earn you credit. It may be the only time in your life that will happen while you are earning money, because the Smithsonian also pays a small stipend and houses you, leaving board as your only problem. So if your interest in the environment can be married to an academic interest or to your chosen field of study, Smithsonian may well offer you an unusual opportunity.

Sterling College: The Grassroots Project

Sterling College
Craftsbury Common, VT 05827
(802) 586-7711
Contact person: Sarabelle Hitchner, director of admissions
Program length: full year
Cost of program: $12,500
Financial aid: available
Housing: dormitory

Age range of participants: high school, PG, college, and up

Number of participants: 50–60

Application process: essay; transcript; 2 references; interview strongly encouraged

Application due date: rolling admissions

Program location: Craftsbury Common, Vermont

The Grassroots Project at Sterling is a one-year college-level curriculum designed, in the words of the admissions director, to "shape a liberally educated adult: a thinking, problem-solving, responsible, disciplined, and caring citizen." Chances are, your response to this kind of statement is: "Sounds great, but can they really do it?" The answer is a resounding yes. Sterling has come up with a successful recipe for creating an interested, responsible, and interesting student. The way they do it is a simple no-nonsense approach to academics and to the world around the project: rural Vermont.

The philosophy behind the Sterling program is the old-fashioned American work ethic. But Sterling's founders have combined that dependable idea with the notion that students are more responsive when they can see and understand exactly what and why they are learning. To implement this philosophy, Sterling has come up with a curriculum that combines academics with real-life experiences. Students at Sterling learn in and out of the classroom.

Academics at Sterling are focused and strongly rooted in and around the environment. This is an environmental-education facility, and students need to be comfortable with that aspect of Sterling. The core curriculum includes, among others, Conservation Skills and Studies, Ecology, Resource Issues, Farm and Forest Workshop. These courses are supplemented with a wide selection of such electives as Forestry Techniques, Comparative Farming Operations, and Fish and Wildlife Management. Students use nature as a proving ground for what they are learning. The staff communicates a strong concern for quality and task orientation. What you do may be your choice, but you must commit yourself. A typical example of this teaching method is shown to students by leading them on a canoe expedition, first having them make their own paddle. If the paddle is not ready on the day of departure, you miss the journey. And because the you know that your success depends only on you, the time and energy put into the project is exceptional.

Sterling is in the northernmost part of Vermont. It is closer to Montreal than to Boston, and is an hour's drive from Burlington and an hour and a half's drive from Montpelier. You must drive about fifteen miles on Sunday to get the *New York Times*, and, as that one index of civilization indicates, the campus could be described as rural. Yet, the fact that it is so removed from the world makes Sterling possible. There is a strong community within the college that allows the high standards and firm belief in the work ethic to exist in an undiluted form. Students become involved at Sterling in a way that they never have elsewhere because there are few viable alternatives to what everyone else is doing. Sterling has realigned peer pressure in a startlingly positive context. Students have a stake in what they are doing and so perform tremendously. As a result they learn that they can succeed, and that hard work does reward them.

Suisun Marsh Natural History Association

1171 Kellogg Street	Age range of participants: varies
Suisun, CA 94585	Number of participants: varies
(707) 429–HAWK	Application process: application;
Program length: minimum 6–8	letter of interest; resume; 3
weeks	references
Cost: summer position is salaried;	Application due date: rolling
nonsalaried during remainder	admissions
of year	Program location: Suisun, midway
Financial aid: none	between Sacramento and San
Housing: provided	Francisco, California

Suisun Marsh is dedicated to "preserving wetlands, educating the public regarding environmental values, and offsetting mans [*sic*] impact on wildlife by returning displaced, injured, or orphaned rehabilitated wild animals to the wild. The center is located on a seventeen-acre parcel of land that is being restored to wetlands and developed for public access trails." Interns will be given in-house training and structured work experience in wildlife rehabilitation. Much of this training will come from Suisun's own veterinarians. In addition, the association also carries on large-scale environmental-education program.

This is an unusual opportunity for anyone interested in working with wildlife, particularly in a medical or rehabilitative capacity. Interns may receive compensation, depending on the time of year, but most important is the experience of hands-on activity with "more than fifteen hundred wild animals annually."

The Quebec-Labrador Foundation

Atlantic Center for the	Age range of participants: 16 and
Environment Internships	up
39 South Main Street	Number of participants: varies
Ipswich, MA 01938	from year to year; usually
(508) 356–0038	about 50 placements
Contact person: Julie Early,	Application process: application;
director of intern operations	recommendations; essay;
Program length: semester,	interview
summer, and full year	Application deadline: rolling
Cost: none	admissions
Stipend: available	Program locations: New England,
Housing; provided	Atlantic Canada

QLF offers internships in Newfoundland, in Quebec on the so-called North Shore, and in northern New England in order to provide rural communities with some skilled service and pass on some specialized form of knowledge. Examples of this include QLF-sponsored water-safety and environmental-education camps for the rural communities in the North, as well as various

QLF-staffed teaching and field research positions. Participants often live in homes within the community in which they are stationed and speak on the experience as an intense one. They find themselves undergoing a cultural as well as a professional immersion. "The Atlantic Center was one of the most positive experiences of my life. And although the job itself was challenging and exciting, it was the people who made last year so magical."— "Your success is not just measured by your work in the North. It is measured as well by the quality of and desire for expertise that you instill in the people." QLF internships are offered at a variety of levels. There are options for high school students as well as for people with graduate degrees. It is important to note that QLF interns are placed in separate locations, and, depending on the needs of the community, not necessarily at the same location with other interns. QLF interns have a high rate of return, and alums are given first preference for internship opportunities. Graduates are very enthusiastic and rate QLF as one of the best experiences possible. "As a QLF intern, you create a spirit of dedication that travels far beyond, beneath, and through the Atlantic region."

Touch of Nature Wilderness Programs

Southern Illinois University
Carbondale, IL 62901
(618) 453–1121
Program length: semester, year, summer
Cost: none
Financial aid: none
Housing: provided
Number of participants: varies by program

Age range of participants: college
Application process: application with fee; usually transcript and/or essay; teachers' recommendations
Application due date: rolling admissions
Program location: Carbondale, Illinois

Interns involved with the Wilderness Programs at Touch of Nature should expect to work with groups of adolescents in what is termed a "bridge" program designed to "develop responsible behavior by trying something new and coping with controlled physically and psychologically stressful situations." In addition, interns may also be involved in Southern Outdoor Adventure Recreation (SOAR), a program for college students and adults seeking recreational adventure. Both programs are based at the Touch of Nature facility, located within the Shawnee National Forest. However, both programs spend a good deal of time on major expeditions or funded trips at various locations around the United States.

In return for their work and training, interns may expect to gain some college credit, assuming the approval of their parent institution. Interns also are housed by SIU, and those seeking an apprenticeship rather than an intern opportunity will be paid a small stipend.

Internships are designed according to the requirements of the individual. "You live in a cabin with other people, but you have your own room. There

is tons of space, [the facility is] . . . right on a lake and a state park and
outdoor activity abounds!" Interns also find their fellows rewarding: "[They
are] . . . really great people and a diverse staff."—"You can learn a lot from
the other staff members. Everyone seems to have a different strength."—
"What matters is your willingness to learn." Best part is the "diversity of
the staff. I didn't have a lot of wilderness skills and there were people there
who really knew their stuff. Also it's a very close staff. You do most of your
socializing with the staff. There aren't major personality clashes. It's a really
healthy place to work. Problems get aired and taken care of because you
have to live with each other."

Wildlife Environmental Science Internships

Chesapeake Wildlife Sanctuary
17308 Queen Anne Bridge Road
Bowie, MD 20716
(310) 390–7010
Program length: minimum 6
  weeks, up to a semester
Cost; none; stipend in summer
Financial aid: none
Housing: provided
Age range of participants: 16 and
  up

Number of participants: varies
Application process: application;
  transcript and/or curriculum
  vitae; 3 references; statement of
  purpose
Application due date: rolling
  admissions
Program location: Bowie,
  Maryland

If you want to care for sick, injured, and orphaned animals and take a
personal interest in every patient the Chesapeake Sanctuary admits, this
internship is for you. Here you are part of "a large team all sharing a
similar goal, to get that patient, whether a common sparrow or a deer,
healthy and strong so it could be safely released as quickly as possible." You
may "never in a million years [have] imagined [your]self *capturing* and *force-
feeding* wild birds of prey," but that's what you'll have to do at the Chesapeake Wildlife Sanctuary. "My main goal throughout my internship was to
learn about wildlife, especially birds. The Chesapeake Wildlife Sanctuary
was an ideal setting for the fulfillment of this goal. I was constantly exposed
to the business of running the sanctuary and learned much about that
process. I was able to work on my speaking abilities by helping with some
lectures to school children. . . . Through hands-on work restraining, feeding, and medicating these . . . animals, I learned that it was work I wanted
to do, not just work I thought I wanted to do."

You will be given in-house training by a dedicated staff, who also will
provide you with special workshops in advanced wildlife rehabilitation. In
return, you will be expected to work a normal week, with added on-call
time on evenings and weekends if you are in residence at the sanctuary.
You must complete an approved project and submit a paper of publishable
or presentable quality reflecting that project. From the reports of previous
interns, this isn't too much to ask. "The Chesapeake Wildlife Sanctuary's

reputation and philosophy of concern for all species enticed me to come from Kansas to spend my senior externship here. It has been a profitable experience."

ENVIRONMENTAL JOBS

Environmental Opportunities
Route 2, Box 16
Walpole, NH 03608
(603) 756–9744

The Job Seeker
Box 788
Warrens, WI 54666
(608) 378–4290

If you are interested in finding a job in the environmental field, these are two job listings you should be aware of. Both are published bimonthly and break the jobs down into categories including: administration, ecology/fisheries/wildlife, environmental education, horticulture/agriculture, miscellaneous, organizational, outdoor education, overseas, parks/recreation, research, teaching, seasonal, and internships. The subscription rate for each publication is $46 for a full year (24 issues), $28 for 6 months (12 issues), $15 for 3 months (6 issues), and $21 for the "Summer Jobs Special" (9 issues). Both *The Job Seeker* and *Environmental Opportunities* will send samples of their newsletters to interested potential subscribers.

Community Service Programs

If you have considered giving your time out to service for others, you've come to the right place. Below are listed a variety of opportunities organized to provide either service to the community or specific help for individuals or groups in need. For the most part, the organizations listed below have been selected because they provide opportunities for a designated period of time and usually with provisions for room and board. Many faiths have organizations similar to some of those profiled below. If you are a church member, be sure to investigate what your church offers in the way of organized opportunities for service. Often, there will be a church organization operating domestically as well as abroad. Of course, there is always a need for volunteers at the American Red Cross and with dozens of other organizations that exist near you. Soup kitchens and shelters for the homeless usually are desperately understaffed. So if you simply wish to help, begin by looking at home. It's likely that you will find many worthwhile opportunities to help others.

The California Conservation Corps (CCC)

1530 Capitol Avenue
Sacramento, CA 95814
(916) 445–8183
Contact person: staff
Program length: 1 year
Cost: none
Financial aid: stipend provided
Housing: provided
Age range of participants: 18–23
Number of participants: 2,000
statewide

Application process: application form; must be a California resident, not currently on parole or probation, and willing to work hard
Application due date: rolling admissions
Program location: throughout California

The California Conservation Corps is a state-funded resource agency that provides aid to government agencies such as the National Park Service. As the name implies, CCC's major interest is with the handling of environmental management. CCC is involved in outdoor maintenance work of all kinds and is a response team in environmental emergencies such as fires or floods. The organization was developed by former governor Jerry Brown as a way to get young adults involved in the care of California's environment. Corps members receive room, board, insurance, and a small wage in exchange for their work. To that end, corps members are required to take two courses: Career Development and Conservation Awareness. The Career Development course is designed to teach corps members the essential interviewing and resume skills to ensure placement after their year with CCC is finished. The Conservation Awareness course is designed so that corps members can gain a fuller understanding of the problems they are dealing with in the field.

CCC members are primarily "urban kids with a high school degree," though a degree is not a requirement for the program. If a student does not have a high school degree, general education courses are available. For those who have graduated from high school, CCC has college level courses available through local community colleges. CCC members are assigned to one of seventeen base camps throughout the state of California. While a corps member may list a preference for a particular base location, the ultimate decision is in the hands of the Sacramento office. At the base camp corps members can expect to sleep in barrackslike conditions, four to a room, and share communal bath houses. Meals are served cafeteria fashion, and three good meals are provided daily. While the housing is not luxurious, it is comfortable.

CCC provides an opportunity for young adults to give some time and energy toward the care of the California land. In return, corps members can expect to learn a great deal about the management of the environment as well as employable skills to take to the "real" world.

Casa Juan Diego

Houston Catholic Worker
4818 Rose Street
Houston TX 77270
(713) 869–7376
Contact person: Mark Zwick
Program length: varies with the
 individual
Cost: none
Housing: provided

Age range of participants: college
 graduates preferred
Number of participants: varies
Application process: letter of
 application;
 recommendations; interview
Application due date: rolling
Program location: Houston, Texas

Casa Juan Diego is a house of refuge, and its volunteer workers provide hospitality, teach classes in English, distribute food, and assist wherever possible the 10,000 or so who appear each year there. To join that group of volunteers, you must want to help. You also must be able to speak Spanish. Those are really the only requirements for service at Casa Juan Diego.

You need not be Catholic, but you must be willing to accept the poverty and pacificism of the center. As its director, Mark Zwick, has noted: "We let people be." Those people are often refugees from Central and Latin America or Spanish-speaking battered women and children. The center houses and feeds them for an average of two weeks, counseling them however possible during that time. An average day might include coordinating the entire house, managing the kitchen, or editing a newspaper the Casa publishes. Important here is a love and respect for Hispanic culture and a desire to use one's skills to help others. Equally important in this situation, because of the presence of so many in one building, is the willingness to be part of a team concept. In return for one's voluntarism a small stipend of $10 per week and room and board are provided. Since the Catholic Worker Movement, of which Casa Juan Diego is a part, believes in life with the poor lived in a simple way, volunteers should expect little monetary compensation. The real return, says one volunteer, is in providing for others.

Catholic Volunteers in Florida

Box 702
Goldenrod, FL 32733–0702
(407) 677–8005
Program length: year
Cost: none; room and board, medical insurance, and a $100 a month stipend provided
Financial aid: none
Housing: available; specifics vary from site to site
Age range of participants: 21 and up

Number of participants: 10–50
Application process: application; essay; references; medical forms; interview and orientation sessions
Application due date: rolling admissions
Program location: San Pedro Retreat Center, Winter Park, Florida

Catholic Volunteers take seriously the injunction to minister to others. As their brochure points out, the organization seeks to "promote social justice by direct service to those persons who do not have access to educational, cultural, social, and economic resources." There should be little question in the mind of any potential recruit that this program demands a full-time commitment. In addition to a minimum of an eight-hour day involved at shelters, food banks, prison release centers, Catholic social services, low-income health centers, the volunteer is encouraged to become involved in both church and community after hours. In short, then, this program demands devotion to bettering the community and to enhancing one's personal vision.

CVs need not be Catholics themselves. But they must be willing to be active spiritually in their faith outside the workplace. Weekends, for example, are often occupied by retreats/workshops. As one young woman, who directs a shelter for homeless families, says: "I'm just living out my faith.

We're all called to service in some way—in different ways, but in some ways." CVs are housed in a variety of locations: from rooms with families to apartments in the community. They are paid a stipend in addition to their room and board, but, since simplicity is an expectation of the program, no benefit is meant to deter the volunteer from that goal.

Clearly, this is a program for the exceptional individual. It demands spirituality, a willingness to devote a year of one's life to service, and real dedication to social justice.

City Volunteer Corps

842 Broadway
New York, NY 10003
(212) 475-6444
Contact person: recruitment director
Program length: full year or part-time basis
Cost: none
Financial aid: none
Housing: none
Stipend: $81 per week; $5,000 scholarship awarded at the successful completion of a full year

Age range of participants: 17–20
Number of participants: up to 500
Application process: application form; completion of a weeklong training program
Application due date: rolling admissions
Program location: New York City

CVC is the brain child of former New York City mayor Ed Koch. Founded in 1984 by a special grant from the mayor's office, CVC was created to promote the ideal of community service. Described by a staff member as an "urban peace corps," CVC strives to involve New York youth in the maintenance and care of all aspects of city life. CVC projects include repainting urban areas, building playgrounds, working with the mentally handicapped, and doing projects of all forms that will enrich the city and city life. City Volunteers wear a special uniform and are assigned to teams of ten to fifteen. There are no real admissions criteria, but all perspective volunteers must complete a weeklong training camp in upstate New York. While a wonderful idea, CVC is not without its problems. The program is at the current time operating at only two-thirds of capacity and the dropout rate, according to a staff member, is "higher than we like to see, but coming down." The participants tend to come from similar backgrounds, and there is not a particularly strong sense of community within the corps due to the large number of volunteers. Similarly, the rolling starting and ending dates create a sense of flux within the program. However, CVC is doing tremendous community service projects for the city of New York and is worth investigating if one is interested in a year of community service in the Big Apple.

City Year
11 Stillings Street
Boston, MA
(617) 451–0699
Contact person: Kristin Atwood
Program length: full academic
  year
Cost: none
Stipend: $61 a week; $5,000 at
  end of the full year in the
  form of a savings bond or
  scholarship to the school of
  your choice

Housing: none
Age range of participants: 17–21
Number of participants: 50
Application process: interviews;
  recommendations;
  application; essay
Application due date: rolling
  admissions
Program location: Boston,
  Massachusetts

City Year is a working combination of lots of ideals. Here's why. Envision this: fifty kids, divided into teams of ten, spending a full academic year doing good works (for example: working at a homeless shelter, working with the elderly, refurbishing playgrounds, reclaiming vacant lots). Imagine that this group of kids came primarily (though not exclusively) from the city and its environs and was a melting pot of races, economic classes, religions, and backgrounds. Imagine that they all got along, really liked each other. Imagine also that once a week they have a day of academic enrichment that focuses on the problems of Boston. For example, they spend several days learning about the problem of the homeless and brainstorming about how to handle it. Now imagine that at the end of the year they received compensation for their good work, a $5,000 scholarship to the school of their choice or a $5,000 savings bond.

Yes, this program really exists. City Year was created as a year of community service for kids seventeen to twenty-one, funded entirely by private donations from Boston-area businesses and individuals. Since there is no housing provided, City Year exists primarily for kids from Boston and the surrounding communities. While this lack of housing is a disadvantage for those not from the Boston area, it means focusing the kids from the city on the city's problems and possibilities—and that's a great thing. This year is about giving back to our neighborhoods, to our city. And it seems to work wonderfully.

Here's how you'll spend your day. City Year operates from 8:00 A.M. to 4:30 P.M., Monday through Friday. On Monday morning you will meet in the 11 Stillings Street office, a wonderful huge warehouse space, and break into your teams. (You will have the same teams all year long, but will often do things as a whole group or in groups of two teams.) From here you will go out to your first project. The projects are chosen by City Year specifically with their students in mind. They are usually about two to three weeks in length, though some, such as helping out at the Boston Food Bank, will be frequent visits ongoing throughout the year. What you will do in each project will be very different, but one thing will remain the same, you will be helping people and making a difference, and you will have a great time.

What strikes the visitor in the camaraderie, respect, and fun these kids have for each other and with each other. This is a program that brings people together and makes friendships that last a lifetime. Simultaneously, this is the kind of program that shapes lives. "I didn't know my own capacity, or that of fifty people, to help so many people in Boston. We're working with people every day—homeless, mentally retarded, beaten mothers . . . there are people here, not in Africa, who need us. We're helping our own lives and learning from each other every day." Another alum said: "Yes, you're going to see things you might not have believed . . but they're things you should believe, if anybody is ever going to understand and help the cities of this country. Getting closer to that understanding is what City Year did for me."

Committee for Creative Non-Violence

425 Second Street, NW
Washington, DC 20001
(202) 393–4409
Program length: 6 months and up
Cost: none
Housing: available, and board
Age range of participants: 18 and
  up

Number of participants: varies
Application process: resume;
  interview; references
Application deadline: rolling
  admissions
Program location: Washington,
  D.C.

Committee for Creative Non-Violence sounds like anything but what it is: an advocacy group for the poor and homeless. Clearly, its philosophical background is Gandhian, but its principal functions are more mundane: operating a huge shelter for the homeless and lobbying anyone who will listen in Washington, from Congress to the array of public agencies that deal with poverty and homelessness. CCNV takes a more activist role in their consistent attempts to shine the spotlight of public attention on the homeless. Your role in all this: to help out wherever possible. You will live on site and you will work harder than you might have imagined. Your colleagues will be international in origin but commonly dedicated to making the lives of CCNV's clients as rich as possible.

Daughters of Charity, Associates in Mission (DC-AIM)

7800 Natural Bridge Road
St. Louis, MO 63121
(314) 382–2800, ext. 274
Contact person: Therese Saggau
Program length: year (12 months)
  or summer
Cost: none

Stipend: available: including food
  allowance, health insurance,
  housing
Housing: apartment or house with
  other DC-AIM volunteers or
  housed at job site

Age range of participants: 21 and up

Number of participants: unlimited

Application process: resume; interview; references

Application due dates: June 15 for August placement; November

15 for January placement; and throughout the year as placements arise

Program locations: Midwest and southwest United States

DC-AIM is doing some very wonderful things. It is a mission of volunteers who "use their talents to empower the poor in many areas of the United States." The men and women involved with DC-AIM work for very little pay as social workers, teachers, therapists, counselors, youth ministers, maintenance workers, computer programmers; in fact, DC-AIM has placements in every conceivable occupation. And while the financial rewards may not be great, the personal gains are significant. One former volunteer says of her time with DC-AIM: "The work is demanding, the pay low, and the adjustments many, but I have never regretted for a moment being here. My experience living on an income equal to the people I serve helps to make me more empathetic and effective in my service." This is a program that does very special things, but also requires a very special sort of participant. If you are thinking about a career in religion or social work and would like to try it out, or if you just have a great desire to help people, DC-AIM may be a program for you to look into.

Frontier Nursing Service—Courier and Volunteer Program

General Delivery
Wendover, KY 41775
(606) 672-2318
Contact person: Carrie Michels
Program length: 6–8 weeks; available throughout the year
Cost: $100
Financial aid: cost can be waived if strong financial need is shown
Housing: dormitory

Age range of participants: 18–22
Number of participants per session: 3–8
Application process: application, with short essays; 3 recommendations; must be able to drive standard car
Application due date: rolling admissions
Program location: Kentucky

The Frontier Nursing Service was started in 1925 by Mary Breckenridge as a way of providing prenatal and birthing care to women in rural areas of Appalachia. It has since grown to include a forty-bed hospital, a school of midwifery and nursing care, several nursing centers, and a home health service agency. The emphasis at FNS focuses on helping people and on promoting proper health care.

The Courier and Volunteer Program was begun in order to provide help for the full-time staff with the day-to-day running of the organization. Couriers are the backbone of the organization: They take care of all the errands that need doing, do mail rounds, take supplies to where they are needed or welcome visitors to FNS at Wendover. They are responsible for helping with the FNS vegetable garden, doing chores around the "Big House" at Wendover, and helping with the bureaucratic paperwork. But they also help nurses with patients, gain exposure to alternative modes of health-care delivery, and "observe the approach to health care that is so unique to FNS, i.e., sensitivity in relating to people–especially when they are from a culture different from what one is accustomed to—and continuity of care." In short, while none of the tasks of the courier are glamorous, the sense of helping is enormous. As one alumna of the program pointed out: "There's so much to do here that you can't help but be useful. But please tell everybody that the overwhelming amount of work means that no one will lead you by the hand. It's the self-starters who make this job work out."

The Student Conservation Association

Resource Assistant Program
Box 550
Charlestown, NH 03603
(603) 826–4301
Contact person: Marsha Warren
Program length: 12–16 weeks, year round
Cost: none
Financial aid: none
Stipend: provided; see below
Housing: provided
Age range of participants: 18 and up; average age is 21

Number of participants: 800 total for the year
Application process: application form, including short answers, questions; transcript; 3 references
Application due dates: September 15 for early winter; November 15 for late winter; January 15 for spring; March 1 for summer/June 1 for fall
Program location: United States

The Student Conservation Association places individuals in outdoor-related volunteer positions in national parks and private natural-resource agencies all over the country, including Alaska, Hawaii, the Virgin Islands, and Puerto Rico. Resource assistants work alongside paid staff at their assignment site and are expected to put in a forty-hour week. There is no pay, but SCA resource assistants are provided with housing, a stipend to cover food expenses, and an allowance to cover travel costs to and from the assignment site.

SCA places individuals in locations according to their background and choice. Not everyone who applies is selected to take part in the program. An applicant must have shown a real interest in nature and possess certain skills, depending on the position. Positions range in scope from trail clearing and general management of a park area to environmental research at a private foundation. Positions are usually twelve weeks in duration. SCA publishes a listing of the many opportunities available each season.

SCA provides interested individuals a chance to try their hand in the natural-resource management field. Experiences will vary greatly, but if the word of graduates means anything, SCA is providing great opportunities.

One SCA grad called it "a wonderful experience," and another alum said that he was "very glad [he] did the program." For anyone with the inclination to spend a semester—or a summer—in a wilderness setting, this program will have some choices to offer. Beyond that, SCA is one way to find out whether you might find have a bent toward environmental education.

COMMUNITY SERVICE ABROAD

PROGRAM LOCATION: UNITED KINGDOM

Community Service Volunteers (CSV)—Overseas Program
237 Pentonville Road
London N19NJ, England
01–278–6601
Contact person: staff
Program length: summer, 10–16 weeks; year round, 4–12 month commitment
Cost: placement fee of $700 for the year program; $300 for the summer program; airfare to and from England.
Stipend: full board; food allowance of 19 pounds per week; pocket money of 16 pounds per week

Financial aid: none
Housing: homestays
Age range of participants: 18 and up
Number of participants per year: 2,000
Application process: application; references; interview
Application due date: rolling admissions

CSV is a clearinghouse for connecting volunteer placements with people interested in volunteering in the United Kingdom. Projects at CSV range from working with the handicapped in their homes to helping out at shelters in London. You name it and they do it. CSV assigns individuals to the projects. Once there, you will have the support group of other CSVers, either right at hand or close by. But what is most striking about CSV is the way you will notice your own personal growth during the course of your stay. One volunteer said of her experience: "I must admit I was quite shocked at the beginning. Jan's disabilities were more than I expected. But after a while I found I could just be myself, and Jan became a person I could respect and enjoy the company of." The purpose of this program is to change lives, and what seems to be apparent is that both the volunteer and the project recipient are changed—for the better.

Frontier Foundation
2615 Danforth Avenue, Suite 203
Toronto, Ontario
Canada, M4C 1L6
(416) 690–3930

Program length: minimum 3
  months
Cost: travel expenses plus $30
  Canadian
Financial aid: none
Housing: provided
Number of participants: varies by
  program

Age range of participants: 18 and
  up
Application process: application
  with fee; essay; 3 references
Application due date: rolling
  admissions
Program location: Canada

Frontier Foundation wants volunteers willing to "tackle the social problems of others," which translates into hard work in rural Canada. If you are to gain anything from Frontier Foundation, you must be prepared to "laugh at mosquitoes" and give up the amenities of suburban living. The foundation is dedicated to helping others in Canada and elsewhere, usually by building (literally) communities across rural lands. You'll be working with other volunteers from around the world—some two thousand since 1964—to build and rebuild housing for homeless Canadian citizens, many of them native people.

Frontier Foundation is interested in obtaining your honest labor and wholehearted enthusiasm for helping those in need. That help usually takes the form of construction. The foundation has sixteen portable sawmills and spends most of its time and energy erecting housing across Canada. It is instructive not only because of the experience you will get in construction but because of your exposure to and interaction with the people you're helping, but you must also be prepared for living on site. Depending on the season, foundation staff members live in rudimentary dwellings or camp out at the location at which they work.

What is most appealing about this work is surely the contribution you will be making to the disadvantaged and to the more general causes of mutual respect and understanding, added to a healthy measure of practical job experience.

World Horizons International, Inc.

1427 2d Avenue
New York, NY 10021
(212) 439–6292
Contact person: Judith Manning,
  executive director
Program length: summer; 6 weeks
Cost: $2,400–$2,800
Financial aid: available
Housing: dormitory or homestays
Age range of participants: 16–18

Number of participants per
  program: 10–12
Application process: application
  form; 4 references; essay; $25
  fee
Application due date: rolling until
  May 15
Program locations: Belize, Costa
  Rica, Alaska, Hawaii, Nevada
  (Indian reservation)

World Horizons is a nonprofit organization that sends students to the Caribbean, Alaska, Hawaii, and Nevada not for nature tours or R and R but for hard work. Students can expect to spend their days working with the poor and less privileged, not lying on the beach. World Horizons exists to "help kids realize that they can make a difference in developing countries," and it is a terrific way to spend the summer. Students can expect to spend three of their six weeks working with the local people on a major construction project, such as a school or a hospital. They spend the rest of their stay involved in an independent internship in a field that they are particularly interested in. Some examples of internships have included tutoring children, working with the elderly, involvement in a archeological dig. World Horizons offers students the chance to make their summer vacation matter, both to them and to the world at large. One word of caution: It is important to remember that this is not a luxury tour. You are going to work, and to help, and to make lifelong friends.

Work Camps

Among the more exciting ideas that dash through the minds of the breaker-to-be must be the possibility of going to foreign lands and being there in a kind of adult version of summer camp. For a minuscule sum and some period of hard work, usually manual labor, you can find yourself living with and making friends with your peers from countries around the world, performing a most useful service and having an unusual vacation. Where in the world would all this take place? They are called work camps, staffed by an international population and aimed at performing some community-development project that requires short-term, intensive work by unskilled volunteers.

There are four principal clearinghouses for work camps. They are listed below in order of accessibility rather than in alphabetical order, particularly since the first two listings are the most inclusive:

Volunteers for Peace
Belmont, VT 05730
(802) 259-2759

In return for a phone call or a letter, Volunteers for Peace will send you its newsletter, chock-full of information on work camps around the world. There is a membership fee involved here—$10. That will bring you the catalogue. Registration fees for camps vary as to location.

Service Civil International, USA
c/o Innisfree Village
Route 2, Box 506
Crozet, VA 22932

Here the fee is $25 for a listing of work camps in the United States and $50 for work camps abroad.

See CIEE, p. 70, for more information about work camps you can connect with. You will note that in order to use CIEE services you must have been enrolled in school within the last six months.

Nothelfergemeinschaft der Freunde e. V.

Generalsekretariat
Auf der Kornerwiese 5
D-6000 Frankfurt 1, Germany
Country code + 069-71111
Program length: varies
Cost: none
Financial aid: none
Housing: provided

Age range of participants: 18 and up
Number of participants: varies by program
Application process: application
Application due date: rolling admissions
Program location: Germany

The Nothelfergemeinschaft der Freunde e. V., or Association of Friends, Helpers in Need, is an organization designed to bring volunteers to places in which their service will be of help. Each camp may last three or four weeks and operate in Germany during summer and autumn. Elsewhere (Israel, Turkey, Poland) camps continue through December.

If you join one of these groups and become a member of the International Service for Peace, you should expect to find yourself in a truly international community. You should expect also to be doing some heavy outdoor work: in agriculture, construction, and forestry, for example. There are also jobs working with the handicapped and the elderly, working in kitchens, in gardens. But clearly one of the goals of the group is universal understanding. If all this appeals—and if you are willing to surmount the predictable language barriers (or if you can get along in German or French)—all you need do is write for an application.

Lesotho Work Camps Association

Box 6
Maseru 100, Lesotho
Country code + 314862
Program length: summer or winter
Cost: $75
Financial aid: none
Housing: provided

Age range of participants: 16 and up
Number of participants: 20–30
Application process: application with fee
Application due date: rolling admissions
Program location: Lesotho, Africa

Like other work camps around the world, the Lesotho Work Camps Association offers you a chance to volunteer some thirty to forty hours of your time per week for between one and four weeks. You might be planting trees, building schools or roads, helping the very young or the very old. You also will be living communally with other volunteers from around the world, preparing meals, living and playing together. And that's really the value of the work camp: to share an experience while helping the community. The work-camp application is fifty cents. Not much for such an opportunity.

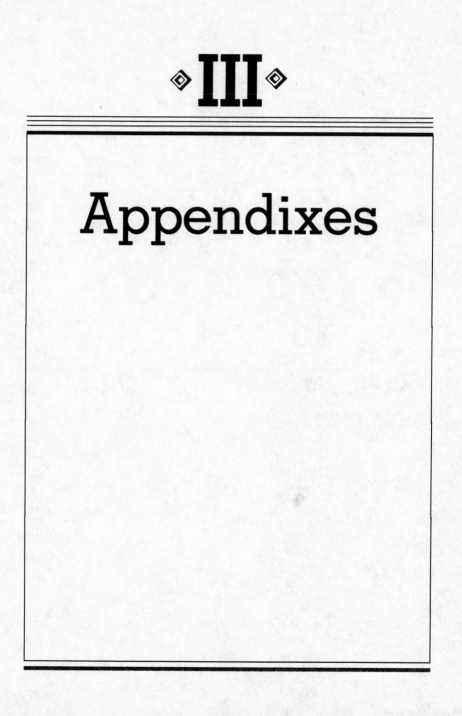

III

Appendixes

Resource Information

This section is meant to help you find things: jobs, opportunities, ways to get places, places to get. You might describe it as that drawer or pocket or box into which you shove all the stuff you don't know where else to put. But look through it, and you might find something useful. We have tried to cross-reference this material elsewhere in the book. The most important parts are also indexed.

U.S. ADDRESSES OF FOREIGN EMBASSIES

Below you will find the addresses of every foreign embassy located in the United States.

Afghanistan
Office of the Embassy
2341 Wyoming Avenue
Washington, DC 20008
(202) 234-3770

Algeria
Office of the Embassy
21118 Kalorama Road
Washington, DC 20008
(202) 328-5300

Antigua and Baruda
Office of the Embassy
3400 International Drive, Suite 2H
Washington, DC 20008
(202) 362-5211

Argentina
Office of the Embassy
1600 New Hampshire Avenue
Washington, DC 20009
(202) 939-6400

Australia
Office of the Embassy
1601 Massachusetts Avenue
Washington, DC 20036
(202) 797-3000

Austria
Office of the Embassy
2343 Massachusetts Avenue
Washington, DC 20008
(202) 483-4474

The Commonwealth of the Bahamas
Office of the Embassy
600 New Hampshire Avenue, Suite
  865m
Washington, DC 20037
(202) 944-3390

State of Bahrain
Office of the Embassy
3502 International Drive
Washington, DC 20008
(202) 342-0741

People's Republic of Bangladesh
Office of the Embassy
2201 Wisconsin Avenue
Washington, DC 20007
(202) 342-8372

Barbados
Office of the Embassy
2144 Wyoming Avenue
Washington, DC 20008
(202) 939-9200

Belgium
Office of the Embassy
3330 Garfield Street
Washington, DC 20008
(202) 333-6900

Belize
Office of the Embassy
3400 International Drive
Washington, DC 20008
(202) 363-4505

People's Republic of Benin
Office of the Embassy
2737 Cathedral Avenue
Washington, DC 20008
(202) 232-6656

Bolivia
Office of the Embassy
3014 Massachusetts Avenue
Washington, DC 20008
(202) 483-4410

Republic of Botswana
Office of the Embassy
4301 Connecticut Avenue, Suite 404
Washington, DC 20008
(202) 244-4900

Brazil
Office of the Embassy
3006 Massachusetts Avenue
Washington, DC 20008
(202) 745-2700

State of Brunei
Office of the Embassy
Watergate, Suite 300
2600 Virginia Avenue
Washington, DC 20037
(202) 342-0159

People's Republic of Bulgaria
Office of the Embassy
1621 22d Street
Washington, DC 20008
(202) 387-7969

Burkino Faso
Office of the Embassy
2340 Massachusetts Avenue
Washington, DC 20008
(202) 332-5577

Burma
Office of the Embassy
2300 S Street
Washington, DC 20008
(202) 332-9044

Burundi
Office of the Embassy
2233 Wisconsin Avenue
Washington, DC 20007
(202) 342-2574

Republic of the Cameroon
Office of the Embassy
2349 Massachusetts Avenue
Washington, DC 20008
(202) 265-8790

Canada
Office of the Embassy
501 Pennsylvania Avenue
Washington, DC 20001
(202) 682-1740

Cape Verde
Office of the Embassy
3415 Massachusetts Avenue
Washington, DC 20008
(202) 965-6820

Central African Republic
Office of the Embassy
1618 22d Street
Washington, DC 20008
(202) 483-7800

Chad
Office of the Embassy
2002 R Street
Washington, DC 20009
(202) 462-4009

Chile
Office of the Embassy
1732 Massachusetts Avenue
Washington, DC 20036
(202) 785-1746

People's Republic of China
Office of the Embassy
2300 Connecticut Avenue
Washington, DC 20008
(202) 328-2500

Colombia
Office of the Embassy
2118 Leroy Place
Washington, DC 20008
(202) 387-8338

Comoros
Embassy of the Federal and Islamic
    Republic of the Comoros
336 East 45th Street, 2d Floor
New York, NY 10017
(212) 972-8010

People's Republic of the Congo
Office of the Embassy
4891 Colorado Avenue
Washington, DC 20011
(202) 726-5500

Costa Rica
Office of the Embassy
1825 Connecticut Avenue, Suite 213
Washington, DC 20009
(202) 234-2945

Côte d'Ivoire
Office of the Embassy
2424 Massachusetts Avenue
Washington, DC 20008
(202) 483-2400

Republic of Cyprus
Office of the Embassy
2211 R Street
Washington, DC 20008
(202) 462-5772

Czechoslovakia Socialist Republic
Office of the Embassy
3900 Linnean Avenue
Washington, DC 20008
(202) 363-6315

Denmark
Office of the Embassy
3200 Whitehaven Street
Washington, DC 20008
(202) 234-4300

Republic of Djibouti
Office of the Embassy
1430 K Street
Washington, DC 20006
(202) 347-0254

Dominican Republic
Office of the Embassy
1715 22d Street
Washington, DC 20008
(202) 332-6280

Ecuador
Office of the Embassy
2535 15th Street
Washington, DC 20009
(202) 234-7200

Egypt
Office of the Embassy
2310 Decatur Place
Washington, DC 20008
(202) 232-5400

El Salvador
Office of the Embassy
2308 California Street
Washington, DC 20008
(202) 265-3480

Equatorial Guinea
Office of the Embassy
801 Second Avenue, Suite 1403
New York, NY 10017
(212) 599-1523

Estonia
Office of the Consular General
9 Rockefeller Plaza
New York, NY 10020
(212) 247-1450

Ethiopia
Office of the Embassy
2134 Kalorama Road
Washington, DC 20008
(202) 234-2281

Fiji
Office of the Embassy
2233 Wisconsin Avenue
Washington, DC 20007
(202) 337-8320

Finland
Office of the Embassy
3216 New Mexico Avenue
Washington, DC 20016
(202) 363-2340

France
Office of the Embassy
4101 Reservoir Road
Washington, DC 20007
(202) 944-6000

Gabon
Office of the Embassy
2034 20th Street
Washington, DC 20009
(202) 797-1000

Gambia
Office of the Embassy
1030 15th Street, Suite 720
Washington, DC 20005
(202) 842-1356

Germany
Office of the Embassy
4645 Reservoir Road
Washington, DC 20007
(202) 298-4000

Ghana
Office of the Embassy
3512 International Drive
Washington, DC 20008
(202) 686-4520

Great Britain
Office of the Embassy
3100 Massachusetts Avenue
Washington, DC 2008
(202) 462-1340

Greece
Office of the Embassy
2221 Massachusetts Avenue
Washington, DC 20008
(202) 667-3168

Grenada
Office of the Embassy
1701 New Hampshire Avenue
Washington, DC 20009
(202) 265-2561

Guatemala
Office of the Embassy
2220 R Street
Washington, DC 20008
(202) 745-4592

Guinea
Office of the Embassy
2112 Leroy Place
Washington, DC 20008
(202) 483-9420

Guinea Bissau
Office of the Embassy
c/o the Permanent Mission of
Guinea Bissau of the UN
211 East 43d Street, Suite 604
New York, NY 10017
(212) 661-3977

Guyana
Office of the Embassy
2490 Tracy Place
Washington, DC 20008
(202) 265-6900

Haiti
Office of the Embassy
2311 Massachusetts Avenue
Washington, DC 20008
(202) 332-4090

Holy See Apostolic Nunciature
Office of the Embassy
3339 Massachusetts Avenue
Washington, DC 20008
(202) 333-7121

Honduras
Office of the Embassy
4301 Connecticut Avenue, Suite 100
Washington, DC 20008
(202) 966-7700

Hungary
Office of the Embassy
3910 Shoemaker Street
Washington, DC 20008
(202) 362-6730

Iceland
Office of the Embassy
2022 Connecticut Avenue
Washington, DC 20008
(202) 265-6653

India
Office of the Embassy
2107 Massachusetts Avenue
Washington, DC 20008
(202) 939-7000

Indonesia
Office of the Embassy
2020 Massachusetts Avenue
Washington, DC 20036
(202) 293-1745

Iraq
Office of the Embassy
1801 P Street
Washington, DC 20036
(202) 483-7500

Ireland
Office of the Embassy
2334 Massachusetts Avenue
Washington, DC 20008
(202) 462-3939

Israel
Office of the Embassy
3514 International Drive
Washington, DC 20008
(202) 364-5500

Italy
Office of the Embassy
1601 Fuller Street
Washington, DC 20009
(202) 328-5500

Jamaica
Office of the Embassy
1850 K Street, Suite 355
Washington, DC 20006
(202) 452-0660

Japan
Office of the Embassy
2520 Massachusetts Avenue
Washington, DC 20008
(202) 234-2266

Jordan
Office of the Embassy
3504 International Drive
Washington, DC 20008
(202) 966-2664

Kenya
Office of the Embassy
2249 R Street
Washington, DC 20008
(202) 387-6101

Korea
Office of the Embassy
2370 Massachusetts Avenue
Washington, DC 20008
(202) 939-5600

Kuwait
Office of the Embassy
2940 Tilden Street
Washington, DC 20008
(202) 966-0702

Laos
Office of the Embassy
2222 S Street
Washington, DC 20008
(202) 332-6416

Latvia
Office of the Embassy
4325 17th Street
Washington, DC 20011
(202) 726-8213

Lebanon
Office of the Embassy
2560 28th Street
Washington, DC 20008
(202) 939-6300

Lesotho
Office of the Embassy
2511 Massachusetts Avenue
Washington, DC 20008
(202) 797-5534

Liberia
Office of the Embassy
5201 16th Street
Washington, DC 20011
(202) 723-0437

Lithuania
Office of the Embassy
2622 16th Street
Washington, DC 20009
(202) 234-5860

Luxembourg
Office of the Embassy
2200 Massachusetts Avenue
Washington, DC 20008
(202) 265-4171

Democratic Republic of Madagascar
Office of the Embassy
2374 Massachusetts Avenue
Washington, DC 20008
(202) 265-5525

Malawi
Office of the Embassy
2408 Massachusetts Avenue
Washington, DC 20008
(202) 797-1007

Malaysia
Office of the Embassy
2401 Massachusetts Avenue
Washington, DC 20008
(202) 328-2700

Mali
Office of the Embassy
2130 R Street
Washington, DC 20008
(202) 332-2249

Malta
Office of the Embassy
2017 Connecticut Avenue
Washington, DC 20008
(202) 462-3611

Mauritania
Office of the Embassy
2129 Leroy Place
Washington, DC 20008
(202) 232-5700

Mauritius
Office of the Embassy
4301 Connecticut Avenue, Suite 134
Washington, DC 20008
(202) 244-1491

Mexico
Office of the Embassy
2829 16th Street
Washington, DC 20009
(202) 234-6000

Morocco
Office of the Embassy
1601 21st Street
Washington, DC 20009
(202) 462-7979

Mozambique
Office of the Embassy
1990 M Street, Suite 570
Washington, DC 20009
(202) 293-7146

Nepal
Office of the Embassy
2131 Leroy Place
Washington, DC 20008
(202) 667-4550

Netherlands
Office of the Embassy
4200 Linnean Avenue
Washington, DC 20008
(202) 244-5300

New Zealand
Office of the Embassy
37 Observation Circle
Washington, DC 20008
(202) 328-4800

Nicaragua
Office of the Embassy
1627 New Hampshire Avenue
Washington, DC 20008
(202) 387-4371

Niger
Office of the Embassy
2204 R Street
Washington, DC 20008
(202) 483-4224

Nigeria
Office of the Embassy
2201 M Street
Washington, DC 20037
(202) 822-1500

Norway
Office of the Embassy
2720 34th Street
Washington, DC 20008
(202) 333-6000

Oman
Office of the Embassy
2342 Massachusetts Avenue
Washington, DC 20008
(202) 939-6200

Pakistan
Office of the Embassy
2315 Massachusetts Avenue
Washington, DC 20008
(202) 939-6200

Panama
Office of the Embassy
2862 McGill Terrace
Washington, DC 20008
(202) 483-1407

Papua New Guinea
Office of the Embassy
1330 Connecticut Avenue
Suite 350
Washington, DC 20036
(202) 659-0856

Paraguay
Office of the Embassy
2400 Massachusetts Avenue
Washington, DC 20008
(202) 483-6960

Peru
Office of the Embassy
1700 Massachusetts Avenue
Washington, DC 20036
(202) 833-9860

Philippines
Office of the Embassy
1617 Massachusetts Avenue
Washington, DC 20036
(202) 483-1414

Poland
Office of the Embassy
2640 16th Street
Washington, DC 20009
(202) 234-3800

Portugal
Office of the Embassy
2125 Kalorama Road
Washington, DC 20008
(202) 328-8610

Qatar
Office of the Embassy
600 New Hampshire Avenue, Suite
1180
Washington, DC 20037
(202) 338-0111

Romania
Office of the Embassy
1607 23d Street
Washington, DC 20008
(202) 232-4747

Rwanda
Office of the Embassy
1714 New Hampshire Avenue
Washington, DC 20009
(202) 232-2882

Saint Christopher and Nevis
Office of the Embassy
2501 M Street
Suite 540
Washington, DC 20037
(202) 833-3550

Saint Lucia
Office of the Embassy
2100 M Street
Washington, DC 20037
(202) 463-7378

São Tomé and Principe
Office of the Embassy
801 Second Avenue, Suite 1504
New York, NY 10017
(212) 697-4211

Saudi Arabia
Office of the Embassy
601 New Hampshire Avenue
Washington, DC 20037
(202) 342-3800

Senegal
Office of the Embassy
2112 Wyoming Avenue
Washington, DC 20008
(202) 234-0540

Seychelles
Office of the Embassy
820 Second Avenue, Suite 203
New York, NY 10017
(212) 687-9766

Sierra Leone
Office of the Embassy
1701 19th Street
Washington, DC 20009
(202) 939-9261

Singapore
Office of the Embassy
1824 R Street
Washington, DC 20009
(202) 667-7555

Somali Democratic Republic
Office of the Embassy
600 New Hampshire Avenue, Suite
710
Washington, DC 20037
(202) 342-1575

South Africa
Office of the Embassy
3051 Massachusetts Avenue
Washington, DC 20008
(202) 232-4400

Spain
Office of the Embassy
2700 15th Street
Washington, DC 20009
(202) 265-0190

Sri Lanka
Office of the Embassy
2148 Wyoming Avenue
Washington, DC 20008
(202) 483-4025

Sudan
Office of the Embassy
2210 Massachusetts Avenue
Washington, DC 20008
(202) 338-8565

Suriname
Office of the Embassy
4301 Connecticut Avenue
Washington, DC 20008
(202) 244-7488

Swaziland
Office of the Embassy
4301 Connecticut Avenue, Suite 441
Washington, DC 20008
(202) 362-6683

Sweden
Office of the Embassy
600 New Hampshire Avenue, Suite
  1200
Washington, DC 20037
(202) 944-5600

Switzerland
Office of the Embassy
2900 Cathedral Avenue
Washington, DC 20008
(202) 745-7900

Syria
Office of the Embassy
2215 Wyoming Avenue
Washington, DC 20008
(202) 232-6313

Tanzania
Office of the Embassy
2139 R Street
Washington, DC 20008
(202) 939-6125

Thailand
Office of the Embassy
2300 Kalorama Road
Washington, DC 20008
(202) 483-7200

Togo
Office of the Embassy
2208 Massachusetts Avenue
Washington, DC 20008
(202) 234-4212

Trinidad and Tobago
Office of the Embassy
1708 Massachusetts Avenue
Washington, DC 20036
(202) 467-6490

Tunisia
Office of the Embassy
1515 Massachusetts Avenue
Washington, DC 20005
(202) 862-1850

Turkey
Office of the Embassy
1606 23d Street
Washington, DC 20008
(202) 387-3200

Uganda
Office of the Embassy
5909 16th Street
Washington, DC 20011
(202) 726-7100

**Union of Soviet Socialist
  Republics**
Office of the Embassy
1125 16th Street
Washington, DC 20036
(202) 628-7551

United Arab Emirates
Office of the Embassy
600 New Hampshire Avenue, Suite
  740
Washington, DC 20037
(202) 338-6500

Uruguay
Office of the Embassy
1918 F Street
Washington, DC 20006
(202)-331-1313

Venezuela
Office of the Embassy
2445 Massachusetts Avenue
Washington, DC 20008
(202) 797-3800

Western Samoa
Office of the Embassy
820 Second Avenue
New York, NY 10017
(212) 599-6196

Yemen
Office of the Embassy
600 New Hampshire Avenue
Suite 840
Washington, DC 20037
(202) 965-4760

Yugoslavia
Office of the Embassy

2410 California Street
Washington, DC 20008
(202) 462-6566

Zaire
Office of the Embassy
1800 New Hampshire Avenue
Washington, DC 20009
(202) 234-7690

Zambia
Office of the Embassy
2419 Massachusetts Avenue
Washington, DC 20008
(202) 265-9717

Zimbabwe
Office of the Embassy
2852 McGill Terrace
Washington, DC 20008
(202) 332-7100

MEDICAL INFORMATION

The International Association for Medical Assistance to Travelers (IAMAT)
417 Center Street
Lewiston NY 14092
(716) 754-4883
Membership fee: donations accepted
Program location: worldwide (not in USSR)

In return for a request (and preferably a donation to support the activities of IAMAT), you will receive a membership card entitling you to access IAMAT's directory of participating physicians around the globe. These doctors have agreed to be listed by IAMAT in order to guarantee you affordable, qualified medical care from physicians who speak English. IAMAT also supplies a variety of informative pamphlets, some of which pertain to immunizations and to the healthfulness of consumables in other lands.

Access Foundation
1-800-876-2882
Access will provide you with a variety of information about disabled access

in return for a $25 membership fee. This organization screens opportunities around the world for the disabled and chronically ill.

HOME EXCHANGES

Better Homes and Travel
Box 268
185 Park Row, Suite 14D
New York, NY 10038
(212) 349-5340
Registration: $50
BHT provides a list of possibilities in exchange for fee and completed information form. But prospective exchangers should be flexible. Options often are limited.

Intervac or U.S./International Home Exchange Service
Box 190070
San Francisco, CA 94119
(415) 435-3497

Intervac is an international exchange service that will provide you with three annual directories of international home exchange listings (each in the language of the home country) for $35. Directors are published in February, April, and June. An entry in one is $35, which entitles you to all three books. This organization's catalogues contained 7,300 listings last year.

Teacher Swap
Box 4130
Rocky Point, NY 11778
(516) 744-6403

Despite its restrictive title, TS recognizes a wide range of people as "teachers," including the Sunday school variety. This organization publishes an annual directory, which costs $40; you may be listed for $34. If you submit your entry by October 1 (the deadline is March 1), you will get a bonus of next year's directory and supplement, as well as this year's.

Vacation Exchange Club
12006 11th Avenue, Unit 12
Youngton, AZ 85363
(602) 972-2186

VEC publishes two issues per year, February and April, and offers about 6,000 listings. You may list in one volume for $24.50; adding a photo will cost $9. If you send in an entry before November 30, you will receive both volumes for $35.

AIRFARES

The following agencies are among the best places to look for reduced airfares. However, remember to make sure you understand all conditions before purchasing your ticket. You get what you pay for, here as everywhere else.

Council Travel (see CIEE, page 70)

International Student Exchange Flights
5010 East Shea Boulevard, Suite A104
Scottsdale, AZ 85254
(602) 951-1177

Student Travel Agency
17 East 45th Street
New York, NY
(212) 986-9470

Now Voyager
74 Varick Street, Suite 307
New York, NY 10013
(212) 431-1616

Now Voyager provides a distinctive service: courier flights around the world. You have to join the organization, and that will cost you $50 for a year's membership. What do you get for that? You get a chance to fly to your destination (if you can wait for it to appear and are flexible enough to go when it does) and you do so for very little money. For example, at the time of writing, a trip to Hong Kong for two weeks was $199 roundtrip. The catch? Your flexibility, your willingness to travel alone, and your willingness to travel light. You are allowed only carry-on luggage. Now Voyager urges you to call them on a touch-tone phone after 6 P.M. Their information line operates twenty-four hours a day, and will tell you all you need to know about available flights. One last note: You must be over eighteen to belong to Now Voyager.

FOREIGN TRAVEL INFORMATION

For current advice to travelers to your intended destination, contact:

Department of State
2201 C Street NW
Washington, DC 20520

For an up-to-the-minute status report on any country you are preparing to enter, contact:

Citizens Emergency Room 4811
Department of State
Washington, DC 20520
(202) 632-5225

Visa requirements of foreign governments obtained from:

Superintendent of Documents
U.S. Government Printing Office
Washington, DC 20402

Alphabetical Listing of Programs and Organizations

◊ ◊ ◊

Listing of Programs by Cost

Listing of Programs
by Location

◇ ◇ ◇

Bibliography

◇ ◇ ◇

BOOKS

Abroad and Beyond: Patterns in American Overseas Education, Craufurd D. Goodwin and Michael Nacht. New York: Cambridge University Press, 1988. This volume is for those individuals and institutions evaluating or considering programs abroad. Despite the volume's mixture of kitschy style and dissertation prose, the authors do a good job of analyzing the genre of semester- and year-abroad programs. Worth reading if you're anxious to get a grasp of the big picture.

Academic Year Abroad, E. Marguerite Howard, ed. New York: Institute of International Education, 1989. This volume is the standard for study-abroad programs. Whether you plan to take a summer, a semester, or year aboard; whether you plan to study a discipline, learn a language, or embark on a new academic experience, *Academic Year Abroad* should be your first stop. And, while you're visiting among its 358 closely printed pages, don't miss the essay on reading study-abroad literature, by Lily von Klemperer, who, before her death, was one of the few authorities on study-abroad programs. Also important to note in this volume are the considerable listings of programs that originate abroad. That's information hard to find elsewhere.

Advisory List of International Educational Travel and Exchange Programs, 1991, H. David Fry *et al.* Reston, Va.: Council on Standards for International Educational Travel, 1987.

Archaeological Fieldwork Opportunities Bulletin: 1991, Galina Gorokhoff, ed. Boston, Mass.: Archaeological Institute of America, 1988. Behind this self-explanatory title lies a world of opportunities for archeological fieldwork. The sites listed range from the United States to New Guinea. Positions advertised are usually volunteer, although each bulletin does contain a number of paid positions as well as a variety of educational situations. Most sites are seasonally occupied; here again exceptions exist, mostly in warmer climates. Each bulletin also includes other useful information: affiliated institutions, state and national archeological organizations, and a useful bibliography.

Before You Go to Asia: A Primer for Personal Adventure without Spending a Lot of Money, John McCarroll. San Francisco: Laurel Publishing Co., McCarroll's iconoclastic approach delivers more or less what this book's subtitle promises. Travel tips, particularly on health and safety, are invaluable. His comments about countries and places to see should be taken as all comments in all guidebooks: as one person's opinion. But the cost alone—$8.95— makes this volume a worthwhile buy.

Bridging the Global Gap: A Handbook to Linking Citizens of the First and Third Worlds, Medea Benjamin and Andrea Freedman. Cabin John, Md.: Seven Locks Press, 1989. If your interest is in internationalism, in exploring connections between your world and the Third World, then you should read this book. It is both anecdotal and directive. Not only have the authors collected a variety of accounts of connections being made between American citizens and people in Latin America, Africa, and Asia, they also outline methods to further those connections. One example of the latter is alternative trade, the establishment of an importing company that returns the profits to the originators of the goods. This volume also contains 100 pages of resource material, including organizations, print, and other media dedicated to internationalism.

Directory of Low Cost Vacations with a Difference, J. Crawford, ed. New York: Pilot Industries, Inc., 1989.

A Directory of San Francisco Bay Area & Silicon Valley Internships. Stanford, Calif.: University Resource Services, 1988. This directory contains over 100 internships and paid positions throughout northern California. Each internship is described in detail, with information about qualifications. Most positions are for upper division college students.

Explorer News: Foundation for Field Research Quarterly Report, vol. 5, no. 1. Alpine, Calif.: Foundation for Field Research, 1989. This periodic bulletin serves two purposes: it details the expeditions undertaken by the Foundation for Field Research, often with photographs, and it serves as the organization's vehicle for connecting with you, the potential consumer.

The Insider's Guide to Foreign Study, Benedict A. Leerburger, Reading, Mass.: Addison-Wesley, 1987. This book should be entitled *The Statistics to Over 4,000 Academic Adventures Abroad* because that's exactly what it is. The problem with this book is that the author gives no information about the programs listed other than the fact that they exist. Reading this book is like reading the telephone book—you can get the names and numbers only.

International Jobs: Where They Are, How to Get Them, Eric Kocher. Reading, Mass.: Addison-Wesley, 1979. All college graduates who want to work abroad should take a look at this book. While it is not by any means a complete listing of international jobs, it will get you started thinking and applying to some places. The book is primarily a listing of companies over-seas who hire young Americans. Each listing gives a brief description of what the company does and to whom to write to for more information on jobs. The author includes helpful essays on how to go about searching for a job overseas. The listings are organized by field and indexed alphabetically by company name. The only drawback to this guide is that there should be more information about the companies and jobs listed.

Thee International Schools Directory, 1989. Petersfield, Hampshire, England: European Council of International Schools, 1988. A worldwide directory of primary and secondary schools, each with statistical and descriptive information.

The National Directory of Internships, Sally A. Magliore, ed. Raleigh, N.C.: National Society for Internships and Experiential Education, 1987. Listed within this guide are the names, phone numbers, and descriptions of hundreds of internships in the following fields: The arts, business and industry, clearinghouses, communications, consumer affairs, education, environment, government, health, human services, international affairs, museums and history, public interest, sciences and women's issues. As you can see, there is something here for everyone. The listings include a brief description of the internship, eligibility requirements for the position, and application deadlines. The guide indexes the opportunities separately by field, geo-graphical location, and organization name for easy usage. *The National Direc-tory* can be purchased through NSIEE; 122 St. Mary's Street; Raleigh, NC 27605; (919) 834-7536.

1988 Internships, Katherine Jobst, ed. Cincinnati, Ohio: Writer's Digest Books, 1987. This guide comes out every year and contains a listing of thousands of internship opportunities in every conceivable field. It provides brief descriptions of the job, as well as eligibility requirements and applica-tion procedures. In addition, it offers readers sample cover letters and resumes and articles that help you to choose the internship that's right for you and to prepare for your interview. The guide contains several indexes that list opportunities by geographical location and in alphabetical order. It can be purchased at local bookstores or by directly contacting Writer's Digest; 1507 Dana Avenue; Cincinnati, Ohio 45207.

1989 Summer Employment Directory of the United States, Pat Beusterien, ed. Cincinnati, Ohio: Writer's Digest Books, 1988. This annual directory has helpful instruction about preparing to find a summer job, as well as an exhaustive listing of positions, broken down by state and area of interest (i.e., conservation or recreation). There are also small sections dealing with Canadian and international opportunities.

1989 Directory of Overseas Summer Jobs. David Woodworth, ed. Oxford, England: Vacation-Work, 1989. This is a useful directory of job offerings for anyone who wants to spend a summer overseas working in a hotel, restaurant, resort, or doing other sorts of service work, such as typing. The listings are broken down by country and then subgrouped by field. This book comes out yearly and can be found in local bookstores or by writing Writer's Digest Books; 1507 Dana Avenue; Cincinnati, Ohio 45207.

Our Classroom Is Wild America, Michael J. Cohen. Freeport, Maine: Cobblesmith, 1989. This volume has been the prerequisite for admission into the National Audubon Society Expedition Institute. It is also a highly idiosyncratic description of the program, its philosophy, its process, and its goals. Worth reading—indeed, required reading—if you're interested in the program; a fascinating perspective on one man's approach to education and to educating us about our environment if you're not.

The Student Guide to Mass Media Internships (1988). 2 vols. Ronald H. Claxton. San Marcos, Tex.: Intern Research Group, Department of Journalism, Southwest Texas State University, 1988. This is the most complete guide for internship opportunities in media-related fields of print and broadcast. It lists thousands of opportunities in media in locations throughout the country; and provides brief descriptions of the internships and information about application requirements. The guide is organized by field and then subgrouped by state. If you are looking for a position in media, this is where to start. The guides can be ordered directly from the Intern Research Group, Department of Journalism, Southwest Texas State University, San Marcos, TX 78666.

Study Holidays: An Authoritative Guide to European Language Learning. London: Central Bureau, 1988. The advantage of this volume is that it contains courses that teach you every conceivable European language. These programs are not generally academically oriented, rather the majority are language courses to be taken for the pleasure of learning a new language. The disadvantage is that the volume is directed toward the British. Therefore, the specific information is likely to be of less use than the listings of the programs themselves.

Summer Jobs in Britain 1988, Susan Griffith, ed. Oxford, England: Vacation-Work, 1988. Susan Griffith, who writes regularly for *Transitions Abroad,* has assembled a guide to summer jobs in Britain. She has included helpful information about working, making one's own opportunity, visas, and work permits, as well as geographical and topical guides to possible positions. This volume is detailed and easy to use.

Taking Off: Extraordinary Ways to Spend Your First Year Out of College, Lauren Tarshis. New York: Fireside (Simon & Schuster), 1989. If you've just graduated from school and you don't know what you want to do, Lauren Tarshis can provide you with some suggestions for an interim year between college and "the real world." The book is divided into several sections, including "Opportunities Abroad," "Volunteer Opportunities," and "Opportunities in the Outdoors," in which several possibilities are described in great detail. While this book won't provide you with all the options, it will give you some solid information on a few (i.e., teaching English in China) that you might want to think about after graduation.

The Teenager's Guide to Study, Travel, and Adventure Abroad. Marjorie Adoff Cohen. New York: Council on International Education Exchange (St. Martin's Press), 1987. If this is your first time going abroad then make sure you don't miss this book. Especially worth reading are the essays at the beginning that lead you through the ins and outs of going overseas and picking a program. The rest of the book contains a listing of programs that offer teenagers opportunities (primarily during the summer months) abroad. Each entry contains a brief program description and information about cost, admission requirements, and living arrangements.

Volunteer!, Marjorie Adoff Cohen; Adrienne Downey, ed. New York: Council on International Educational Exchange (CIEE) and the Commission on Voluntary Service and Action, 1988. This is the most comprehensive published listing of worldwide volunteer positions, providing descriptions of the volunteer organizations and the positions as well as data on the application requirements, living arrangements, finances, and application due dates. A special section devoted entirely to work camps concludes this guide. *Volunteer!* is updated every year and is available in bookstores or through the Council on International Educational Exchange.

Whole World Handbook, Marjorie Adoff Cohen; Margaret E. Sherman, ed. New York: Council on International Educational Exchange (CIEE)/E.P. Dutton, 1981. This is *not* a listing of opportunities abroad, rather, it is a handbook, perhaps the most extensive "guide to study, work, and travel abroad." If you are planning to travel abroad, this volume should be read and packed in your on-board luggage.

Working Holidays: Britain and Abroad: 89. London: Central Bureau, 1989. Obtainable through the Institute of International Education or directly from the Central Bureau, this book details jobs and volunteer positions all over the world. Like its companion volume, *Study Holidays*, it is written from the perspective of Great Britain. Nonetheless, it is an indispensable resource for work in and outside Great Britain, with detailed job descriptions provided in almost all cases.

MAGAZINES AND PAMPHLETS

Transitions Aboard. (Bimonthly magazine.) Although *Time Out* would have been written without *Transitions*, it would not have been half as informative. We are indebted to Clay Hubbs, founder and editor of *Transitions*, for the work he and his staff have done over the years to make this magazine work so well. You can find references to its articles sprinkled throughout this book. *Transitions* is a funky, mostly participant-written guide to travel, work, and study abroad. In its more than thirteen years of existence, it has managed to catalog and discuss almost every kind of overseas program. And in almost every article, there's a gem or two of valuable information. No school or library professing to have a travel section should be without it. For the student and adult going abroad, this magazine is a treasure. To subscribe write to *Transitions Abroad;* Box 344; Amherst, MA 01004-9970.

Exploroptions. This series of pamphlets listing summer programs is published periodically by Cindy Ware, its author and editor. In addition to containing useful information about the hows, whys, and what to dos of summer programs, Ware has excavated an enormous number of summer options, collected in a topical format. To date, she has listed summer programs abroad, in archeology and anthropology, in outdoor adventure, in the arts—both performing and graphic—in marine biology and environmental science, in academic study, in work and volunteer/internships, in the social sciences, in writing, and in sports. Each listing contains vital information, such as age, application deadline, etc. *Exploroptions;* 30 Alcott Street; Acton, MA. 01720. See also Cindy Ware, *Summer Options for Teenagers* (New York: Arco,1990).

TravelBooks Catalogue. This catalog gives a sampling of the books available at or through TravelBooks; 113 Corporation Road; Hyannis, MA. There may be more convenient bookstores; there may be more encyclopedic ones when it comes to travel, but this store and this catalog are extremely helpful. They also have a toll-free number: 1-800-869-3535.

"Money Sense Overseas," obtainable from *Travel Tips;* 3602 W. Glen Branch; Peoria, IL 61614. This succinct pamphlet provides information about money "as a commodity" and has a sheaf of helpful hints about obtaining and dealing with foreign currency. For instance, don't carry large amounts of cash, but do carry some one-dollar bills. They are universal currency. This pamphlet is free for a stamped, self-addressed nine-inch envelope. The reason for such a bargain? The parent company, Unicon Enterprises, wants to sell you a money converter. You will get the flier with your pamphlet. Judge its usefulness for yourself.

Index